Born Expatriated

SARA S. VILLARREAL BISHOP

Born Expatriated
by Sara S. Villarreal Bishop

ISBN-13: 978-0-6152-0165-8

With the utmost thanks and gratitude to the Megs for sticking with me through endless edits and unending revisions; to the two who inspired it in the first place, Susan and Denise; and to my mom, for helping me articulate what to do in the first place. But mostly to the two little people who made it possible.

TABLE OF CONTENTS

1. Welcome!

Parenting is the blind leading the blind. Also, like the proverb of the three blind men and the elephant where one felt a rope, one felt a tree and another felt a hose, it's all a little different. We all have the same wondrous and amazing infant, and see and feel entirely different things. Please don't forget that, especially if something in here doesn't work for you. This is meant to be a tool, not a how-to book. The book is divided into two parts, first the things that are specifically helpful for a U.S. diplomat living abroad, and secondly the style and choices we made that helped us live in these circumstances. The first half isn't so much parenting as expatriate survival methods, while the second half is the parenting choices that made our lives overseas easier. The book covers parenting, short cuts, hints, products and a whole lot more. Because it is so broad, there may be a great deal that is just not relevant to your situation, particularly in the second half.

This book is geared towards U.S. Government, Embassy based or supported, employees, but it is still pertinent to all expats. Foreign Service babies are a paperwork circus because of the natural bureaucratic inclinations of government. Throughout this book I will refer to the Foreign Service, Embassy and State Department, but please extrapolate your particular organization or titles since I am relating only my experiences. In reading this it will sound like the process was grueling and difficult, but it wasn't that way. I met and worked with numerous great folks throughout. However, since I don't want to make the long-winded, politically correct variations every time, I will always say Foreign Service, Embassy and State Department. It could just as easily be Peace Corps, office and organization or Brigade.

Once when I was a new parent, I posted a question during a live "chat with the expert." I was new, so it could have been anything, but the question was particular to living overseas, jet lag and infants. I don't remember the exact question, but I remember the answer. The expert told me that the forum was for average parents and children, and this was a special circumstance and I "would be best served by being referred to my pediatrician." Now, that was a nice safe response, except that my pediatrician was also twelve time zones away! Not only that, this expert WAS a U.S. pediatrician, so ... shouldn't the answers be similar at least? One of my first thoughts was, "Gee, I wish there was a book out there for this special circumstance!" I was the first one in our group of friends that had a baby[1], and when we were getting ready to depart post, one of them said, "Could you write a little primer for me?" I continued to occasionally get questions, and finally decided that, yes, I could write something. It won't be perfect, and it won't fit everyone, but it will show the choices we made and hopefully, show some other expats that there are choices out there that can make our somewhat unusual circumstances slightly less complicated.

I am sorry to say that there is no one book out there. There probably won't ever be, because not only is every child different, but every mother is different, every father is different and every environment is different. That's 256 possibilities right there, without figuring in any other variables! This book is meant for expats, particularly U.S. Government employees; if you know what that means, you probably are one. It is coming from an Embassy life and means perspectives and experiences from having lived in Second and Third World countries. This is what has worked for me, and some others, as Foreign Service parents and American expatriates from a country that doesn't know what expatriate means. We travel overseas, a lot; we might be assigned housing rather than choosing it; we sometimes have staff; we might have a weight limit on what we can ship; we might have restrictions on what we can ship. We are winging it in a not-prepackaged, not-fast, not-at-all-convenient, sometimes dangerous and always interesting world.

No matter how many times you hear this, this is not a cliché, it is a truism: Advice is worth what you pay for it. These are choices that we made for our family, and they worked for us. I've been asked to share, and am happy to do so. That said, in every book I've read about child-care, parenting or behavior, I've always been able to read critically and take at least one thing from each book, even the scarily militant ones, and use it in my home. I hope that in this book, there is one thing for you too.

May something make your life easier, make your child smile, or save you some time, effort or money. Congratulations and welcome to this wonderful new world. This is going to be fun ... trust me....

---

[1] Except for those fabulous friends who's kids had grown. Thank goodness for them too!

PART I

In which I relate some expatriate survival methods to make this circumstance slightly less intimidating.

2. We're WHAT?!

First things first; you are so lucky to be pregnant overseas. This is the best of both worlds. If you are in a Second or Third World country, you don't have the fast food convenience and preservative laden boxes of pre-made foods (oh how I miss them) or ready-to-heat meals at your fingertips. You probably can go to an open-air market for your fruits and vegetables; your bread probably molds within a few days because it is fresh baked and finding a rock in it isn't so odd. You are almost forced to eat healthier. But, the best of the other world is that you will also probably go back to the U.S. for your delivery, which can be infinitely preferable to local medical care.

Since it is so red-tape oriented, you have got to get organized. I opted to buy a three-ring binder, with some paper and pocket folder inserts for it. However, one of the closable covered folders that can be separated into sections, or a legal expandable portfolio all work just as well. Stick a page of labels in the back and label the sections/folders with the following:

> a. Medical Mom
> b. Medical Baby
> c. Finance/Insurance
> d. Work
> e. Hospital
> f. Social Security
> g. Passport/Travel

If you've been diagnosed "pregnant" while overseas, most of your monthly visits will occur at your assigned post or on the local economy and you need a place store these records for easy transport back to your U.S. OB-GYN. If your pregnancy begins in the Continental United States (CONUS), you can transport your appointment pages and all the relevant documents back to post. The actual Department of State regulation (2007) is provided in Appendix 1. For us, we're trying to organize beyond that and within it.

BINDER SECTIONS

A. MEDICAL MOM

On the title page of this section, write down your OB or midwife's name, address, phone number and e-mail, as well as the contact information of the place you will be staying pre- and post-delivery (hotel, apartment, family, friend), and write it large. Under that keep two or three pages of blank paper for a correspondence log.

Be sure to get a copy of your authorization cable and keep it in this section. If you have any questions prior to departure, be sure to ask your Med Unit. You are going to receive some hand-outs and pamphlets from the Med Unit, including the Comprehensive Guide to Pregnancy, and the OB Travel Booklet. They're both available on the MED website. Be sure to call Medical/Foreign Programs (MED/FP) upon arrival at the MedEvac site, and log it as correspondence. MED/FP will walk you through the administration and State Department medical parts of the MedEvacs and are a great resource themselves.

> Sometimes it can be difficult to get into a medical practice at seven months pregnant. Try to contact a doctor in the U.S. as soon as you get the news.

All of the information that you received prior to departure will go into this section of the binder, as well as your points of contact, both at MED/FP and back at post. A copy of your prenatal exams and medical information will go here, as it has documented your pregnancy thus far and may be the primary means of showing your U.S. doctor information.

Sometimes it can be difficult to get into a medical practice when you are seven months pregnant. Like it or not, they are taking a risk accepting a patient that they haven't seen until delivery time, and while you are at the end of a process, they are just starting to get to know you. It can feel a little like being lost in a sea of paperwork, so I strongly recommend that you contact your OB, or find one, as soon as you find out that you are pregnant. While you are overseas, communicate with them by e-mailing copies of your monthly visits, and calling with questions and such. This will make you a 'real' person. Don't hesitate to make yourself heard. Remind yourself that you are making up for six months of monthly visits and that you are certainly less of a bother, challenge or difficulty than their present-in-person patients. So don't be embarrassed or hesitant to speak up, even if it is in e-mail or a phone call rather than in person. If you are more cautious, you can ask your health unit to fax critical and pertinent information such as monthly visit summaries and test results on a regular basis.

The Health Information Privacy Protection Act (HIPPA) makes our lives a wee bit more challenging. Most doctors and their offices will not communicate private information via e-mail because it is not 'secure'. You may communicate the information to them, but they are likely to respond very vaguely. This is not because they are stubborn or rude, they're being held to a standard that is very difficult for the long-distance patient to work with. I tended to use e-mail to make 'an appointment' for a phone call at a specific time (usually first call of the doctor's morning), since a phone conversation with the actual patient meets their privacy standards.

If you don't have an OB in the U.S., one of your more important choices will be choosing him or her! Your insurance is going to play a key role – you do not want to choose someone and later discover that they are not part of your insurance plan if you cannot afford to self-pay for the services. Most insurance companies offer lists of their 'partners', physicians and hospitals, and you can begin there. Set aside a few hours and send some preliminary e-mails – mine always began with "I am an American citizen living overseas. I have received regular medical care from a U.S. licensed (Physicians Assistant)(Family Nurse Practitioner)...." And the note went on from there.

Responsiveness to e-mail correspondence was an important detail for me, and was helpful in determining who I wanted to make a 'phone appointment' with for an initial interview.

Responsiveness to e-mail correspondence was an important detail for me, and was helpful in determining who I wanted to make a 'phone appointment' with for an initial interview. One woman I know called several times to each practice that she was interested in and spoke with a different nurse each time, asking the same question. Their responses helped her gauge how she wanted to proceed. I have been told that if you choose a teaching hospital, especially one that is known internationally such as Bethesda or Boston's Brigham and Women's Hospital, they are well versed in dealing with expat mothers. Hospitals in towns with a significant military presence are also slightly more tuned to the 'living overseas' challenges than a hospital in rural Wisconsin.

There are also federal regulations that you will have to work within, as well as your organization's policies. An important note regarding Foreign Service parents is that currently the State Department's default OB Medical Evacuation

(MedEvac) point is a U.S. destination. It is a major process to deliver outside of the United States, even if it is somewhere that would seem logically allowable like London or Tokyo. If you intend to deliver somewhere other than the United States, be clear from the outset with your Medical Unit, and start the process (an appeals process) immediately. This is particularly pertinent to those spouses who have family outside of the United States and quite reasonably, would prefer to be with family than in a hotel in the Washington DC Metro area. If you choose to have your baby outside of the U.S., and haven't communicated that you are returning to the U.S., after thirty-four weeks of pregnancy, you will have to sign a waiver with the Medical Unit that the birth will be at your own risk.

Additionally, if you do have your child overseas, there is a largely held belief that any child born overseas will be 'paid in full', but the single fact of a foreign birth is not a guarantee. The cost of some things, like deliveries and tests, are more expensive overseas than in the U.S. The overall cost of having your baby where you live (in this case, overseas) is less because of no payment of per diem and lodging because you are not on a MedEvac. However, the actual medical costs overseas may be more than the allowable amount (based on insurance and other reasons) and you will end up paying significantly out-of-pocket. Since these regulations change all the time, check with your health unit, but I am confident in stating that Medical's preference is to send you to the U.S. for your delivery.

For both the liability reasons, and financial reasons, if you intend to deliver somewhere other than the U.S., be clear from the outside with your Medical Unit and start the appeal immediately. Keep the records of that appeal, such as copies of e-mails, in this section, Medical Mother, of the binder.

B. MEDICAL BABY

I put the pictures of the ultrasounds here. I put my list of potential pediatricians/family practitioners here. As I formulated interview questions so that we could choose a doctor,[1] this was where those thoughts and notes, and finally the list of questions themselves, were kept.

I also put the pamphlets on the testing recommended, and the testing we chose, in this section, as well as information relating to it, such as results. There is a standard battery of tests that are generally recommended for a pregnant person. Part of being informed is knowing why tests are recommended and if this is right

8

---

[1] One place to start for doctor interview questions is http://ttcdreams.com/doctor.html

for your family. Part of being heard is making those choices and voicing them. Having all the information in one place, allows for well-informed decision-making, regardless what choice you make.

My son was born with newborn jaundice for the first few weeks. This is where we logged the test results, and how long he slept on the glow-bed each day. Copies of the recommendatins, and quite a few Internet articles on it (we were new parents, we didn't know anything) were all kept here.

Copies of paperwork that refer to the child only is kept here in the Medical Child. Otherwise I kept all medical, prenatal, information in the Medical Mom section.

A little personal perspective: I am a minimalist when it comes to medical care. As an anthropologist, and a zoologist, I feel that birth has been happening a long time and that humans tend to over-think things. To the horror of our first Medical Unit, I chose not to take any test other than the 'triple-test' for neural tube deficiencies, and even that was only because it was a blood test. For me, as a Hispanic female, the risks were fairly minimal, and as a blood test, it was non-invasive. I declined all the other offered tests, particularly the invasive ones like amniocentesis, partially because the test results would not have changed our decision to carry to term or not, and we personally did not feel like knowing would help us prepare or not. It was a balance of risk versus benefit. I also declined as many ultrasounds as I could get away with because way back in 2000, I had the great luck to swim with wild dolphins, and underwater, sound-waves coming at your ears is LOUD. I could see on one ultrasound the baby just jolt initially from the sound, and decided that there was nothing that ultrasound could tell me personally, and therefore only took the two that the doctor requested with medical explanations. Again, communication with your health care provider is key. So, two ultrasounds total per pregnancy for me. That said, I had recently read an article that showed that the sound frequency of a cat purring was the same frequency that facilitated bone growth (broken bones, not new growing ones) and decided that my children and I would have pre-natal purr-therapy. Daily, I made a point to sit with a purring cat on my belly, and even now, the children think that is awfully funny.

"Dolphins and Purr Therapy"

C. INSURANCE/FINANCE

Again, on the first page put your contact information, particularly if you are lucky enough to have one agent you deal with rather than a call-center. Behind the contact page, keep the blank pages for a correspondence log. These pages can be supremely helpful if they become necessary because you're not digging through the margins of everything else trying to find your references. Date, name of contact and a brief summary can end up being very important.

Ask your insurance company to explain clearly (preferably in writing) how the pregnancy is paid for. Is it paid as you go, or more likely, at the post-partum visit in one lump sum? Ask when your child is covered individually and how long before you have coverage of the infant. Some insurance companies will bill the mother and child together until discharge, some insurance companies use the time of birth to begin billing separately. All of this is important because usually you are the go-between between the hospital's billing clerk and the insurance.

Additionally, as an OB MedEvac, I had to explain to that billing clerk that my insurance was the primary responsible party, but the State Department was the secondary responsible party and we only paid the annual deductible and co-pay. That said, it was MUCH easier to do in a hospital that had dealt with military than it was in a small Mid-western town that did not have any military (let alone international) exposure (neither of my children were born in the DC Metro area).

Forms change, people move on, policies adapt – this is not a static process or an unchanging environment and you may feel like this is the first baby to ever be born to parents living overseas.

Other issues under insurance and finance are things like adding your children to your orders. Check with your Human Resources folks to see what is needed for that. You will need to add the child's name to your life insurance forms (although most states default to your children being your beneficiaries, not all do).

A few examples of choices that we made regarding insurance and financial information are life insurance and investments. While there are a wide array of choices for you to investigate, we insured our little ones immediately with a Universal Life policy, changing our family's insurance dynamic and requiring a great deal of time in communicating with the commercial insurance company. They will call back to verify the information – they have the unenviable task of ensuring that you are not insuring for financial gain. How gruesome is that! I kept this information in the Insurance Finance section of the binder for easy reference.

Please note, to return to post, regardless of your Embassy affiliation, all family members to include mother and child, are required to have the following for things:

1. Medical clearance pertinent to the post

2. The Agency pays into ICASS (sort of an Embassy co-op fund, what percentage your agency pays determines the level of administrative support that the Embassy provides the personnel)

3. Health insurance that is recognized overseas

4. MedEvac insurance (for all other agencies other than U.S Department of State)

Additionally, we also started Coverdell Educational Investments for both children, with a monthly allotment beginning at birth. For lack of a better place, and because it dealt with money, in an investment kind of sense, we kept it here in the Insurance/Finance section. We also reviewed our personal investments, and with the birth of children, decided to change from the more risky plans to slightly more stable plans as a part of a 'major lifestyle change' review recommended by the insurance company.

D. WORK

Where do I always begin a binder section? With contacts and correspondence of course! One page is a list of all the contacts that I had, or were recommended, in the State Department, the Medical Unit, shipping, country desk, etc. I also kept a copy of my spouse's original travel orders, as well as a copy of the orders sending me home on OB MedEvac.

All State Department personnel, including dependents, will need a Medical Clearance. Yours is revoked the second that you depart on MedEvac. You will have your Medical Clearance form filled out by your OB and the child's by his or her pediatrician. The clearance form is provided by the State Department and in the comments section, must include the phrase, "Infant is fit for travel." If there are or were any problems, such as newborn jaundice, be sure to ask that they also comment, "Newborn jaundice is resolved." The Office of Medical Services will assume that the problem is not resolved if it does not specifically read otherwise[2], rather than visa versa. Keep a copy of this and hand-carry it back to your Med Unit at post. Per a good friend, double- and triple-check who you have to fax it to, as well as the fax number. Find out if they're going to be on leave around your due date and who their back-up is if they are. Ask them to

---

[2] Think about the implications of if they assumed it was cleared up; you return to post and it isn't. Depending on the problem, can your post handle it?

please expedite the Medical Clearance due to travel. You're not asking for a special favor here; these are just the magic words for getting the clearance processed in 3-5 working days instead of 3-5 weeks. Depending on the person, you may be able to scan and e-mail the documents versus faxing.

Forms change, people move on, policies adapt – this is not a static process or an unchanging environment and you may feel like this is the first baby to ever be born to parents living overseas. Patience, grasshopper, it will come and your goal is not to fix the process, but go back home with your new family member. These people can, and will, help you, but you must be patient.

E. HOSPITAL

If you are a MedEvac outside of the DC Metro area, you are going to want to be particularly careful to document your hospital correspondence, because the whole "responsible party" (first insurance, then State Department) issue can be difficult to communicate.

Pre-register! You have the opportunity to get all of your information, allergies, etc., on record before you even get to the hospital for delivery!

Put your admission procedures here – and pre-register. You will have the opportunity to get all of your information, contacts, insurance, allergies, etc., on record before you are actually admitted to the hospital to have a baby. So if you are blessed with a quick delivery, you're not going to be spitting out portions of information between contractions or begging your best friend to make your spouse leave the room before he alienates the nursing staff. It doesn't feel like it when you are pre-registering, sitting there answering their 347 different questions, but it actually does speed things up a little bit and it is one less thing to think about when the time comes. I strongly recommend that you take a hospital tour. Call Labor and Delivery, or Maternity at the hospital that your OB delivers at and they will tell you when it is offered. Plan an additional half-hour for pre-registration on the day of the tour and not only do you know where to go (which can get surprisingly confused without the hospital tour: some places say the ER, others want you to go to a particular nurses station), but you're in their system.

In the Hospital section, I put my packing list. Things got put on and crossed off as I thought of things and then thought better. There are all kinds of lists and recommendations. One recommendation I followed was to pack a bag one month prior to the planned delivery, and I am very glad that I did so. I treated myself to some things, since most of the toiletry items were duplicated in my own travel bags, but I figured this was a special occasion and went ahead and bought small travel sizes of the more indulgent things and thus also saved having to find my usual toiletry bag in the middle of the night. I left the bag packed and in the closet and we were able to grab it and go without a thought.

Otherwise, what I thought I needed, and what I actually packed were only sort of similar to the lists. Remember, less is more. All of it has to be transported by HAND, usually by one person (that would be the daddy usually), if you transfer rooms and again when you depart.

A basic list, in no way all-inclusive, is:

Pajamas (I got special ones and wore the same ones for both babies[3])

Slippers with no-slip soles or sticky socks

Toiletry kit to include lipstick and powder but especially lotion and Chapstick[4]

CD player with CD or iPod with speakers

A book

Magazines for when you can't concentrate enough to read the book (think "*People*" not "*The Economist*")

A onesie for baby, or footie if it is winter

Baby socks

Underwear

Sanitary pads (in case not provided)

Baby carrier

Birth Plan on 3x5 card, two copies*

Elastic waist pants and comfy shirt

Phone list

Ah, regarding that compilation CD, it does end up being rather subliminal. I sadly can't hear *Enya* now and enjoy it, so choose your music carefully!

If your baby is going to be born overseas, contact the hospital and see what it is that you will need to bring because some things (sheets, hospital gown, etc.)

[3] www.pajamagram.com
[4] I strongly recommend Burt's Bees mama items in their travel size.

are not provided.

The birth plan on a 3x5 index card will be addressed shortly. But there are two copies so the nurses can have one and your spouse or partner can have another; just in case he needs something that looks like a plan.

Most baby-books and websites will have very comprehensive lists for what to take to the hospital. But less is definitely more — we had to move from the neonatal infant room to a maternity room and had to schlep all of the stuff with us. I'd taken way too much the first time, including a pillow, of all things. Remember, if you are there for any length of time (unusual in the U.S.), either before or after the birth, your spouse or partner will likely be VERY grateful to have a useful errand to run (just be forgiving when it isn't exactly what you were thinking of).

Also in this Hospital section, I kept a copy of the letter regarding payment and contact information at the State Department. When you receive your OB MedEvac instructions and your orders, draft a one-page cover letter that outlines how the hospital or doctor's office is supposed to submit the bill to your work organization. Outline each step and be liberal in including it with each and every bill you resubmit for payment. Send the entire pack, bill, letter and forms, *every time*.

Regarding Birth Plans, I think that these are great mental exercises. They make you focus and think. My mother, a neonatal nurse said, "You can have a birth plan or a birth." The birth belongs to the child, they will choose how it happens, not you. And, by the way, it's going to happen no matter what. But you can figure out those things that are important to you. Discuss with your doctor, read, check out the web, but in the end, the nurses will find it much easier if you've been able to get your birth plan on a 3x5 index card that does not contain more than three or four things that are truly important to you.

For reference, my Birth Plan points were:[5]

> 1. I did not want to take drugs unless the pain was hindering the progress of labor.
>
> 2. In order to allow me to move around and walk, I did not want to remain hooked to monitors unless it was medically necessary

[5] Just so you know, my son did NOT read the plan. I ended up getting just one point.

(monitors may be necessary, but they can be taken on and off until you are in the third stage, at which point they are on and you don't care).

3. I did not want an IV unless it was medically necessary. I was willing to have an IV catheter placed in my arm so it would be immediately available as a compromise.

4. I did not want to have a catheter, enema or shave. The catheter would be allowed only if medically necessary (e.g. surgery).

You might have noticed that all my points were things that I did *not* want. I did not personally feel that I knew all of the available choices and couldn't decide between them. I did know that I wanted to keep the birth as natural as possible, and therefore identified those things that might impair that. Your OB may have a birth plan program that is preferred, although I found the online quizzes and questionnaires to be most helpful in helping me define what few points I wanted to articulate. And I knew that I wanted to avoid surgery if possible.

F. SOCIAL SECURITY

Your child will need its social security number sooner rather than later. This process very much depends on the state! In some states, it is relatively easy. For instance, with some communication with the nurses and staff, you may be able to expedite the Birth Certificate. Then, by going to the County Records Office with your child's birth certificate, they can issue the number right there. In other states, it may be a smidgen harder. You may need to ask that the hospital **not** file for a social security number automatically if their automatic process is longer than your timeline allows. You may need to keep checking for when the birth certificate is filed (thank goodness for the Internet), before you can even apply, and then it may need to be in person. In some states, the father cannot apply for a child's social security number without the mother present, even if he is listed on the child's birth certificate.

So, long story short, check what the procedures are for filing for a social security number and birth certificate. Interestingly enough, sometimes those bassinets that are in the labor and delivery rooms have stuff in them, including information on just this! Open those little drawers and look in there – it might be just extra diapers and cloths for cleanup, or you may be lucky enough to have a whole binder full of information or welcome gifts from companies. Otherwise, the maternity ward nurses can usually point you in the right direction and they are a good place to start asking questions.

Either way, in the Social Security section of the binder, keep all that information, including phone numbers, business hours and location. You will need to know the sequence of events that have to happen to GET a social security number, for instance whether the birth certificate is processed, you take it in and they mail back a social security card, OR can you go in and have one printed. Sometimes, with a carefully cultivated point-of-contact, you can go into the office and even though the card hasn't been mailed, if the number has been issued, they might quietly print out the actual number on a piece of paper, if you appear in person and they know that it is because you NEED to get ....

G. A PASSPORT TO TRAVEL

Some of you will require Diplomatic Passports, which have a special desk in DC for processing, and some will need a Tourist Passport. If you use the Diplomatic Travel office, you will also get the appropriate visas for the child's travel. That said, don't get only the Diplomatic Passport; also get a Tourist one. Some posts require that you have both. Check with the Consular Affairs website or your Consul General regarding the new timelines. Take several extra pictures home either way for the visa applications and other credentials in your child's future.

You may be in a city large enough to have your own Passport Office. As things stand now, subject to change of course, passports are currently processed through the Post Office. Diplomatic Passports require a special form, and the postal clerk/passport clerk will review it, accept payment and it is mailed from the Post Office itself. I always include a pre-paid, self-addressed, Express Mail envelope for the return, purchasable right there at the counter. These are not forms that are filled out and mailed from home. The Post Office processing may change in the future, given the Homeland Security changes taking place. However, currently call your Post Office, confirm times, locations, which window, which clerk if possible and check if you have to have both parents present. Also re-confirm whether both parents have to be present, and what would be required if they cannot be. It may be a notarized letter, or there may be a different requirement. This is particularly important if both parents won't be present for the entire MedEvac period.

To get a passport, your child will need a passport photo! Now, I've heard differing reports, some saying their digital photograph was sufficient, but here's the official word, from a Consul General. Either a professional photograph or home digital camera photograph will work for passports. The baby's head has to be exactly the right size in the photo, the picture cannot be altered to blow it up to make the head the right size or shrink it to the right size. The background color must still be white, all white. The baby's eyes must be open. The baby (who cannot hold his or her head up, by the way) must be looking straight ahead. Oh, and no one's hands can be visible in the photo! So, if your baby is not cooperative, the first recommendation is to wait until after nap and try later. Then, what we did (twice) was put boy baby in a blue onesie and a pink onesie for girl baby[6] and place the child in a car seat with a sheet draped on it. Put your hand up the baby's onesie and cup that tiny little chin between your thumb and forefinger and have someone else take the photo. All of this happened at the Insta-Photo guy across the street from the Main Post Office, where the Passport Office was located, because it was part of his business to make sure the "passport photos" really were correct. Another recommendation I've received is Sears! They take pictures all the time and have the patience and practice to pull it off. If you are willing, you can do a white sheet on a bed, standing above the child but not throwing a shadow, but remember that unaltered head-size is critical on the photos. It isn't as frustrating or strange as it sounds, but it makes for some interesting stories!

Confirm times and locations, clerk or window and if both parents must be present.

I not only sent the application for passport, with photo and documentation by USPS Express mail, I included a pre-paid, self-addressed USPS Express mail envelope for return. Remember to write down the tracking number before they seal up that envelope. You can do the same with Federal Express, send it FedEx and include the pre-paid return FedEx envelope. Those tracking numbers will save you a lot of time and concern.

Then you wait. This is the hardest part, waiting for the passport. However, at the same time, you will have the distraction of trying to arrange your travel, which is why I keep Passport and Travel in this section of the binder.

Immediately after birth, planning for a departure of approximately eight weeks after delivery, you will begin corresponding with whichever travel agency your

[6] Throw political correctness, and not wanting to put girls in pink and boys in blue, right out the door. This actually is helpful down the road when the child no longer looks like the picture and a foreign passport control officer is peering out at you at 3am trying to determine if they are looking at a boy passport or girl passport since the names are as foreign to them as Traktorbek is to you.

organization works with. My recommendation, and the recommendation of others, is to book the shortest possible route with the fewest number of connections. The chapter on Travel will cover this in considerably more detail. If possible, upgrade to Business Class for both of you. If not, beg and plead if you have to, for the bulkhead section and request the airline have the bassinet/baby bed available for you. Confirm this seating and availability every time you call and particularly 24 hours before departure.

Some folks have run into issues where they are not 'allowed' the bulkhead seat if their child has a paid seat, and the State Department does require that all travelers on Diplomatic Passports have paid, assigned seats. A little honey goes a lot further than vinegar when talking to the Purser (skip the stewards and stewardesses) when trying to work this out. One note on the bulkhead bassinets: use the security straps – if there is turbulence in flight (your child is not in the bassinet during landing and take off), the baby must be secure. Low and loose, but definitely around that little body so no one has to catch the child (happened, but thankfully, not to me).

The airlines could care less and will occasionally try to pull the 'overbooked' card and say your child must be a lap-baby so another, paying customer, can be assigned the seat. First of all, your child's seat was paid for, by the U.S. Government no less, so bumping him or her is no more acceptable than bumping you. I've discovered that I've lost my embarrassment-gene while traveling with small or infant children. I've gotten further with a smile and understandingly saying, "I understand your difficulties. You may rebook both of us (or all three of us!) and place us in a hotel at your expense, but I need a receipt for all changes since the U.S. government paid for both of our tickets and I will need to document the change." Suddenly it isn't as easy as the child being held by the mama, and they pick a less complicated customer. I've had an American airline move my son from Business to economy (to sit next to his grandmother), forget to feed him, and never refund the difference in cost. I've had them attempt to turn my children into lap babies. I've even been forced into missing flights and then required to endure a forced layover of four days, because the post we were traveling to had only two flights a week. You are a paying customer; you just happen to pay every time they take taxes out of your paycheck.

Some other things that have come up when it comes to traveling back to your post are a letter of release from the non-present parent (usually Dad) and a

Power of Attorney. Believe it or not, some airlines will not allow you to fly with your child, particularly out of the country (and gods help you if you're going to a 'stan), if the other parent doesn't know about it – in writing. I say, how would they know if he knows or not? They'd don't, so they assume that he doesn't either. A letter from the father, stating that the family really does all live out-of-U.S., together even, and that mother is bringing baby HOME, not stealing it, may be necessary. So, if Daddy is going to be departing before mother and child, get that letter written and have it notarized. You may not be asked for it, but then again, you might be! We were asked for it both times. My children have traveled in many instances with their grandmother and not been asked for it (apparently borrowing your grandchildren is not frowned upon). We also had on hand a specific Power of Attorney, a document that basically states that if one parent wasn't present, the other was allowed to travel internationally with the child(ren). It sounds bizarre, but it is a scary world that we live in apparently. An example of the Power of Attorney is in Appendix 2, for your reference.

If both parents are not traveling back with the infant, a notarized letter of authorization may be needed.

If your child is born overseas, there are procedures in place for registering the birth and receiving a U.S. passport. As soon as you receive your local birth certificate, you must take that and proof of citizenship of the parents, to the nearest U.S. Consular office. They will file a Consular Report Birth Abroad (CRBA), apply for passport and social security number. You should check with your Consular office regarding the procedures and timelines prior to the birth of the child if possible.

And that is what the binder does; it organizes a whole bunch of chaos. It doesn't contain it all. Something else always comes up, but it also gives you ONE thing to carry around, fitting conveniently in a diaper bag, instead of digging for notes or finding sticky notes in the bottom of your purse (pre-diaper bag incarnation).

This was the actual letter that Husband wrote to authorize our travel from U.S. back to our first post. Names have been changed to protect the innocent (that would be me), and yes, it really was written on April 1, 2002, on Embassy letterhead, notarized and faxed direct to the airline (and I carried a copy), because we found out on March 31, 2002 that we needed it to fly on the 3rd of April.

1 April 2002

I, Buffalo Bill, Third Secretary, Vice Consul of the Embassy of the United States of America in First Post, Former Soviet Republic, husband of Annie Oakley, father of Little Bill Hickock do grant them my permission to travel from the United States of America, to our residence in First Post, Former Soviet Republic. Please speed, assist and aid them in any way possible, as they are good and kind people, who are very worthy of your efforts.

With all due sincerity,

Buffalo Bill

Third Secretary
Vice Consul
Embassy of the United States of America
First Post, Former Soviet Republic

Subscribed and sworn to before me this first day of April, 2002

Billy Bob Smith
Consul of the United States
Consul General
First Post, Former Soviet Republic.

While I recommend neither such sarcasm nor such formality, a letter is helpful and sometimes required.

"Authorization Letter"

Meanwhile, back on Planet Pregnancy...

GETTING AHEAD OF THE GAME (because it is a game!)

Eventually one of the thoughts you may have after getting over the shock of a positive pregnancy test, is realizing how much you don't know. If you are of a certain demographic, you'll immediately think, "I need a class!" on childbirth, CPR, parenting, breastfeeding, you name it! There is just so much we don't know! You can't control it, but once again, you can organize it. The list of parenting books that we found most useful, complete with commentary, is in Appendix 3, because otherwise the list derails the end of this chapter. If you are able, read the parenting books three times as much as you read the pregnancy books, and do it while you are pregnant. You're just not going to have the same time or focus after the baby is born, and parenting will continue forever.

CHILDBIRTH CLASSES

If you are lucky and you're where you can get classes, I recommend them for the sheer eye-opening quality of it. Like me, you may have distinct opinions on operant conditioning versus paying attention to what your body is trying to do and will recommend that you read, research and ask questions. Your OB may have a preferred method. You may choose a doula or midwife instead. Keep in mind that every method wants you to choose them as the one and only best method out there. I ended up using a sort of modified Bradley Method[7] with one or two Lamaze[8] additions and not a small part of humor. My opinion was that Lamaze teaches the mother to distract herself and detach from the situation, although you should check out their website for their angle on it and discuss with your provider. For me, The Bradley Method focused me on what the body was doing and the exercises are to practice doing it. But, again, read the information and decide for yourself. Both are a bit militant in how they want to be practiced, and I can say with authority, take what you need and disregard the rest, entirely and without guilt. The baby did not read either method or take the class.

Whatever method you choose, I have a friend who asked me to please include the most important bit of advice she received regarding delivery – "do not look at the clock on the wall of the hospital." Let anyone else in the room keep track of time. As an aside, do ask someone, like the nurse (who will have the most wits about her when the time comes, the doctor will be focused, and mother and father will be worlds away), to please make note of the first thing that each parent says when he or she first see the baby. The most amazing things come out of a parent's mouth and it is so difficult to recall.

CPR

Take an infant and child CPR class, which is part of the full American Heart Association CPR certification.[9] It is usually offered at the hospitals on a regular basis and your OB or pediatrician can recommend where to go. If not, try the local Red Cross or American Heart Association. Take it and take it again every time you are in the U.S. or when re-certification is offered. Really. Discuss with

[7] www.bradleybirth.com/FAQs.aspx
[8] www.lamaze.org/Default.asp
[9] www.americanheart.org/presenter.jhtml?identifier=3011764

your pediatrician the importance of taking it due to where you live. The fact that you don't live in the U.S. and are usually well away from, um, shall we say, reliable medical care, let alone emergent care, and don't even have 911 and therefore don't just want this class but need it, will bring your circumstances into focus more than most other things. They will be very helpful if they understand your circumstances. My pediatrician helped me create a very thorough Emergency Kit, more of something you'd see in an ambulance, rather than a standard First Aid Kit (which I also have). Once they are not just hearing but paying attention and understanding, they start processing the complexities. Be patient. Repeat yourself.

Embassies do occasionally offer special pediatric classes, either childcare, CPR, re-certifications, or food handling and preparation. Be sure that the CPR classes are taught by a certified instructor, not just someone who is certified themselves. You can learn it either way, but the instructor is the only one who can offer the test and give you your certification. This information changes all the time! I've taken the test every two years for the past six and seen three different changes. If you have in-home child-care, do express the interest in having the class offered in the native language for them as well. Some Embassies will do this free of charge, but even if it costs money, it is worth it for the safety and well-being of your child.

Take infant and child CPR, part of the American Heart Association CPR certification courses, and keep your certification current.

CHILD CARE CLASSES

Yet another good idea is child-care classes. I didn't take one, but I had some built in. The first time I was living with my best friend and I knew that my mother was returning to First Post with us. My mother was the one who gave the classes when she was a neonatal nurse. The second time around, I stayed with my mother for five months before the birth, with a two-year old toddler, and learned more about child management pre- and post-Daughter than I ever knew before. I still need the annual parental software reboot from my own mother to keep me on track. Not everyone can borrow my mom for a month going back to post (although you might ask, she's probably willing if you buy the ticket!), these classes can range from seminars to the very well-worthwhile full on handling in a daycare.

They are all very informative, but remember, TAKE WHAT YOU NEED AND DISCARD

THE REST! Most will let you walk away with some information that you can put to use. You won't find one magically perfect method, but just because some parts don't fit your family does not mean that all the information is junk. Take what works for you, a little from here, a little from there. You are the parent and, here's the stunning part: you CAN decide. Even if you don't think you can, think you're not qualified, or don't have a clue, you can. You are a parent, and making decisions whether you want to or not. Failure to make a decision is a decision in itself. You can change your mind, adjust accordingly, or try again. So make an informed choice and give yourself permission to trust yourself for a little while.

Regarding the parenting books in the appendix, the most important tidbit I have to is to read them while you're pregnant. This is the only chance you have to not just read, but read and digest, because that time to process information runs out astonishingly fast once you are a parent. I read a lot less in the first four years of being a parent than I did pre-parent, but don't fall for that line that you won't be able to read again for years and years. I continued to read throughout my children's infant and toddler-hood and (more on this later) they do need to see this as a part of your life (if it is).

> In all your reading and research, take what you need and discard the rest! Don't "throw the baby out with the bathwater" and disregard the entire book because of one thing you didn't like.

INTERNET

Another resource appears on the Internet. I personally like the ivillage.com/parenting page, with information from conception to parenting (they sent this neat little weekly note about where the baby was in development and what my body was doing too, without the scary extras). Signing up for newsletters during the pregnancy, mom-to-mom chats and forums, as well as easy searchability make this a convenient resource. My lifestyle, to include the times that I was online and connection speeds (or lack thereof), and the information spectrum gave me all the flexibility that I needed. The sites that sent information on a daily or weekly or monthly basis are nice because it is 'easy' information. If you value your privacy, you will need to confirm whether or not they share your information. You will need to be aware of their 'source' (are they sponsored by a drug company, are they run by Nestle or Gerber). Most sites are saturated with advertisements as well and you will discover all kinds of things that they think you need.

Don't discount the information available, but remember that the Internet is not censored – you might be reading a right-wing or left-wing radical sites just as easily as the American Medical Association; so it is up to you to keep that in mind. Schools and universities are good resources, but they do publish their students' non-peer reviewed papers as well. Just because it is on some sort of NGO (.org) or academic site (.edu) doesn't make it right – it just may have more peer review or scrutiny. Take it all with a grain of salt and choose carefully.

Parenting.com, the folks who publish Parenting magazine, and Parents.com (ditto the magazine part), also have web-based resources. The Parenting website has the Ages and Stages area that I liked in the magazine (I didn't subscribe, but the magazines were passed around at post with one caveat, "Don't tear things out!"), and a Pregnancy Planner. I found the organization of the Parenting magazine to be slightly more modern, short little blurbs of articles, tips and hints, text box format and less time intensive. The Parenting website is point-and-click easy. *Parents*, the magazine, has been around longer, and is really well organized, with articles broken down by Food, and You and Play, Health, and Age-by-Age Advice up to 12 years old. The web-community of *Parents* is less 'friendly', but still perfectly navigable. There are several more websites, parenthub.com and parenthood.com, etc., etc. Talk to your pediatrician or OB to see if they have any recommendations.

When we arrived at First Post, we were barely pregnant, and I was nervous, considering the third world (although it was really second world plus) conditions, environmental factors that I had no control over like pollution and such, and most importantly distance from my family and 'proper' medical care. I spent most of my pregnancy in self-imposed isolation, although not completely. Suddenly I was going from the world of Young Professional Couples to the world of diapers and birthing stories!

Go to a play-group or two before your baby is born if you want some culture shock. It was hard enough not being in the U.S., but you will be seriously culture shocked from not being a mama! Single friends of mine say it is mutual; they go to a book club that has a number of new moms and the conversation deviates to breastfeeding and labor and delivery stories and they feel like the fifth wheels! It took some effort on our part not to lose our single and/or young professional couple friends, but we were pretty persistent and babies are amazingly portable. Remember, your friends don't know what your comfort levels are, and they don't know that you don't know either! So they will worry about waking the baby, interrupting and stuff like that and assume that you'd rather be with 'your family'. You are going to have to communicate with them, a lot, or the associations will slowly wither on the vine.

Yes, others will pop up, but friendships are like plants, they need to be tended and looked after in order to grow. Suddenly dropping 'off people's radar' is disconcerting and annoying, and sometimes a little sad. We fought this by packing the baby up and going too! Breastfeeding was mostly something I did discreetly and avoided discomfiting others simply because they mostly didn't notice! Son went pretty much everywhere we went, and we didn't change where we went much. You discover that initial hesitation, Mama Bear is what I call it, of not wanting to let your child go when someone asks, "Can I hold him?" and that it leads to everyone wanting to hold him and him getting comfortable with that (depending on the child!).

As a result of a lot of tending and effort with Son, we have some sustained friendships because they were all his family. It is harder with a second child, because the toddler child isn't quite as portable as the new baby, but it can be done. You will be naturally categorized into the Young Family group, and automatically copied on that kind of correspondence and activities, but you don't have to belong to JUST that group or lose any of the others. The trick has been belonging to multiple groups, and getting comfortable with the ones we do choose to belong in. Once your children pass from not-in-school toddlers, the parents of babies and toddlers drop you off their radar, again, unless you make serious effort to counter it. It is a never-ending battle of involuntary, but totally appropriate categorization.

"Culture Shock"

3. A Very Short but Very Important Chapter

No matter what, if you are in an Embassy with a Marine Security Guard detachment, be nice to your Marines. I say this not just because they are usually really nice guys, but because if you have an emergency and only have a local phone line, especially if your post policy is not to allow IVG ('tie') line call patches from home, an emergency might arise and they DO have the power to patch your call to a Maryland connection. Post One, in the event of an emergency (such as a poisoning), can help — but it is less complicated if they know you, if you're invariably polite and kind, and of course, if you occasionally feed them. They do need a lot of food!

My personal experience is with Vonage, for which I am ever grateful simply for keeping in touch with family and friends and having a U.S. phone number. Others that I know use Skype and other Internet based phone/computer connections. We signed up for Vonage while in the U.S., and took it (the modem) with us when we moved overseas. You need a digital phone. We like the cordless ones (analog phones such as those provided in most homes do not work), and it fits into the usual phone line–modem–Vonage sequence that is easily connectible no matter where you are. Another family I know ordered it using their Pouch (via APO) address with no problems. This gives me a US phone number, and easy access to 1-800 numbers without relying on Post One (who is happy to help). That said, it is Internet dependent, so if you do not have ADSL or better, it won't work well at all.

On the last page of this chapter is what I call the Print Page. Copy and fill in that page and include your contact info for your child care provider (local and U.S.) and tape it in your Kid Kit (Children's First Aid). Check with your insurance provider because some of them, such as Blue Cross/Blue Shield, have an ask-a-nurse or dial-a-doctor hotline. Include this number.

Talk with your doctor and get his or her input on a Children's Emergency Kit (which looks suspiciously like my Veterinary Emergency Kit). I've outlined in Appendix 4 what is in mine, so you can copy the page and shop if you are so inclined. It is covered in great detail in the Medical chapter.

Make a Kid Kit, which is simple child First Aid. Again, there is an Appendix 4, for the list, and greater detail in the Medical chapter (the chapter most everyone wanted). This one (Chapter 7) is also on hand for what I call Murmuring Mamas; those mothers or nannies that hover and murmur over each bump, bruise, bang, bonk or bing. Sometimes, having some of these things close is enough to forestall a full on panic attack – from the mother (the children tend to take their cue from the mamas).

If you are going to have child-care help (aka, a nanny) take a local map and blow up the section with your neighborhood. Label your American neighbors' homes with a number, then make a list of names and phone numbers for reference. Keep this with your Embassy phone list and protect the information in the same way that you do the phone list. Check with your RSO if you are not sure if this is advisable or not, as it is strictly post-dependent. This was helpful for a variety of reasons, not just area familiarization.

Pack a go bag! It doesn't matter if it is duplicate stuff. Keep passports and important documents on CD with it, as well as back up medications.

When the daughter of one of our American neighbors locked herself out of her home, we had both parents' cell phones, knew their names and had their daughter's name too. Designate one American neighbor as your emergency point of contact, and clearly label them as such. This person should have an extra key to your home if it is available. This is useful whether you're on a compound or in a local neighborhood.

Explain an emergency contact process to your family or household help. Decide who is contacted first and second, put your designated neighbor on the list, and ensure that a point of contact at the Embassy is on the list, in case all else fails. Talk with your designated neighbor about your concerns and cares, and whom they would call in the U.S. if necessary. This sounds extreme, but believe me, when you need this, you are glad it is done and in one place. And if you never need it, the world is a better place.

PACK A GO BAG. It doesn't matter if it is all duplicate stuff. If it is all in the same place, with passports and important documents, it is worth the small expense of duplicating if you actually do need to use it. Scan your important documents to CD and leave the originals in a safe deposit box at home where someone (with a key) could get to the originals if they needed to. Label the CD "Muy Importante" or something and keep it with your passports (tourist and diplomatic), immunization records, mini-medical records (covered in the Medical chapter of course), credit cards (which you are probably not using overseas if you are in a tier 2 or higher place), a calling card (with minutes available preferably), and toiletries for one full day (when sizes change, be sure to go in and switch out the diapers). Include some odds and ends necessities in the Go Bag, and then forget you have it. It makes looking for passports easier for normal travel and it makes it possible to focus on the other gazillion details if you really do have to go. My theory here is that if you have it, you will never need it. From my lips to God's ears, please.

Our CLO recently send around a list, which I will share for you here, because it is relevant and compiled from the State Department website.

ITEMS TO HAVE READY IF YOU NEEDED TO DEPART IN TWO HOURS
In an evacuation, you can usually carry one suitcase.

> Clothes, including clothes for the next season.
> The average evacuation is several months.

Hand carry:

> Passports, drivers' licenses, visa if needed (check all are current), State Dept ID badge
>
> Cash (local and U.S.) – ATMs may not function
>
> Credit Cards, ATM card
>
> Birth/marriage/naturalization certificates and any other legal documents
>
> Medications (prescription and over the counter)
>
> Medical records, immunization cards
>
> Eyeglasses and prescriptions
>
> Current power of attorney
>
> Insurance policies, including auto and title and registration of car
>
> Address book
>
> Computer disks containing current resumés (for family members), photos, written or photo inventory of household effects
>
> Extra cell phone minute cards
>
> Provide a plan for pets left behind
>
> Plan for someone to pay household staff and other bills

Employees are evacuated to their home office (usually DC). Decide where in the U.S. other family members want to go as a safehaven. Anywhere outside the U.S. needs pre-authorization.

The Go Bag is not a substitute for a two-week emergency kit. If your CLO or RSO doesn't have a list immediately available, there are recommendations on the State Department website. While neither the Go Bag or Two-Week Emergency Supply situation are likely to happen in the vast majority of posts, it is a weight off your shoulders to have both, if ever circumstances should warrant.

SUPPLIES TO HAVE AT HOME IN CASE YOU CANNOT GO SHOPPING FOR TWO WEEKS.

Drinking water for two weeks (approximately 1 gallon/4 liters per person per day)

Non-perishable food

Shelf stable milk

Flashlights

Extra Batteries

Candles

Lighter or matches

Non-electric can opener

Battery operated radio

First aid supplies

Toilet paper

Toiletries

Pet food, if needed

Any medication taken regularly

First Aid kit

A supply of local currency

All members of household (including school-aged children) should practice using radios. If you have a car, always keep the fuel tank at least half full.

Copy the below information if you don't already have a calendar or address book that this information can be easily accessed.

- -

1-800-222-1222 Poison Control
This is the number of Poison Control, nationwide. It will connect to the closest available center (VA if calling from an Embassy, within your area code if calling from a Vonage phone).

- -

Write down the number of your pediatrician here, or their 24-hour number:

Dr. _____ at (_____)_____-_____

A calling card, just in case: _____

- -

Ask-A-Nurse 1-800-888-5551
Explain that you are a U.S. citizen currently serving overseas and need some first world, American help because you have little to no health care options where you are (whether it is true or not, it does get their attention) and no, you can't call 911.

- -

Med Unit: _____

Med Unit Mobile: _____

Post One: _____

- -

Mom at work: _____

Mom's mobile: _____

Dad at work: _____

Dad's mobile: _____

4. What to Haul

If you are living with a weight allowance (or restriction, depending on your mood), how much stuff you have can be daunting. To haul or not to haul becomes a crucial question! Infants only SEEM to need so much stuff. So much of that stuff is just so USEFUL. Your primary goal is going to be giving the children a routine and regular life overseas, touchstones of what your family would consider normal, in order to give you the framework for the unending task of actually raising them. And in the end, the stuff sometimes makes that task easier.

I can't dictate what you do and do not need; every family is different. I can, however, tell you what I ran into and you can make informed decisions. Since the entire book is about making informed decisions, it's not a bad place to begin. I have three sections for The Stuff: Things You Simply Must Have, Things That are Bonus Items and Things that Could Be Either Category. Finally, I end with some shipping information, and things TO ship.

THINGS YOU SIMPLY MUST HAVE

> A car seat
>
> Universal wheels/strollers
>
> Baby gates
>
> Bins & bungees

A car seat is a must. These are critical for keeping your child safe in countries that don't have driver's education classes, traffic laws, or safe and reliable transportation. Car seats also make airline travel, and arrival at destination, more manageable, and are well worth checking as luggage or actually taking onto the plane as an infant seat. When purchasing a car seat, check for the FAA approved sticker, and when actually traveling, take the instruction manual with you (I tape it to the seat) so you can show the cabin attendants that yes, it is allowed and approved. Infant seats fit easily into the airline seats. Because of the ever-changing seat size on airlines, the forward-facing child seat, over 10lbs, does not always fit. If it does, a seatbelt extender will secure it safely. The booster size, over 20lbs, is not airline approved as it requires a three-point harness. Do keep in mind that in Europe, the airlines generally (but not always) prefer that the infant be held on the lap, with the seat-belt extender around the infant, whether or not an infant seat is present. In the U.S., seat-belt extenders are not deemed safe or appropriate for infants that are lap-babies. This apparent disconnect serves to emphasize the constant need to be flexible.

A stroller of some sort is helpful. I felt that Universal Wheels, which are just frames that the baby carrier clips onto and are made by two companies that I know of, were a definite must for us. Again, when we needed a stroller, it was for transportation from the house to the car, the car to the Embassy, or the car to someone else's house, and back again. The ease of the Universal Wheels' collapsing and opening, and simply leaving it in the trunk, made it ideal for those purposes. At our Third Post you were taking your life in your hands to walk anywhere near traffic, and sidewalks were as potholed as the roads. A stroller of some type is an absolute must for airports. I bought a fancy jogging-type stroller, with all the bells and whistles when returning to our First Post, and due to the climate and type of city, we hardly used it at all, as Son was an infant, even though the infant seat snapped on. When Son was a toddler, we were still not in places where we could use it as a stroller; you know, taking him on a stroll. There was nowhere to walk TO at our Second Post. We used the Universal Wheels much more often. Whatever you choose, ensure that the stroller (also known as an airport-transportation-device) has hard plastic or hard rubber wheels, not inflatable ones.

Another item that I can't recommend strongly enough is baby gates. There are several types, but I recommend the "old-fashioned" ones that are wooden with a lever. I am astonished at how durable these are compared to the hard plastic ones. Too much levering on the plastic ones and SNAP!, they are no longer usable as safety gates. When the kids had out-grown baby gates[1], I was able to continue to use them to block off fireplaces and keep cat boxes safe from the puppy. I also have gotten great mileage out of the "play yard". This is several sections of hard plastic baby gate that snap together and can form a 'yard' for a child to play in, outside. We've used it now to contain infants during toddler playtime, to provide a visual barrier to toddlers during play groups, and most importantly now, to reinforce fort walls and drape blankets over. Not all posts can or will provide built-in baby-gates for your stairs. Don't assume that they will, so plan accordingly. You may be pleasantly surprised, but you will keep your children safe regardless.

[1] Outgrowing is also known as the mastering of the power to open the gates by themselves.

Toys are a practical requirement when you have children. Toys and books are going to be a part of your life now whether you buy them or simply receive them as gifts. Keeping them under control is addressed later in the book (in a chapter called Controlling the Chaos), but we chose to make Fisher Price Little People our tried and true constant toys. Son has a bin of Matchbox toys and Daughter now has a bin of ponies. Many families choose many different means of maintaining some sort of control over their toy population, but I see a lot of bins everywhere.

Bungee cords are a must-have. It is funny, but they are so useful, and stay useful for a long time! I keep one in the outside pocket of our largest carry-on. When traveling with the stroller part of the car-seat/stroller combination, they help hold things together. When moving with the luggage cart, they keep things from traveling faster than you do, allowing you to focus on keeping your child safe. They can also secure the car seat or booster while you go from home or car to airport check-in. It doesn't seem like that distance from the car to the counter is all that far; but it is when you are trying to keep things from collapsing and keeping a hand on a child.

THINGS THAT ARE BONUS ITEMS

Changing Table

Portable crib

One bonus item is a changing table. Although it is convenient, it isn't necessary. I've known people to do entirely without, and others who used the concave changing pad on a dresser or counter-top. The actual table is lovely, but it is also extra weight.

A portable crib like a Pack-n-Play is lifestyle dependent. I found this to be a nice extra, but it didn't fit our lifestyle at all – it was too heavy and too unwieldy to easily pack! We ended up leaving it in the U.S. for when we visited and used it like an extra crib rather than a playpen. I did not find it large enough for use as a playpen but for napping we had familiar props like blanket, pillow and eventually a favorite "baby" (stuffed animal), so it made our naps portable. The infants don't particularly care where they nap, for the most part, as long as the setting is safe and secure. Once they are crawling, this is more challenging, but if you are on a schedule, you can at least plan your outings.

Breast pump

Bouncy chairs/swings/ExerSaucer

Crib

A breast pump must be on a list somewhere. Since I've had people swear that they saved their sanity and since I didn't use them at all, I decided that this was the first and foremost "it depends" item on the list. I had one child who wouldn't even consider a bottle, no matter how badly his daddy wanted to help feed him or how patiently and repeatedly we tried. I never even tried to pump with the second child. That said, I have been told that a good breast pump is worth its weight in gold. Working moms out there swear by it; especially when having to struggle, for the first time, to get an Embassy to offer an appropriate nursing room setting. I have been told that Medella is a trusted brand. Their website has listings for suggested retail locations and available discounts.

There are a variety of brands of breast pump to choose from. Use your own judgment to make your own choice – whether it is via published product reviews, asking at the hospital or your doctor, or a friend's recommendation. Before buying, define why you are buying it. Is it an occasional supplement or will it help you pump daily? Do you need something portable or will you be in one place every time you pump? Do you need something with a motor, and if so, do you need a transformer? Once you've answered the why questions, you can find a pump that fits your needs.

Children do need distractions. Bouncy chairs and swings and other containment devices can be wonderful, but you might not be able to predict which your child will prefer before you meet your child! Bouncy chairs and swings do not have a terribly long life-span; they keep your child occupied until they are a year old or less, give or take a few months. There are well-published things to remain vigilant about – not just the swings and chairs that have been recalled, but also the weight of the child, the straps, and the toys that dangle down. Most of them come in small enough boxes to be able to be shipped via Diplomatic Pouch or APO/DPO. But which one works depends on the baby!

My son loved both, as long as he was introduced to each slowly. There was no plunking him in and turning him on, it had to be a slow process. He is a Cautious

Child and it was a multi-step process, but then it was lovely. He had a great portable one, that really did break down flat! My daughter, who could be described as Spirited under most circumstances, couldn't stand either because she felt trapped (which IS the whole point). Another similar containment device was the ExerSaucer, which I found incredibly useful for crawling children. I could take a shower and get dressed (rather fast regardless) without worrying if Son was up or down or Daughter was asleep or awake. I parked it in the bathroom with me, and then we moved on to the bedroom, ExerSaucer and all, and had conversation the whole time.

Another item that could be a Must Have or a Bonus Item is a crib! The crib itself is, of course, a necessity, but whether or not to ship it and haul it is the question. With Son, the Embassy provided a crib, but not everyone has that luxury, and then you can run into the challenge of European sizes versus U.S. sizes (EVERYthing in the U.S. seems to be supersized, including cribs). My U.S. crib sheets fit fine on the European size baby mattress, which is thinner and longer than the U.S. version. You will need to check dimensions and know your own comfort level for how sheets fit. I used sheet bungees (I don't know what they are really called) to hold the sides of the sheets together and reduce slipping. The Embassy crib worked fine and before we left First Post we purchased a child's bedroom set. This set could be used at toddler height and morph into a Big Boy Bed as he got older. We had made the conscious decision that part of the weight that we would haul would be Son's bedroom set so that he would always have 'his bedroom', regardless of the house it was in. With Daughter, there was no Embassy crib available, and we purchased a convertible crib. We went with the more expensive convertible crib for the longest use so it would be 'her bedroom' and a familiar item. These purchases will allow us to move the furniture around and still get the longest use from the furniture without having to replace it. She will eventually require some additional furniture, but they are still sharing a room at this point, so we haven't reached that point.

TOYS AND TRADITIONS

Haul the toys and kid books. Really. These items get out of control quickly, but if you are diligent about meeting the space requirements when it comes to the actual moves, there are always children who need toys at the posts you are assigned to, or as a donation to the CLO office and/or Medical Unit. With more than a ton of books to my name[2], I am a firm believer that you can't have too many books. One thing about books though, not only is it beneficial to read to

---

[2] Literally two thousand pounds of books not in my household effects, they are mostly in storage, but we regularly move well-over than twenty boxes of books per move.

the children young, even as an infant, but, to instill a culture of reading, they will need to see you reading also. A friend of ours was distressed that her teenage daughter wasn't a reader in spite of everything having been 'done right' to set the child up to love reading. The mother certainly loved to read. But the mother usually read in bed, so the child had never seen reading as something one just did.

To try to keep a handle on things and avoid toy-overload, we have two family traditions. First is Toy Trade. This involves their own toys, not inter-family trades, and requires that they put away some of their toys to take others out. To keep clutter down, Toy Trade is usually done weekly (when they were little) or as needed as they hit pre-school ages. On Sunday we did a Big Clean of the playroom and traded toys at the same time. Not all of our toys are out at once. Some of them remain on the shelf and we keep around four or five things out. Son always wants his cars available and now Daughter is heavily invested in playing with her ponies. Everything else rotates. Children can be taught that things on the shelf are not available to play with, and when they are older, they can be taught to put something UP in order to take something else down. This means that I now have the flexibility to trade something outside of the Big Clean days. I also have the flexibility to insist that they wait, dependent on what I am trying to accomplish (e.g. if I am asked nicely with manners, the reward is the trade, if they are whiny and rude, we wait).

Since both of my children are winter babies, most of their new toys would arrive in one thirty-day period and the month from December 23rd to January 23rd would be incredibly expensive. If we hadn't come up with some sort of solution, it would have been overwhelming. Therefore we created the tradition of Family Fun Day. This is a large birthday party for the entire family (yes, parents celebrate their birthdays on this day also). This way we only gift twice a year, once at the end of December and once again around June 21st or so. Family members had a bit of a hard time with it initially, but if a birthday gift arrived around Christmastime (and their real birthdays[3]), we wrote a thank you card and said we were holding it for Family Fun Day. Then we wrote a real thank you card when we opened the gift.

I sincerely believe that the best part of both Christmas and Family Fun Day is that one of the integral parts of it is the children think that we have to give away toys in order to get NEW toys. Before each event, we sit down together and pick a toy or two, which they take to the CLO or donate to an orphanage. We are

38   [3] On their real birth-dates they got a birthday cake and a small gift from the family, but we don't have a party, just a small acknowledgement.

also very lucky not to be bombarded by commercials, which is helpful in keeping the Gimmies down to a manageable level.

THINGS WORTH THE SHIPPING

A few things that are worth the hassle of ordering, mailing and shipping, while at a post, not as a part of your household effects shipment. One of those things is children's' magazines. I have subscribed to magazines from Carus Publishing[4] since the children were born. This isn't about managing stuff, but I also doubt that you will keep them ALL the issues. To avoid ending up with a mountain of kids magazines, donate to the CLO or Medical Unit for their waiting room, a local English language preschool or any orphanage. You can also share with a family that subscribes to a different children's magazine like *Highlights* for Children.[5] Carus Publishing offers *Babybug* for infants, which is a mailed board book. *Ladybug* and *Click* are for children to age 6, *Ladybug* being a literature approach and *Click* being a science approach. They love getting their own magazines, although we are having to be more careful about sitting together and reading them, rather than leaving them to be read at will. The magazines contain crafts and activities that can be done together. I've also tried the Scholastic book programs[6], which I enjoyed, but I had trouble keeping up with the address changes and ended up ordering books via amazon.com or other sites instead of remaining in the club.

Additionally, if you haven't joined amazon.com's "Amazon Prime" membership, it is a good thing for anyone ordering books, DVDs or, now just about anything household oriented. Many websites besides amazon.com have these types of programs, and if you have things you ship on a regular basis, read into their offers to see if it meets your needs.

NetGrocer has been a life-saver for this family. We found that too many of the things that the family likes in terms of comfort foods or familiar toiletries cannot be shipped in the Consumables allowance. A year or two's supply of Cheerios doesn't taste the same by the end. We place a monthly order.

A note on the 'clubs', such as the Disney DVD club, Scholastic, etc.; remember to ask a customer service representative if they have a program for military or other overseas participants. Scholastic waived the automatic mailing of each month's selection if you were overseas, although it was necessary to use an APO/DPO address to participate and some posts might not have that option.

---

[4] www.cricketmag.com/shop_magazines.asp
[5] http://www.highlights.com/jump.jsp?itemType=CATEGORY&itemID=345
[6] www://clubs.scholastic.com/cool/login.jsp

While this story would actually be more appropriate in the Food chapter, it also involves shipping, so I will include it here. Besides, my children asked me to please include this story (probably because it makes Mama look silly).

I am an avid NetGrocer user. While you cannot use it to circumvent your consumables order, there are things like ... well ... dried soup that are best purchased at this particular post via NetGrocer. Once, when returning from the U.S. and suffering the worst jet-lag I have ever experienced because my children de-lagged at different paces for the first time ever, I was desperate for easy dinner ideas. I went to the large grocery store, a western style one, with goods from Europe and Turkey and bought, among other things, dried soup (the kind where you add 500ml of water and bring to a boil). This was a trusted brand of soup too, not something unpronounceable, something that I had used when living in Europe.

I'm not entirely sure how long it took for the soup to transit to where we were, and it never occurred to me to look for an expiration date. That night I went ahead and prepared soup, with fresh biscuits to take the edge off of it being an easy dinner idea. Son and Daughter washed hands and sat down, and Daughter said, "I don't think that I want to eat this."

"It's ABC soup, sweetheart. I think you'll like it."

"Do the worms like it?"

"What worms?" I asked, thinking this was something they'd read or seen during the day.

"The ones in my soup." She answered.

I hightailed it to the table and sure enough, she had ABC soup, with worms. Thankfully the meal worms had been boiled and were probably just protein at this point. But, as she pointed out, they still had eyes.

"You do not have to eat Worm Soup!" I told them. And they thought that it was the funniest thing ever that Mama had made Worm Soup.

I ship in my dried soup now.

"Worm Soup"

5. Eating and Food – the Mama

We tend to value a doctor's opinion for a variety of reasons. The best advice will come from a physician who you have learned to trust, with whom you have an open and free dialog, who has taken the time to get to know you and is willing to take the time and effort to communicate as well as listen. This kind of doctor is hard to find, but well worth the effort. My primary physician was outside of our insurance plan for a long time as well, but we decided that it was worth the extra effort of filing the paperwork ourselves. The bottom line is that you need to know that you have choices, and you have the right to exercise them. Hopefully, you will have informed choices resulting from communication with your doctor or primary care provider, but don't be afraid to ask questions.

A trusted physician has told me that medicine in the United States is changing to a liability-shy business. He said, "Doctors are required to tell ALL of their patients that there are no compromises on avoiding drugs of any type, not just illegal drugs, or alcohol during pregnancy, because nothing can be open to interpretation. Interpretation equals liability in this country." Because of my personal history of extraordinarily low blood pressure (even when pregnant), he said that if I wanted to, I could continue to have my single cup of coffee in the morning or glass of wine in the evening. The key to his recommendation was our understanding of the definition of 'moderation.' He also said that since I placed such a strong emphasis on my sleep,[1] and since I was also good about hydrating, if I had a cold I could take a half-dose of NyQuil to help me sleep and fight the cold more effectively.

This is merely a personal example of communicating with your doctor; it is not a recommendation to drink caffeine or alcohol or take over-the–counter medications. I am not a doctor and I cannot and will not and do not recommend that you even CONSIDER these kinds of things without a long and frank discussion with your doctor. And trust me, it will be long and it will have to be frank, because you will get the party line: liability-shy. They don't have the flexibility to open their minds. I pointed out that if I had a cold, I lived in a place where I most certainly could be exposed to tuberculosis, and therefore recovery was of utmost importance to me. He knew that sleep and water were the two primary keys in the recovery of my immune system and I asked him what COMPROMISE we

---

[1] My belief is that if you are rested, you can handle anything. If you are tired, everything, including sickness, can become overwhelming. I continued to get eight hours of sleep nightly, and only for a small time in the Fourth Trimester mode of brand-new-infant did I have to settle for less.

could come to that was safe for me and for the baby.

All of these choices are up to you, but you should make them with all the information available to you. There are women out there who make awful choices regarding over-the-counter drugs, cigarettes, alcohol and illegal drugs, in spite of well-published recommendations otherwise. I'm not recommending that you do anything that you're not comfortable with. You are going to have to be comfortable enough with your decisions to be able to just smile graciously when someone 'corrects' you because of THEIR beliefs and choices. You are not in control of what your body does anymore. That infant is; you are just along for the ride. Being the ride, you have to make responsible choices for the two of you. Many people were not comfortable with my choices, even if they were in moderation, particularly Americans. Most importantly though, I was comfortable enough with my choices to thank people for their concern and move away. Pushy babushkas (grandmothers) in the Former Soviet Union will make you get over not wanting to be impolite very quickly.

Practice moderation in your pregnancy diet and if you haven't before, take the time and effort to now make it balanced moderation.

One word covers nearly all of my Food and Mama choices: MODERATION. Really. Eat a balanced diet; now is the time to make sure that you get those vegetables. And don't eat anything to excess – either item or quantity. Got a craving? Indulge it (if you can; if you're in, say, a country that HAS decent pickles, or strawberries in winter). If you have a craving for DIRT or chalk, that is a medical issue that needs to come to your doctor's attention. Food allergies DO develop during pregnancy. Don't borrow trouble, but don't ignore when milk now gives you serious cramps or meat makes you vomit. If this continues for more than you're comfortable with, do mention it to your doctor; it is not silly. However, if it is a food craving, give yourself permission to indulge it ... in moderation! Got an aversion (I didn't get cravings, but, man, did I get aversions!); then avoid it! My aversions were to meats, which is not such a good thing to lack entirely. So in order not to be immoderate, I had to make an effort to get my protein elsewhere to balance that out. My personal choice was neither vegetarian nor organic. I don't think that a drastic change in diet (unless medically called for such as with gestational diabetes) is an appropriate thing during pregnancy. Stick with what you know; and if that is vegetarian or organic, more power to you! You have more willpower than I!

Towards the end of your pregnancy, you aren't going to be able to eat three solid meals a day. Keep in mind that this is almost like practice for nursing – five or six small meals a day keeps the blood sugars up, nutrients flowing and since your poor stomach is completely squished, deals with the rapidly decreasing space. This is a good habit to remain in and again, in moderation, a little indulgence goes a long way. Towards the end of one pregnancy, and during nursing, I regularly had one piece of cold chicken as a mid-day snack or before nursing. Nothing major, not a bag of chips or box of Little Debbies, but certainly not something I would make an effort to have in the house during other periods of my life!

You'll remember that I said that one word covers NEARLY all of my eating choices? Well, the only thing I do not recommend consuming in moderation is water. Don't moderate that. In fact, while you are pregnant, do your utmost to drink three liters (yes ladies, LITERS) of water a day. A liter is approximately a quart, so that means you're drinking nearly a gallon of water per day. By day, I mean a 24-hour period. This isn't as bad or as extreme as it sounds once it is broken down. One liter should be drunk between the time you wake up (let's say 6am to keep things simple) and noon; the second from noon to 6pm and the third from 6pm to 6am. Setting the liter bottle by your bedside helps (sipping all night long or chugging it at 2am, whatever works for you). This has the additional benefit of making it MUCH easier to add another liter (yes, really) when you are nursing. Water makes milk. Drinking more milk will not increase your milk production. Water and proteins make milk, not more milk – you are not a hose, you are a factory. Remember, we are something like 90% water, AND water is the only substance that can move through cell membranes via osmosis. Water also has NO additives like sugars or sodium. So the new official word out there might be that we can now receive some of our 'water' in soda, juice, milk, coffee or sports drinks, but that is for a non-gestating, non-nursing person. You're BUILDING a baby, and if you are 90% water, so is that child, and it needs that essential building block. I am sticking to what I know, and soda, juice, milk, coffee or sports drinks all require digestion for the water to get into your system. Water can do it by passing through cell walls directly. You and your baby need WATER.

> Many small meals at the end of pregnancy is almost like practice for nursing.

One of my choices, which might not be yours and which you might not agree with, was to allow myself one cup of coffee or one cola and a glass of wine if I wanted. This is not a usual choice for women in the U.S., but it is more common than not outside of the U.S. In the former Soviet Union, it is safer to drink beer than water, cheaper too, and moderating alcohol is not even discussed. Of course, their fetal alcohol syndrome rates are terrifying. In Europe, a glass of wine is even recommended, as is weissbier in Germany. I flew back to the U.S. for the OB-MedEvac and during one of the U.S. carrier flights, I asked for a glass of red wine. The flight attendant was appalled and said, "I can't give that to you! You're pregnant!" A number of thoughts crossed my mind, from saying that there was no liability issue, to asking her to mind her own business. Instead I smiled and said, "Yes, I am, but it is a European pregnancy." I don't know why, because this was an inane answer, and anyone who would have thought it through would have called me on it. Instead she smiled back with the wide, professional hostess smile and said, "Oh! That's wonderful!", and poured my glass of wine!

"European Pregnancy"

6. Eating and Food – Little People

There is a consultant of every flavor when you have a baby, but not one of them will answer all your questions before you can think of them. Lucky for me, my mom was a neonatal infant nurse at a time when this meant lactation consultant, new mom teacher, nurse to mom, and everything a new baby and mother might need – before they all became different nurses. Being my mom, she had no problem telling me what to do. And I can tell you what she told me!

Every consultant has an agenda, whether it is the lactation consultant sponsored by La Leche League or the nurses' assistant whose position is sponsored by Pampers and is required to show you how to diaper using on a certain set of products (which you simply must have). Food and feeding is easily the most complicated, and most simple, issue and could take a book of its own.

You will not emotionally scar them or stunt their potential by changing methods or ideas.

There are plenty of experts out there that talk about the "fourth trimester." Our babies are born when they have gestated in the womb for nine (or ten) months. We can't carry the baby more than nine months for emotional, mental and more importantly, physical reasons, so we provide a great deal of care and nurturing to a baby that is almost ready to be born. If our bodies (and minds) could handle it, they would gestate for another few months. Even if you start and stop a different method every week, it is sort of like a free pass, they're eating, sleeping and growing for that "fourth trimester." Period. So don't worry if you don't start as you mean to go on or you change your mind and change your method.

Nursing: I define "nursing" as when your child sucks his or her food – not whether s/he is breast or bottle-feeding, which is entirely your choice. For us, expat Americans, breastfeeding is easier just because it is portable, requires no mixing, does not have to be warmed or cooled, and is user-friendly (some of the formula mixes and things are downright confusing). That said, breastfeeding takes practice; it is not an intuitive, instinctual, automatic thing. Neither you nor your baby has done this before, and frankly, it is not necessarily a no-brainer. so...

For breastfeeding, you will need PATIENCE. You, your child, and every other bird, reptile and mammal on the planet, is born with a yolk sac.[1] Babies have a store of extra fat (on the back of their neck), which will do well for them for almost three days, and colostrum is a fabulously powerful thing. Colostrum is that watery pre-milk that your breasts will offer while the milk-making machine kicks into gear. It is potent; a little bit goes a long way. So, you have a few days to practice and be patient while the two of you learn how to do this thing. Relax. Take a deep breath. And here are a few "try this" kinds of ideas:

Try what you know for a few minutes, and then stop if you have to and relax in place. Trust me, you smell good to the baby and Baby is going to want to nuzzle and cuddle and that can lead to some really educational surprises – like milk! Try the different holds; Son was a cradled baby; Daughter preferred to lay down to nurse. There's even a football hold! Try cupping your breast with your palm and having your nipple come between your pointer and middle finger, pressing forward, not pinching, to guide the nipple to the right place. Try using your thumb to put a little bit of pressure on the baby's chin, with the same hand cupping your breast if you have to, and let a drop get on the lips or tongue. Believe me, if you don't try too hard, it will come. If it doesn't, you're likely to stress and tense up. If the act of nursing doesn't 'just happen', relax. Take a deep breath. Nuzzle Baby yourself and smile and coo, enjoy the smell, and the warmth and closeness. And try again later. Once they get the hang of it, it's all good. You have three days, easy, before Baby gets "hungry", although the baby may eat well immediately if s/he gets the hang of it sooner. Lie to the lactation consultant if you have to, "Oh, we're doing fine," if you find her intrusive (I did); or make friends, pick her brain and ask a lot of questions. Remember? There is no perfect fit or perfect answer. This is from me to you to reassure you that the baby won't starve, especially in those first days. It can take four to six weeks for the two of you to get into the routine of nursing. Breathe. Patience.

You have a few days to practice and be patient.

Breathe.

Something else that you may or may not hear, is that nursing can be physically uncomfortable. Your nipples are not used to being gnawed on (and if they are, I don't want to know). Suction is uncomfortable over extended periods of time. You might get raw or you might not. You might require nipple cream (which is not as exciting as it sounds), or you might not. Keep the nipples warm and dry;

46   [1] Including fish! I had no idea until I just checked that, but it makes sense.

include nipple pads if necessary. They will toughen up enough to do the job.

Additionally, I can say with authority and confidence, if you have your child supplemented with a bottle, you will not sabotage either your milk supply or your child's ability to nurse from the breast. Depending on your temperament and the child's, it might take an extra day or two to re-establish a routine that you prefer, but all is not lost if you deviate. I had a long, hard labor with my son and asked that he please be allowed to sleep in the nursery that night and given water if he woke. They were horrified, and said he'd never breastfeed if I did that. I told them that I was willing to take the risk but that the baby's mother needed to sleep so she could take care of him the next day.

I was a timed nurser; I basically nursed my children ten to fifteen minutes to a breast, both breasts, with a burp in the middle and after. I didn't worry about fore-milk (the richest milk that comes first) or hind-milk (the skim milk behind the main feeding). But there are differing theories, and some mothers do only one breast one feeding and only the other the next. Some mothers nurse until they feel empty. You will find what is comfortable for you. My routine was important, and my children knowing what was going to happen was important to me, so I went with ten to fifteen minutes per breast.

If you give your child a bottle, it will not sabotage your milk supply or your child's ability to nurse.

PUMPING

A friend recently received a previously-owned pump and Medella did give her some problems when she wanted to buy replacement tubing and attachments. She was told, "The pumps are for one person and not to be shared." Eventually I think she told them that this was the second child and the tubing and other washable parts had been thrown away in the meantime, and was able to purchase replacement parts. I've also been told that microwavable steam-sanitizing bags kill 99.9% of the bacteria, so buying replacement parts might not be an issue.

This is a good spot to tuck in a friend's experience with pumping. At nine months old or so, her child liked a 'dream feed', early in the morning, without ever quite waking all the way up, but didn't nurse so much that she'd empty both breasts. Of course, Mama is waking up with very full breasts from a full night of not nursing. So, this brilliant woman pumped while she nursed! Oxytocin is sometimes called the Cuddle Hormone because it gives you a warm cuddly feeling, and it is released when the child nurses. Prolactin is the main milk-producing hormone. Oxytocin is the hormone that causes the milk to 'let down' so that the baby can get it. It is the whistle that starts the factory's production line. A supply-and-demand dance with the baby helps set the production levels.[2] As a result, this mama can get a full five or six ounces more if she pumps while her child nurses, double what she can get pumping without the baby at the other breast! Other women will get in an extra pumping and then pump at the time when the baby is being bottle-fed breast milk at home. This works very well if there is a nursing room available or if you're comfortable pumping at work because it keeps you and the baby, and milk production, on the same schedule. There are many ways to work with pumping.

Feeding = schedule = sleeping through the night!

Feeding Equals Schedule Equals Sleeping (through the night!). Really.

I am not kidding. I do not mean a planned, rigid, schedule, I really don't. With children you have to be adaptable above all else. I mean plus or minus ten or fifteen minutes by schedule. If I have a feeding planned for 1200, I do try for 1200, but sometimes it is 1145 and sometimes it is 1215. Life happens. The only time I watch the clock is when someone starts crying and I watch those incredibly long two or ten minutes tick by as I wait for them to settle back down. What I mean is a flexible general schedule, with the goal of introducing the world's time concepts to these little brains that have no idea that time exists. It is kind of like the most major jet lag we can possibly imagine, and you have the unenviable job of undoing it. We call it a Sorta Schedule. And I kid you not, the many children that I know, six personally, that followed these general guidelines all slept through the night at two months. As an added bonus, for today's readers only, if you didn't begin the Sorta Schedule from the beginning, you too can begin at any time and get the same benefit of sleep! All of these times and rates are based on the child's weight, not the child's calendar age. Babies are individuals! They're different, and a calendar isn't going to tell you whether this is an early bird or a night owl. The sections that follow are incredibly dense and very packed with information. They're also mind-numbingly boring if you're beyond this point. It begins at birth and the feeding times and how to spread them out for sleep purposes until they are ready to wean. It is all covered again in the sleep section, because that is how important I think this is.

Here are my parameters for the big picture, how do we measure success:

[2] http://www.drgreene.com/21_1473.html and http://www.morgenwelt.de/futureframe/9908-oxytocin.htm for more on oxytocin and forming lasting relationship bonds.

First, you have to get them to regain their birth weight. Then you want to ease to three hours between feedings instead of two. By the way, that is three clock hours from when they began nursing, not three hours from when they finish. Three hours is a good interval so you can start to drop feedings but still keep their intake smooth. Incidentally, this probably leads to sleeping through the night because they get introduced to the daily rhythms of the outside world, and the habit in darkness equaling melatonin production and light equaling seratonin production is introduced.[3] Their insides begin processing on something resembling time, establishing a circadian rhythm. No, I don't really know why it works, but it does. After you and the baby are used to dropping feedings, you can start easing them into eating every four hours, which meshes well with society's eating schedule. So, how in the world do you accomplish all of that in just one year without turning into a zombie or putting the baby in charge? That is in the details, dear, and there are four phases.

Phase 1: Birth to regained birth weight; nursing on demand or every two hours

Phase 2: Regained birth weight to double their birth weight; nursing every three hours, dropping feedings as they get closer to double their birth weight

Timed nursing is three hours by the clock from when they start, NOT when they finish.

Phase 3: Double their birth weight to approximately triple their birth weight or appropriate behavior, nursing every four hours.

Phase 4: Introducing solids.

There's a good reason why Phase Three is an approximation. Example: Daughter was 6lbs 7oz when born. She was THREE years old and then only just past 22lbs. We introduced solids at nine months old based on her other reactions: watching us eat, reaching for spoons, opening her mouth when we put food in ours, all indicating she was ready to start solids.

PHASE ONE: BIRTH TO REGAINED BIRTH WEIGHT

Babies lose a little weight when they are born, and this is normal and okay. Everyone will be watching the weight gain to the regained birth weight stage partially because this is the little milestone that shows that they've recovered from the stress of birth (you think it was hard, but it was twice as traumatic for the little one!). Nurse on demand or every two hours until they regain their birth weight. At this point, 10-15 minutes per side is probably more than the baby has energy for (think of sucking on a straw for that long!) and will probably do very well with 4-6 minutes per side in the beginning. And not every baby nurses the same way, some are putzy, some are ravenous, some are thinkers, and some change their minds and try all kinds of styles. This is also known as the 'no sleep for you' stage. Fortunately, it doesn't take terribly long for them to regain their birth weight, and each and every breath that they take is going to wake you anyway. Baby is probably in a bassinet in your room. I agree with the 'start as you mean to go along' mandate, so we avoided the baby-in-your-bed option. However, Baby did sleep in a bassinet or basket in the same room during this period. Everything is so very new, how could I possibly be more than an arm's length away ....

You're not Super Mom, nor do you need to be. Nap. It is a sign of intelligence, not weakness.

Nursing occurs at:

DAY1	6am	8am	10am	12pm	2pm	4pm	6pm	8pm	10pm	12am	2am	4am
DAY2	6am	8am	10am	12pm	2pm	4pm	6pm	8pm	10pm	12am	2am	4am
DAY3	6am	8am	10am	12pm	2pm	4pm	6pm	8pm	10pm	12am	2am	4am
DAY4	6am	8am	10am	12pm	2pm	4pm	6pm	8pm	10pm	12am	2am	4am
DAY5	6am	8am	10am	12pm	2pm	4pm	6pm	8pm	10pm	12am	2am	4am
DAY6	6am	8am	10am	12pm	2pm	4pm	6pm	8pm	10pm	12am	2am	4am
DAY7	6am	8am	10am	12pm	2pm	4pm	6pm	8pm	10pm	12am	2am	4am

And so on, until Baby is back to birth weight. And for goodness' sake, nap when the baby does!

PHASE TWO: REGAINED BIRTH WEIGHT TO DOUBLE BIRTH WEIGHT

Now you will start to ease to every three hours over a week and continue to nurse every three hours until they double their weight. Begin to let them fuss themselves back to sleep, one feed at a time, dropping approximately one feeding about every two weeks (depending on the baby's temperament). Baby should go to their own room around now as it makes the fussing part, and you learning to let them fuss, less difficult for you. The fussing means that they do get fed, but only after fussing and attempting to soothe themselves first, and it is a relatively quick and impersonal feed. I DO mean to let that baby fuss. First, try two minutes of fussing (look at the clock and count; it seems like ten minutes when it is just two). Then go ahead and go in and feed the baby, or if baby is willing to take a bottle, ask Daddy to do it.

First the chart on how long it takes and how to do it

Week One of Phase Two

DAY1	6am	9am	12pm	3pm	6pm	9pm	12am	3am
DAY2	6am	9am	12pm	3pm	6pm	9pm	12am	3am
DAY3	6am	9am	12pm	3pm	6pm	9pm	12am	3am
DAY4	6am	9am	12pm	3pm	6pm	9pm	12am	3am
DAY5	6am	9am	12pm	3pm	6pm	9pm	12am	3am
DAY6	6am	9am	12pm	3pm	6pm	9pm	12am	3am
DAY7	6am	9am	12pm	3pm	6pm	9pm	12am	3am

Week Two of Phase Two

DAY1	6am	9am	12pm	3pm	6pm	9pm	12am	FUSS
DAY2	6am	9am	12pm	3pm	6pm	9pm	12am	FUSS
DAY3	6am	9am	12pm	3pm	6pm	9pm	12am	FUSS
DAY4	6am	9am	12pm	3pm	6pm	9pm	12am	FUSS
DAY5	6am	9am	12pm	3pm	6pm	9pm	12am	FUSS
DAY6	6am	9am	12pm	3pm	6pm	9pm	12am	FUSS
DAY7	6am	9am	12pm	3pm	6pm	9pm	12am	FUSS

Week Three of Phase Two

DAY1	6am	9am	12pm	3pm	6pm	9pm	FUSS	DROP
DAY2	6am	9am	12pm	3pm	6pm	9pm	FUSS	DROP
DAY3	6am	9am	12pm	3pm	6pm	9pm	FUSS	DROP
DAY4	6am	9am	12pm	3pm	6pm	9pm	FUSS	DROP
DAY5	6am	9am	12pm	3pm	6pm	9pm	FUSS	DROP
DAY6	6am	9am	12pm	3pm	6pm	9pm	FUSS	DROP
DAY7	6am	9am	12pm	3pm	6pm	9pm	FUSS	DROP

Week Four of Phase Two

DAY1	6am	9am	12pm	3pm	6pm	9pm	DROP	DROP
DAY2	6am	9am	12pm	3pm	6pm	9pm	DROP	DROP
DAY3	6am	9am	12pm	3pm	6pm	9pm	DROP	DROP
DAY4	6am	9am	12pm	3pm	6pm	9pm	DROP	DROP
DAY5	6am	9am	12pm	3pm	6pm	9pm	DROP	DROP
DAY6	6am	9am	12pm	3pm	6pm	9pm	DROP	DROP
DAY7	6am	9am	12pm	3pm	6pm	9pm	DROP	DROP

And you are sleeping through the night 9pm to 6am! Your baby is approximately two months old, give or take. This means that you can now handle just about anything.

If you are tired, small things are insurmountable; if you are well-rested, you can handle anything.

FUSSING FEED VERSUS DROPPING A FEEDING

Okay, the difference between fussing and dropping. The fussing means that they do get fed, but only after fussing and attempting to soothe themselves first, and it is a relatively quick and impersonal feed. I do mean to let that baby fuss. First, try two minutes of fussing (look at the clock and count; it seems like ten minutes when it is just two). Wake your spouse or partner and make him talk to you for two minutes. After a few days, make it ten minutes for a few nights, then fifteen; it usually only takes three nights (lots in the *Baby Whisperer* about this) for the new pattern to set. Call a friend in the U.S. to distract you if it is during their daytime, most people will have no problem with a two-minute interruption. At double their weight, they can physically make it through the night. You just have to mentally and emotionally help them do it and you have to mentally and emotionally make yourself do it. Remind yourself, "If I do this, the baby will sleep and I will sleep and we will be able to handle anything." I can tell you that if you say that to yourself 150 times slowly, that's two minutes.

Unfortunately, not all babies are the same. We could go in when Son fussed and cork him with a pacifier and he'd go back to sleep. But if I went in at all when Daughter woke in the night, all bets were off. Husband, bless his heart, would get up to get the baby, change the diaper, let me feed in bed, and take baby back (the other child was diapered after, not before, feeding). But every baby is different: some need comforting, some need ignoring, some need something in the middle. After the timed fussing, nurse the baby just a little, not a whole feeding. This will comfort you, and most astonishing, have the added benefit of building trust. Now that child knows that you will come, even if it is not immediate and sudden, instant gratification, you will come. However, as brutal as this sounds, feed, change and tuck. Minimal interaction, you want this to be a sleepy thing.

Inconsolable crying isn't good and painfully wracking sobs mean they want to tell you something, and this is entirely different from fussing or whining.

Dropping the feeding will happen as a natural side-effect. The fussing will go for two, then four, then eight, then sixteen minutes and usually, if you have made it to sixteen minutes, you can go a full twenty and they decide that they're tired out and fall back asleep. Certainly, they're hungry when they wake for the next feeding, but three nights of fussing for twenty (or so) minutes, and the feeding is dropped and nudged into the next. If they're not sleeping after twenty minutes, but you're in the we-want-to-drop-this-feed phase, try a soothing mechanism like pacifier or pats or rubs or whatever, but if you're actually at the dropping-the-feeding part, don't pick that baby up. Some parents say that it is best if Daddy does this, because he doesn't smell like milk and it gives him something to do, which men seem to like. This is of course, entirely up to you. Also, I do not agree with the idea that you should let the child cry regardless. Inconsolable isn't good and painfully wracking sobs cannot be good and is entirely different from fussing. Think of it this way: Can you tell the difference between a puppy's cry to be let out of his or her kennel and the difference between when their tail is stepped on? Listen to your child cry for a second, and think of it as a different language or small-mammal-speak.

Either way, it is a hard thing, but parenting is hard. It is a very hard thing; you want to comfort that child and pop a breast into its mouth to do so, but remind yourself, you're building trust, the baby physically can do it, you and Baby are establishing sleep patterns. Three days is not as long as it seems during those two or ten minutes (the hardest interval for me) of crying in the middle of the night.

Keep in mind that it might take slightly more or slightly less than seven days. Babies don't do calendars. But once the pattern is established, you stay at the Week Four of Phase Two part of the schedule until they are double their birth weight. It could take until they are six months old (not likely, but it could). But you are sleeping, so you can handle it.

PHASE THREE: DOUBLE THEIR BIRTH WEIGHT TO TRIPLE THEIR BIRTH WEIGHT:

During this phase you will be easing to nursing every four hours over a few weeks, adding fifteen minutes here and cutting it there, and will feed every four hours until they triple their weight or show the signs of wanting solid food. The following example is one way, of many different patterns, that you could do this:

Week One of Phase Three:

DAY1	6am	9am	12pm	3pm	6pm	9pm
DAY2	6am	915am	1215pm	315pm	6pm	915pm
DAY3	6am	915am	1215pm	315pm	6pm	915pm
DAY4	6am	915am	1215pm	330pm	6pm	915pm
DAY5	6am	930am	1230pm	330pm	6pm	930pm
DAY6	6am	930am	1230pm	345pm	6pm	930pm
DAY7	6am	930am	1230pm	345pm	6pm	930pm

Week Two of Phase Three:

DAY1	6am	945am	1245pm	4pm	6pm	945pm
DAY2	6am	945am	1245pm	4pm	6pm	945pm
DAY3	6am	945am	1245pm	415pm	6pm	945pm
DAY4	6am	10am	1pm	415pm	6pm	10pm
DAY5	6am	10am	1pm	430pm	6pm	10pm
DAY6	6am	10am	1pm	430pm	6pm	10pm
DAY7	6am	10am	130pm	445pm	6pm	10pm

Week Three of Phase Three:

DAY1	6am	10am	130pm	445pm	6pm	10pm
DAY2	6am	10am	130pm	DROP	6pm	10pm
DAY3	6am	10am	130pm	DROP	6pm	10pm
DAY4	6am	10am	145pm	DROP	6pm	10pm
DAY5	6am	10am	145pm	DROP	6pm	10pm
DAY6	6am	10am	145pm	DROP	6pm	10pm
DAY7	6am	10am	2pm	DROP	6pm	10pm

And continue Phase Three Week Three schedule of five nursings a day, until they are triple their birth weight or you are ready to introduce solids (also known as weaning).

Do remember that babies and Mamas are different. So adjust the actual factual times on the chart to suit yourselves, meaning 7am, 11am, 3pm, 7pm and 11pm if need be or 5am, 9am, 1pm, 5pm and 9pm. Nothing is written in stone with little people (and they're not reading anyway) and if you try to force the issue, both you and the baby will be bewildered and confused. Adapt accordingly and you will survive.

Adapt the schedule for you and your child, if you force the issue, both you and baby will be bewildered and confused.

PHASE FOUR: WEANING OR INTRODUCING SOLIDS

Weaning is when food instead of mother's milk or formula is introduced into the baby's diet. You decide when weaning occurs; either at triple their birth weight, or when you are ready to wean, or when they sit up on their own, or when you have to go back to work. It all depends on different choices for work or food or other variables.

However, when the time comes and you are ready, continue to feed every four hours and gradually drop every other nursing and replace with food. Which feeding you replace is dependent upon the child, whether or not the child is a morning child or evening child. Depending on the child, start solids when they are most active, as this is the time when they are most receptive to change and new stimuli. Notice that only week one is different.

Also, there is the issue of Dream Feed. While the child is now receiving an official four meals a day, four hours apart, there is a Dream Feed tucked in there, sort of to tide them over. It is a nursing, but usually an incomplete one, not a full feeding.

Night Owl Baby

1	8am Nurse	12pm Nurse	4pm Nurse	8pm SOLIDS	10pm Dream Feed
2	8am Nurse	12pm SOLIDS	4pm Nurse	8pm SOLIDS	10pm Dream Feed
3	8am Nurse	12pm SOLIDS	4pm SOLIDS	8pm SOLIDS	10pm Dream Feed
4	8am Nurse	12pm SOLIDS	4pm SOLIDS	8pm SOLIDS	10pm Dream Feed (Can fuss)
5	8am SOLIDS	12pm SOLIDS	4pm SOLIDS	8pm SOLIDS	10pm DROPPED

Early Bird Baby

1	8am Nurse	12pm SOLIDS	4pm Nurse	8pm Nurse	10pm Dream Feed
2	8am Nurse	12pm SOLIDS	4pm Nurse	8pm SOLIDS	10pm Dream Feed
3	8am Nurse	12pm SOLIDS	4pm SOLIDS	8pm SOLIDS	10pm Dream Feed
4	8am Nurse	12pm SOLIDS	4pm SOLIDS	8pm SOLIDS	10pm Dream Feed (Can fuss)
5	8am SOLIDS	12pm SOLIDS	4pm SOLIDS	8pm SOLIDS	10pm DROPPED

Another thing to notice is that I don't say days or weeks or months, just steps 1-5, and the length of each step might vary.

FOOD INTRODUCTION

Food introduction is also logical. Your child gets a new food (the first one is a single grain cereal, rice usually) one meal a day on day 1 (I recommend Saturday) of the new solid. If there is no reaction that day, Baby gets it again on day 2 (this would be Sunday). If no reaction, that week Baby's solid is of the new food; something that nanny or both parents can keep track of, but don't make changes, either in time or type, all week. If all is well, you can introduce a new solid the following Saturday. Now, that said, I recommend a good month on the first single grain cereal before introducing more solids because eating is not just a matter of taste. This gives your little person the chance to accept the idea that food does not just come from Mama, but also starts the habit of sitting still (well, still-ish), eating and still burping afterwards. Likewise, this is a whole mastering of using new muscles. The process of nursing is nothing at all like the process of masticating. Learning the difference takes time and you shouldn't be surprised if there is some resistance. It may have nothing to do with 'taste' but with learning. Once you've got this sitting and eating thing down, then move on to food introductions loosely using the chart in appendix 5 (also in the DK *Baby & Child Question & Answer Book* and every other book out there that covers food and weaning).

By "solids", I mean single grain baby cereal. After that first month of forming the eating habit, you can go to a mixed grain cereal. Then a week or more later, add in a vegetable. Then, a week or more after that, add a fruit, and eventually meats. Unless you own stock in Gerber or something, I recommend that you make your own fruit and vegetable puree. The only time I use pre-made jars of baby food was when we traveled. I order enough for the trip from NetGrocer about six weeks ahead of time (unless we're going to civilization, in which case I get enough for the plane trip and first day). *The Super Baby Food Book* is a good book for order of food introduction – which fruits and vegetables first, and at approximately which month. However, keep in mind that Son didn't start solids at all until seven months old and Daughter was nine months old, so I just started at the beginning of the list rather than looking at the months since the book is based on introductions at four months. The book struck me as over-board in some respects, but I've used the order of food introduction for both babies – I literally printed the list of fruits and veggies and went along and checked them off the list as they were introduced. For other things, I just made sure that I wasn't jumping too far ahead on the list (because she includes things like tahini and brewers yeast!). A mnemonic is to start with light colors, white and beige, and make red the last color, going from white to yellow, to green, to blue, then orange and lastly red. The list is included in Appendix 5 and has a column for basics, one for fruit, a third column for vegetables and a final column for dairy and miscellaneous. While the list is thorough, it is by no means all-inclusive. It is also not exactly a practical list if you don't have food choices at the market. Remember the colors and start bland. Check out the book if you want lots of food info. It does have recipes for things like play-dough and the lava volcano cake in it too.

When making baby food, we are talking about the cereals, fruits and vegetables. There are a number of things that need to wait to be introduced after the baby's digestive system is more mature. These things include nuts, egg yolk, honey and strawberries, but that is by no means an all-inclusive list. The food introduction list in the appendix lists a number of the foods that should wait, as do all the child-care books. I particularly like the DK books for their charts.

Back to baby food...

In a blender, mix chopped food and liquid (water or breast milk) until it is finely pureed. At that point the food will pour off the spoon into the baby's mouth and should be only slightly thicker than breast milk/formula (think thin milk shake) or warm honey. As time goes by, food should still be pureed or mashed until it is smooth and lump-free, but can be slightly thicker, like heavy cream. No wheat products until after six months (cookies, melba toast, graham crackers, etc.)

Gradually increase the thickness as time goes on, and switch from a blender to a chopper to increase chunkiness. Then it is time to introduce bite-sized pieces of soft finger foods. Watch carefully and always supervise – do not leave the child alone. The "babysafefeeder" is also a great product because it is a little mesh bag (buy extra bags) that you can stick hard food into like apples, or "goo cubes" (these are rice cereal mixed with apple juice and frozen in an ice cube tray). It helps them to not choke, gives them something to work at and is a nice way to try new tastes when they're at a curious stage. The down side is that they are rather challenging to clean, particularly bananas.

Foods should still be the consistency of fork-mashed, chunky but blended, until molars are present (about two years old). Never leave your baby alone while eating. Once I got to this point, I began letting them try the spoon. It was as messy as all get out, but fun.

To make your own baby food you first need a blender, and then a chopper. KitchenAid makes a nut chopper that works wonderfully. I did it once a week. I purchased 500g (1 pound), each of two or three fruits and two or three vegetables. Either boil or steam your fruits and veggies. While hot, put them in the blender (for little babies) or chopper (for bigger ones) and puree. Add a little rice cereal to take away the bite and to give it some texture. Put a spoon in and get some on the spoon and check the consistency. It should pour off the spoon smoothly, in one stream, but not drop. Later, as they are more used to it, thicken it slightly. Pour into saved empty baby food jars and refrigerate. One full chopper makes five to six baby food jars. Or you can pour them into an American ice cube tray (not the little Euro ice trays) and freeze. Remove the cubes from the tray and place cubes in labeled bags. Each cube is about one ounce, which is a serving. As they get teeth, not by their calendar age, you start making it a little less pureed. Four teeth indicates that they can handle a coarser texture. Incisors mean go ahead and introduce meat if you're at that point. Molars mean make it chunky because they're learning to grind now!

IS THIS RIGHT, ARE WE DOING IT WRONG?

Introduction of food seems complicated, because you are on edge and always watching for a reaction. One wonders, "Is this right?", "Is this wrong?", "Was that a reaction or just gas?", "Was that poop different?" A reaction, food allergy speaking, is different than an intolerance. Infant and Children's Benadryl should be in your Kid Kit regardless. Speak with your pediatrician for the appropriate dose for your infant's weight and have this chart taped to the inside of the Kid Kit.

Children's dosages are not the same as Infant dosages. NEVER give adult medicine or dosages! Check with your doctor before dosing an infant with anything other than infant formula because half of a child dose is not an automatic infant dosage. Check with your doctor!

If there is a reaction to food, either intolerance or allergic or due to immaturity, take away the new food and try again in two weeks, if it is not a severe (need medical attention) reaction. Proteins are allowed through the lining of the stomach in increasing numbers as the lining of the gut matures, so a food that got an intolerant reaction at six months may be fine at seven. If there is a reaction again, put that food on the do-not-feed list for introduction after the baby's digestive system is more mature, like after one year. If this occurs when you first introduce rice cereal, you may consider holding off solids altogether for another two weeks for just that reason: your child's system may not be ready.

ALLERGIC REACTIONS ARE:

• Rash, mild to severe (not just around the mouth) that does not go away within a few hours or that blooms suddenly;

• Diarrhea or vomiting;

• Failure to grow or put on weight;

• Coughing or wheezing (sounds like asthma);

• Anaphylactic shock (very acute allergies) is a sudden blotchy rash all over, puffy face and eyes, difficulty breathing, unconsciousness; any one or some or all of these symptoms require immediate medical attention.

If you are ever concerned about if it is an allergy or an intolerance, ASK! It is a quick phone call, no appointment necessary. And no, it isn't a silly question.

Intolerances are different and can be various levels of an immature digestive system or pure intolerance to a food. Both are treated the same way — take away the new food, and try again in two weeks; repeat if necessary.

INTOLERANCE REACTIONS ARE:

• Mild rash around the lips, goes away quickly or when washed (usually acidic things like tomatoes);

• Diarrhea (generally soon after the meal, otherwise no discomfort).

Two examples: while she was breastfeeding, my sister had to switch to drinking soy-milk because her son was having an intolerance reaction when she drank too much milk. Once his digestive system was slightly more mature, she added back the 'real' milk to her diet, hoping he was now able to tolerate it, or be able to build a tolerance for it. That said, he might have to be lactose-free forever. Similarly, because I do not feed my children much sugar beyond juice and the occasional baked goods, sugary foods, particularly candy, tend to get an intolerance reaction. To minimize it, I increase their water intake if they get something like birthday cake, which helps them digest it. We also do not feed them sweet things late in the day, not because we're worried about them getting wound up or something, but because if they are going to get what is commonly called Toddler's Diarrhea, it is best that they be awake ....

Toddler's Diarrhea, also called chronic non-specific pediatric diarrhea (that name is not helpful, is it?) and is most commonly caused by drinking too much juice, usually fruit juice, which travels through the intestine too fast for water absorption. This is when the child has loose, sloppy stools, but no change in behavior, no fever, no pain. You can increase their water intake or cut the juice with water. My magic number is 100. If there are more than 100 calories in a juice serving, I cut it with water. Believe it or not, you can 'slow down' toddler diarrhea by increasing their fat and protein intake a little. But a moderate diet for your child will help prevent you "running" into this too often.

This brings me to my A#1 rule regarding food and children: food is only eaten at the table. Really. It is simple, easy to remember, quick to repeat and it makes so many other things so much easier. They know that when they eat, they eat at the table. They observe, and then are encouraged to practice, table manners there. There is little to no whining for snacks because the snacks and the children magically appear at the table at the appropriate times. There's no food in the couch or spills on the floor or furniture, which means no bugs in the living room and no animals getting in trouble for yielding to the temptation of an easy target. Toys are magically not sticky. We bend this rule only a little and allowed sippy cups (ones with valves) when they were little and now cups or bottles of water (not juice) in the playroom or when watching a movie. This makes the appearance of popcorn during a movie that much more exciting. The second half of that rule though is that you have to follow it too. They cannot observe you eating anywhere except the table. If you are used to munching on chips in front of the television, well, now you have to wait until they are in bed for that or the whole idea is out the window.

> **Food is only eaten at the table —for so MANY reasons.**

"Not for Son"

"Why is Daddy allowed?"

"Because he's bigger," which translates into "Because he is responsible and somewhat less likely to be distracted and either knock over the juice or miss his mouth."

That works to a certain point, but there comes a point when it doesn't and what you do is twice as important as what you say.

That said, we love outside snacks and picnics.

WHERE TO FEED THEM?

My answer to where to feed them is the same as it would be for the big people in the house: at the table. We didn't do a real, stand-alone highchair, so I am a poor person to ask for a recommendation on those! I do know plenty of people who chose these and loved theirs. Again, you will need to define why you are going to use a high chair, containment or feeding or both? Does it need to be portable? Does it need to be a certain weight? Perhaps you have brand loyalty that needs to be taken into consideration. Once you define why you are getting a highchair, you can start looking for one that meets your parameters and make an informed choice. We chose a wonderful clip-on highchair, also called a table chair. It is a bit tricky with Embassy issued dining room sets, especially as the baby gets older or is chunking up, but it can be done. I don't recommend the cloth table chairs. The firmer, solid ones made for better sitting, less wiggling and they fold virtually flat. Those of you that know us know that it went everywhere; easy for restaurants, no worries about not being in the first-world where they have highchairs in restaurants; comfortable, convenient and familiar for the child. Baby is used to being in it and eating, so the setting changed a little, but we sit, we eat. No problem. I'm big into containment; if I can contain them, I can control them. Sort of.

When Son was too big, we went to this oh-so-simple (like smack yourself on the head simple) booster. It is called a Cooshie Booster[4] and comes with its own bag (we tossed the snack food and cup in the bag too when they weren't quite on restaurant food, for that this-is-taking-so-long-and-my-child-is-hungry period of the restaurant experience). I was tickled that it came in purple too for Daughter and, like the clip-on highchair, we had a set of the boosters in pretty much every location that we visited on a regular basis. Son loved his big boy chair, because he could sit at the table with the adults (which he does anyway), and because it is bigger than the high chair. When Daughter was too big for the high chair, but still too small for the Cooshie, we flipped the Cooshie over and it worked just as well! AND it is light and portable. There's a lot out there, but less is really more in this case.

By the way, there are no special Kid Meals in this house unless you count lunch

[4] www.onestepahead.com

on weekends. They eat what we eat. Now, yes, I will sometimes spice something a little less – less curry, less or no cayenne, plain red sauce instead of arrabiatta. Three bites is magical here – if they try three bites, and don't want to eat more, that is fair, they don't have to eat it. But that is all that they get and there are no substitutions. There is also no snacking or munching later. I don't make them hot dogs or pizza just to get them to eat, because they are not going to fade away. They might be hungry, but they won't starve or be injured by it.

Why do I feel fairly confident about that? According to the Mayo Clinic, WebMD[5], and other sources, our stomachs are naturally about the size of our fist. This is usually in reference to portion sizes for adults, and the huge size of American restaurant portions and dieting. You could eat half or less of that restaurant portion and still fill your stomach (we don't have to clear our plates!). So, the same can be said for a child's stomach size. Remember the infant; three tablespoons of food per meal, one fruit, one veggie, one cereal. That fills the little belly full! Yes, they do get this four or five times a day, but packing it in there does no actual good. So, our two year old had a fist that is perhaps a quarter to a third of a cup in volume. That is not a lot of food, folks! I was quite comfortable putting one heaping tablespoon of each item on her plate, and with allowing her to eat three bites only if it is new or unusual. That just isn't a very big belly.

> Three bites is our magic number —they might be hungry if they don't get more, but they won't starve.

And this brings me to the fact that you are the adult. It was the Big Belly that reminded me. You control the portion sizes, time and quality. You will instill good habits by trying to be appropriate about food choices. And my Big Belly Baby Girl will keep eating as long as there is food in front of her – she has got to be slipping it to the cat or something because I just can't figure out where it goes! She gets that half-a-cup total of food, and if she wants more, she gets a little more of each, no matter how insistently she says, "MUCH please!" We had an Embassy nurse over for dinner one night and she actually said, "You're the first person I've met who gives their children realistic portions" (I said thank you).

Snacks are the same. Applesauce can come in little plastic half-cup containers, and we go through a lot. They are the perfect snack container. I can dump in some raisins, a few graham sticks (either the actual sticks that they make now or parts of a graham cracker), and a few dried apricots or apple slices and add a glass of juice and voilà! Perfect snack size! Or, fill said container with plain yogurt, top with granola, honey or wheat germ and poof! Snack! Or fill said container with Jello, chill and bam! Snack! They're great. They work well for feeding foster kittens too or containing tempra paint or beads. Oh, I can also use them in the laundry to keep the stuff that my spouse and son leave in their pockets.

TEETHING

One last note on food and eating – eventually these little people are going to get teeth in order to be able to do all this eating themselves! I was reminded rather comically recently, as five-year old Son is starting to get an adult tooth and he is grumpy and irritable, and very "mouthy", in that everything goes into his mouth. I am trying to correct him, deal with it, etc, and finally ask, "Do you know why you're so grumpy?" He said, "Yes. My mouth hurts." I did a double-take and checked, and sure enough, that little tooth is trying to get out, and frankly, it looks like it hurts, a little red and irritated and the gums are pushed up with the inward pressure. I said, "Well, I know what to do to make this not hurt so much!" I gave him a half of a dose of the appropriate Tylenol, and a "BooBoo Bear"[6] for him to put on his jaw or right on the gum. The same principle works for infants and toddlers, but they are much less able to articulate it.

Cold packs, an appropriate Tylenol, and something hard, edible or not, for them to chew on, and burp cloths because they're extra drooly, are really the best means of transiting the teething times. This too shall pass, with a tooth at the end! I had the Orajel for teething pain[7], a little Q-Tip looking stick with medicine in the middle to numb the area, and only ever used two.

SUGAR SUPERCHARGE

In spite of what you will read later in the story box at the end of this chapter and later, when the children managed to steal chocolate, we have been relatively successful in limiting the amount of candy and refined sugar that we allowed our children to be exposed to. We decided early on, "No candy." We were fairly militant about enforcing it also, requiring the kids to give us candy when it was presented to them. This happened fairly often, as we were in posts where giving candy to children was an approved interaction with children, regardless of

---

[6] There are little child cold packs out there – from the BooBoo Bear and Boo-Boo Bunnies to Blues Clues cold pack, soft and comforting, but cold. I recommend having at least two in the freezer, on hand, just in case (adults use them too).

[7] They work for cold sores too.

whether you were known to that child or not. Perfect strangers handing your child candy is a major cultural difference for Americans to get used to, let me tell you!

I baked so they did eat sweet things, but I would regularly choose to make graham and honey muffins instead of chocolate chocolate chip cookies or oatmeal raisin cookies instead of sugar cookies. This was a choice for our family that we chose to be consistent in enforcing until they went to school. We lost any semblance of control once they went to school, since we were not present and there were entirely different standards with inconsistent enforcement. However, by then we'd instilled decent habits in the children regarding candy and sweets and were no longer surprised when they requested an apple instead of a cookie. Make no mistake, my children do love cookies. But they also think that candy is too sweet, and I'm not one to argue with that perception!

Halloween presents our family with a particular challenge in this area, and while the Embassy party planners were outstanding in offering small prizes in lieu of candy, it couldn't be avoided forever. One year we had the coincidence of chicken pox, so we managed to only have to worry about addressing the issue with one child, not both. Husband did his best to convince Son to take the toys instead of the candy, but of course he ended up with a significant amount of candy. Given that Son was four years old, we allowed him to keep four pieces of candy. The rest of it was set aside and the following morning, Husband and Son counted the candy. Husband paid Son the equivalent of a quarter per piece of candy and then they immediately went to the store that carried toys and Son purchased the toy of his choice with the money he'd gotten in replacement for the candy.[8] Son thought that was a pretty good deal, and we were certainly pleased to avoid the candy inundation.

I shared that method with a colleague and even though their family had not done that in previous years, they decided to go ahead and give it a try, frankly telling the children that it was just "too much candy," and believe it or not, it went over fine. The compensation of the toy was worthwhile, and they did not remember the "loss" of the candy because the family's attitude towards sugar, candy and sweet things was similar. I don't know how well it would go for children who were used to eating candy, but someone suggested that I include that as a tool for managing to keep their teeth in their heads! The post we were at had a local attitude that "milk teeth" were going to fall out anyway, so there was no need to protect them or keep them healthy.

As you can well imagine, we were a wee bit controlling when it came to what Son ate, how much sugar, and no candy. The challenge for us really came at his first birthday. According to all the food charts, that first birthday is a magical moment and suddenly so many things are allowed! I balked at this relatively arbitrary date – after all, it is the maturity of his insides, not his calendar age, that determines if he can process strawberries or honey. I joked that I was going to have a first birthday party with all the previously Forbidden items. But instead, I just had a birthday party. I went to birthdayexpress.com and ordered a complete Winnie the Pooh first birthday party in a box. It came with banners and balloons, crepe paper and ribbon, plates and napkins and a cake topper too! And we had a real party. We decided that this first birthday was really for the parents – a photo op and celebration for us – we've survived a whole year! All our invitees were adults, although there were a few with children of their own who did bring them. Real food (not just the Forbiddens) was served and a birthday cake too.

Son had not had refined sugar products up to that time. After much discussion, we decided that baked goods were acceptable compared to packaged sweets of any kind and I made him a cupcake. He ate his dinner, we sang Happy Birthday and then I gave him his unfrosted chocolate mini-cupcake.

The look on his face was priceless. He took his first bite, did a double-take, and then looked at us like, "Oh WOW!" and he stuffed the rest of it in his mouth and grinned like there was no tomorrow!

"Chocolate Cake"

7. Medical

While you are in the U.S. having your child, you will have pediatric appointments also. I highly recommend interviewing several pediatricians. We found one in Colorado that insisted that his parents have current infant and child CPR certification, but he was willing to take us even though we might not be able to provide proof of our certification renewal. He also listened to my concerns about vaccinations – even though he felt that the varicella (chicken pox) vaccine had passed his personal threshold into the realm of safe and routine, we had a frank discussion about why I felt otherwise. The fact that he was willing to: 1) discuss it and 2) respect my decision as a parent regardless of what it was, made him a good fit for our family. This was not something that would have come up without an interview, and he was the fifth doctor that we interviewed. Generally, a doctor should be willing to make an "acquaintance appointment" free of charge. As an expat family, I recommend a family practitioner who can see all of you (from Daddy to darlings), as it keeps all your records in one place, makes accessing them and communication considerably easier, and means a lot less explaining to do in the long run.

> A doctor should be willing to make an "acquaintance appointment" free of charge. As an ex-pat family, I recommend a family practitioner.

When you find one, get an e-mail address. During the interview, make sure you bring up, and reiterate *ad nauseum*, that most of your communication will be via e-mail once you leave town. Ask how this will be charged, if at all, and be sure to communicate with them. When your children have annual exams, a problem or a vaccine received overseas, drop a note to be included in their record. Ask about the office's HIPPA policy regarding e-mail, and whether or not they require a waiver of some sort to communicate this way. Send your questions, or at least an update, twice a year. That way when you do get to see your doctor in person, you're not a virtual stranger (just not virtual anymore). Not only that, it is incredibly reassuring to know that you can ask a U.S. physician when your confidence in local or post medical services is shaken or you just need a second opinion.

Record keeping can be a real challenge. Wisconsin has a great program funded by the United Way of Racine County called *Success by Six*, within which they offer a "Health Passport." This thing is fabulous. I wish I could reproduce it somehow and attach it so you could print it and staple it together (providing I wouldn't get sued if I did that). It comes in a plastic sleeve and the book is a lay-person version of your child's medical record – what to expect at which visit, shots, length and weight charts to age six. It also fits the standard International Certificate of Vaccination yellow form. I keep this little red passport, the shot record and schedule of vaccines together and take them to our doctor's visits. Check to see if something similar is available locally since many states have similar programs.

The footnote contains a link to the version from British Columbia that is printable and usable in the same manner.[1] On the whole, it is a very useful tool for parents, including easy vaccine tracking and growth chart tracking. Additionally, it goes through 14 years old and has a wonderful chart of fever medications by weight.

A word on Poison Control; in the U.S., they are not recommending the use of syrup of Ipecac, which causes vomiting. That said there are a lot more options in the U.S., including 911. I am not a doctor, so check this with your well-informed pediatrician, but if you are within fifteen minutes of ingestion of pills (since most liquids, particularly corrosive ones, should not be vomited back up), syrup of ipecac can get the pills out of their system before they start getting broken down. For us, this can be a real lifesaver since stomach pumping is generally not an option where we live. Activated charcoal absorbs the toxic material.

A note: a **big huge** PAY ATTENTION note:

> 1. Do not just give syrup of ipecac. First call your Med Unit and have it ready if the doctor instructs you to give syrup of ipecac.
>
> 2. Syrup of ipecac still requires a doctor's supervision and instruction, particularly regarding dosages.
>
> 3. Once you give a child syrup of ipecac, activated charcoal won't be an option until all the vomiting has stopped and the activated charcoal may be more important.

Vomiting begins anywhere from ten to ninety minutes after taking the syrup

[1] http://www.healthservices.gov.bc.ca/cpa/publications/childpassport.pdf

and I strongly recommend going outside if it is an option. They are going to vomit at least two or three times, and have the hiccups for about twenty-four hours straight! For the full day after, keep them on the oatmeal and BRAT[2] diet, just to give that poor little tummy a chance to recover.

RESOURCES

Be careful when using the Internet for medical "research." For starters, ensure that you are using an area designated for patients or parents, not the medical professional. Many sites are for the medical professional. Two sites recommended by *Parenting* magazine[3] are kidshealth.org and intelihealth.com. I also like WebMD.com, but be sure to get on the Patients site, or you will be mightily confused mighty fast.

Ask-A-Nurse 1-800-888-5551 is a free service in the U.S. When you call, you will be connected to a service in Tennessee. If you prefer to look for a local, or home state version, check the Ask-A-Nurse website or ask your pediatrician. Explain that you are a U.S. citizen serving overseas and the reason that you are calling. Make note that they cannot diagnose, but they can make recommendations for home care. Be very clear that you do not have access to 911 or physicians that meet U.S. standards. They are most useful, helpful, nice folks and if you are worried that your child, who has had a 102 fever for three days and now has spots, might or might not have chicken pox (versus measles), they can certainly help you determine whether or not to seek the health care of your Med Unit or RMO. They can also clarify what your Med Unit may have (or not have) said. I also have the number for our "local" U.S. hospital, that has HealthLink nurses available 9am-9pm, which is the middle of the night for me, so I can call and see if I need to wake up our local physician and get to the Med Unit, or if it is something that I can monitor at home and wait until morning.

Your most important resource is your pediatrician and your Med Unit. Develop a relationship with both, be interactive and proactive and above all, trust your instincts and articulate your opinions. A lot of times I have had something explained to me, causing me to revise my opinion and honestly, as long as I have been respectful in my interactions, I've never had anyone fault me for it. I'm willing to adjust my perceptions, and I understand that they have access to information that I do not. I don't want to be spoken down to any more than they do and insisting you are correct without hearing their information leaves that impression, however inadvertent.

[2] Bananas, Rice, Applesauce and Toast. We have a personal variation, the BARF diet - Bananas, applesauce, rice and freakin' nothing else.
[3] October 2007

FEVERS

When reading my rules of thumb regarding a fever, which is a temperature over 98.6^F, FOR AN INFANT (under 2 years old), keep in mind that I have a high tolerance for not going to the doctor. That said, I have checked with our Medical Unit to ensure that if this were the only symptom, I wouldn't be endangering you by offering the following chart:

100F	38C	Pay attention			
101F	38.5C	Pay attention	Increase fluids		
102F	39C	Pay attention	Increase fluids	Tylenol	
103F	39.5C	Pay attention	Increase fluids	Tylenol	Call Doctor
104F	40C	Pay attention call doctor	Increase fluids call doctor	Tylenol call doctor	Call Doctor First

Babies run hot; 100^F is not scary .... Okay, that's not true, it is scary, but it is not cause to panic or worry. That said, everyone has their own comfort level. Find yours and stick to it and do not second-guess yourself. If your child has a mild fever but is otherwise acting normal, treating the fever may be for your peace of mind, not for the medical benefit of the child. Medical experts recommend that you call your doctor if your child has a fever and is less than three months old, if the fever has lasted for more than 24 hours (look at the clock, don't guess), or if your child is also vomiting. For any infant fever, speak with your pediatrician or Med Unit because the cause of the fever may be as important as controlling it. You might not know that there are four other infants also with a fever, but it might allow them to pinpoint the cause. Keep in mind, control of the fever is generally done to allow the infant to sleep, and continue to eat and drink, as well as to soothe the parent.

Toddlers have better thermo-regulation, and a lower fever can indicate illness sooner. For instance, at 101^F you would consider Tylenol or Motrin, rather than waiting until 102^F, if you medicate at all and don't try to keep them comfortable in other ways. You may choose to only medicate them for a fever so they can sleep comfortably, since sleep also helps the immune system and all the energy can go to fighting whatever invader bug is trying to encroach on your healthy baby. If they are eating and drinking, particularly drinking, you may choose not to medicate at all.

Accuracy is important, especially when you are reporting to a physician. An ear thermometer is very accurate when done professionally. They are now available for us plain-old-parents. These are wonderful, providing that you get your child used to it and take their temperature three times and get the average. It has to sense off of the eardrum itself, which is easy to miss, especially when you're moving briskly. Just like puppies and kittens, play with their ears, put your pinkie on (not in!) the ear canal, wiggle the lobes, touch and play (and do it with their fingers and toes too!). For taking their temperature with a digital ear thermometer, the averaging method works and if the temperature is high, it is going to show it.

Another parent-friendly thermometer is the forehead, temporal artery thermometer. This uses infrared technology to read the temperature and is much more user friendly and less prone to error. It does need to be at room temperature before taking the temperature to avoid false reading. The child's forehead needs to be dry and not sweaty.

A child's anterior fontanel is the place at the top of their skull where the plates of the skull meet. It is not fused as an infant, but closes within a year. If your child's fontanel is depressed or sunken, it is an indication that the child is dehydrated. If it is puffy or significantly elevated, it is an indication of intercranial pressure, and a medical professional should be consulted immediately.

Recent research regarding fever phobia[4] and other studies, seem to show that children who have fevers as small children have healthier immune systems. The study concluded that parents need more education regarding fevers. Fevers are the body's defense, and it is a sign of a working immune system. Fevers mainly cause discomfort and while parents worry that a fever can lead to seizures, brain damage or death, this is much more rare than we fear. This is not to say that occasionally a fever may need to be treated, but don't reach for the acetaminophen immediately upon seeing 99^F or 100^F temperature. Let your baby's immune system practice kicking some invader butt, and keep them comfortable with lighter clothing, calmer play, damp washcloths or sponges (but never an alcohol wipe since it can be absorbed through the skin) or a nice lukewarm bath in a warm room.

[4] Crocetti M, Moghbeli N, Serwint J. Fever phobia revisited: have parent mis-conceptions changed in the last 20 years? Pediatrics 2001; 107:1241—1246.

Temperature conversion chart for fevers:

$$40^{C} \ldots .104.0^{F}$$
$$39^{C} \ldots .102.2^{F}$$
$$38^{C} \ldots .100.4^{F}$$
$$37^{C} \ldots .98.6^{F}$$

The other area where accuracy is of utmost importance is dosages of medication. Purchase a syringe, measured dropper, dosing spoon or medicine cup in case the medication doesn't come with it and don't use standard tableware. It isn't a bad thing to get used to using just the one measured dropper, and check your measurement twice before you give it. There are different strengths of acetaminophen (Tylenol) or ibuprofen (Motrin) medicine based on the brand you buy and whether it is infant or children's dosages. Always read the label carefully so you give the right amount. Milligrams (mg) are not the same as liquid milliliters (ml). Again, check with your pediatrician or Med Unit to ensure they adjust the following recommendations for your child or your preferences. There is a dosage Appendix 6 for Tylenol and Motrin. Do not give your child aspirin.

Because of where you probably are, you can't usually ship liquid Pedialyte, which is an electrolyte solution used to help prevent dehydration. Lucky for you, there are several powders now. My favorite is called Kaolectrolyte Electrolyte Replenisher and it comes in grape or bubble-gum, but Gerber makes a powder too. I keep this stocked in my basement – three boxes at all times, and when I take the second, leaving only one, I order three more. We do the same for Kid and Infant Tylenol, Kid and Infant Tylenol Cold, and others, because the medications may expire if ordered in a consumables shipment. If you do order medications or things like Pedialyte in your consumables, remember that it DOES expire, so pay attention to expiration dates. Don't be afraid to ask for the Med Unit to carry a take-home version of Pedialyte or its equivalent.

By the way, I am going to mention something again. Water. This is what the child needs to remain hydrated. The Kaolectrolyte or Pedialyte is so that they don't sweat or burn it out too fast and to remain hydrated.[5] Remember, we are something like 90% water. I am sorry but juice, soda, milk and sports drinks are not water. If you can't get the Pedialyte (which is not yummy) into a child,

---

[5] Electrolytes help the muscles communicate, via charges signaling the sodium/potassium pumps in the cell walls. The entire gut is operated by sodium potassium pumps in the muscle cells which are the gate-keepers that allow water to move across cell membranes. Lack of electrolytes causes cramps and the muscles to stop working.

try diluted juice or flat clear soda, also diluted. Adult sports drinks, such as Gatorade, are not a good option because there is too much sodium and sugar for their little bodies. Unless they have cholera, when they need that extra sodium and sugar, opt out of the adult sports drinks. Instead, cut the Pedialyte with water or juice. I have even mixed it with Jello powder, just a smidgen, to make it more palatable. Flat clear soda is a better option than adult sport drinks for a child. Water is the only substance that can move through cells through osmosis, traveling through cell walls, without digestion, without breaking down, without help. If an adult sports drink is all you have available, please use it, but dilute it at least half and half with water.

Patience is the key to re-hydrating or keeping a child hydrated. It is better to go slow and get a teaspoon of appropriate liquid into your child every fifteen minutes, than to try to get them to drink a whole cup of water. Remember that if they're vomiting or have diarrhea, this is not just about staying hydrated during a fever, this is about fighting a bug, and fever plus vomiting means inform your Med Unit or pediatrician. If you can tell them you're getting a teaspoon of Pedialyte into them every fifteen minutes, believe me, their level of respect changes and you are taken with an entirely different type of seriousness. You're not a Murmuring Mama; you're informed! If they are vomiting, imagine that there is a large "Push to Vomit" button sitting at the bottom of their stomach. Any significant weight on the button, and it is pushed! A little water won't set it off, but a lot will. Go slow and keep the fluids going in. The incentive for doing this is avoiding an IV to re-hydrate your child. If a child is so dehydrated that they cannot find a vein, they will place an IV in their long leg bone to rehydrate, and this is a whole different level of intervention.

Fever plus vomiting equals inform your Med Unit.

For all of these things, find your threshold and don't change it for anyone! Do what you are comfortable with. If you are not comfortable about something, recommendations or prescriptions, is it okay to speak up and say that this makes you uncomfortable. You are not a pain in the tuchus, you're an involved parent. Remind yourself of that. Worst-case scenario, you seek a second opinion; best case scenario, you get an answer.

INJURY

Infants have a fontanelle. This allows their brain to grow, and also allows for a certain amount of flex. This is why bonks and bumps, so common for the top-heavy short people, would hurt us a lot more than it seems to hurt them. This isn't a recommendation to drop them on their bean or anything, but when they do bump, a little comfort, sometimes a pacifier (sucking is an infant's soothing mechanism), and a distraction can be all that is needed. For big bonks, I give half of the appropriate dose of Children's or Infant's Tylenol. Remember, they are not the same thing, each is formulated differently and dosed differently.

By the way, your child will fall off the bed and/or couch or both. It is as scary as all get out, but it doesn't make you a bad parent. They are generally more frightened than hurt. So give them a good once over and comfort your baby and yourself. Don't panic. Breathe. And don't drop them on their bean – or down the stairs.

Terrifying but true, Daughter went down nine wood stairs at Second Post, at less than a year old. I did not know she could open the child-gate lock, and my only warning was hearing the lock click. Then there was a sound like a box of shoes rolling down the stairs – it never occurred to me that it was Daughter. I was on my way already due to the click, and was at the top of the steps, seeing her sitting on the ninth step down, when she gathered enough air to let out a scream that could break glass. I don't think I touched a single stair on the way down – but did gather myself enough to know not to snatch her up in case something, like her neck, was broken. It wasn't likely since she was sitting, but it did occur to me. But I looked at her, got on the stairs below her, and reached out as she screamed at top volume, and ran my hands up her legs, along her arms, around shoulders, feeling fontanelle, wiggling fingers and toes. Nothing. StuntBaby was born. The RMO was a few houses away and we called on the spot. He listened and said, "Tylenol. And if she is stiff, has pain anywhere, or severe bruising, call immediately and bring her into the Embassy tomorrow." He knew my thresholds, bless him, and advised accordingly. Not a mark on her, bruise or otherwise.

"Stunt Baby"

VACCINATIONS

Ah, vaccinations. Lovely things. First, you can go to the CDC website and via their vaccine schedule planner, get a printable record for your child's immunization schedule based on their birthday. This does not include what we need for some of the more interesting places that we live overseas, but the website is very easy to navigate to find that information. Print your child's schedule and keep it with their shot record. Yes, this is a third record of shots, but it is more of a convenient reference. The Office of Medical Services, in the State Department, has a list of vaccines required by post. This is useful if you are going to travel to a post like India or Africa. If you can't check it, your Med Unit can.

Only healthy babies should be vaccinated — if there are sniffles or sneezes or Child has what is going around, reschedule. There aren't any vaccines out there that have a window of opportunity of a week or less. Overall, there is not a lot that you can do to 'help' with vaccines, but I do break them up so that they don't receive more than two at a time (one per leg). Three is the most I will do at once, and then only if I cannot possibly go back for the third shot at a later date. This means that if there are five shots due in February, I go in on the first week, providing that there are no lingering coughs or colds, again on the 10th and again for the last one on the 20th. And, here's the commercial again, before we leave the house, I give a dose of Tylenol. Fortunately, there are not too many vaccination-times that come so many at once.

When I arrive at the doctor's office overseas, I double-check that the vaccines are drawn up before we get into the exam room. This can be an issue in the U.S. because their vaccine protocol isn't as flexible as it can be in a Med Unit overseas. If you request it, they are generally happy to help. I will also get the dose of Tylenol now, if I've forgotten.

As they get older (Son was two when we did this), they know what is going on. I had him yell, as loud as he could (coordinating this with the nurse first of course) when they went to stick him. "Yell loud honey, but don't move." And oh, boy, did he yell! She stuck, he yelled louder. I told him to keep yelling and she was done. Then he cried a bit, and we acknowledged that it had hurt, but was done, and gave him a cookie (that's code for graham cracker) for yelling so well. My mom used a variation where we squeezed her hand instead of yelling. But do not go about how it is going to hurt and they're going to be brave, because believe me, brave is not what they feel and when they don't feel brave, that little mind thinks it is disappointing you or worse, tricking you (and you're supposed to be all-knowing, so you'd know). Instead, acknowledge it perfunctorily and move on, don't dwell on it. I told them it was going to hurt, but only for a little bit, and it is a yelling (or squeezing) test.

Doctor appointments themselves can be trying. I've told people about how I acclimate our pets to go to the vet by going when they do not have an appointment, and for an animal, go when you're buying food, because that is great positive reinforcement. I make the same recommendation for your children – for goodness sake, visit those nice people in the Med Unit when you're not sick! Invite them to dinner! My children aren't afraid of the doctor because they see them at times when they're NOT sick or going to get a shot.

Appointments can be awful, especially in the U.S. where insurance companies have so much control. Luckily, we're not in the U.S., so you can call ahead, verify that things are running on time and go in, have your appointment, and get out! This doesn't seem important until you have a sick child who, frankly, should be home sleeping and not hanging out in a waiting room. We have even gone so far (once) as to say to the doctor or nurse, "You've got fifteen minutes. GO!" after getting in the room. I call ahead to see if they are running on schedule. Always schedule appointments for your child's most awake time, usually after a nap or well before one. Don't try to reverse plan it and think, if I schedule it for when he's due for a nap, he'll get the shot, get tired and sleep. You're right, but he'll probably sleep in the car! Then he's got to be woken up (can't be helped, moving generally wakes them a little), at least enough for him to remember the indignity and then, depending on your child's temperament, all bets can be off and your nap is blown.

Take your kids to visit those nice people in the Med Unit when your kids aren't sick, or invite them to dinner!

Once they are in the 18-month old range, doctor's appointments can be downright entertaining (or excruciating). We started to take James, a little boy doll that my mom gave to Son. James gets his ears looked at and so does Son. Our RMO was great, and he also let Son look in his ears, and then mouth, listening with the stethoscope, etc. If the RMO is visiting and we didn't need an appointment, we'd make one for James. Afterwards, Son would pretend to be the doctor all day. Stuffed animals and little sisters work well for the patients too. If your doctor doesn't do this, do it yourself! "May I show him please?" you ask as you reach for a stethoscope. "Do you want to be the doctor and look in Mama's ear?" Overseas they are not as busy as they are in the U.S., or so controlled by insurance companies and they've got the time. Be pushy about making it not stressful for your child. Remember, this is all just normal stuff, nothing scary about it at all; different and strange and occasionally painful, but normal. Your reactions govern theirs – think normal.

CHILDPROOFING

Childproofing can be a politically correct swamp. There are more products out there than I ever even remotely considered. We have two things in our homes that I consider actual childproofing steps. First is the clear banister guards because the banisters/railings are not always up to snuff or are made of sharp, pointy iron, or are too wide at the top and thin at the bottom, inviting little heads to go in them, slide down them and be stuck. So, the clear banister plastic from One Step Ahead is what we purchased to make that safe. It comes in rolls and installs with a hole-punch and zip-ties. It works for containing kittens too.[6] The other thing that we have are outlet protectors, because 220v sounds like an awful lot to me, and those holes are so tempting and usually at an inconveniently easy height.

Remember, new and different, but normal, not scary.

Otherwise we tried to exercise an abundance of common sense:

Hide your wires under couches, behind furniture, or taped securely. This is useful if you have pets too.

Close your doors. If you don't want to lock things up, close the room and if you have to, put a bell on it. The hobby shops in the U.S. have these wonderful jingle bells that work great as kid-escape (or entry) alarms. I have one on our library/office door because my computer equipment is in there.

Move coffee tables and end tables to corners and walls for the cruising – learning to-walk stage. I didn't have corner protectors, not even on the sharp marble edges of the fireplace. However, in the playroom at Second Post, which did have a sharp marble fireplace, I did put a couch in front of it until we were at a less stumbly age.

Close your toilet lid. Now is the time to retrain your spouse! A lock isn't necessary (and is so frustrating when you need to go!). Your child isn't likely to be off your radar for that long and if it is likely or possible to happen, close the door. Potty training age gets a little iffy here, but hopefully at that age, if your child is cruisin' for the bathroom, you're right there behind him encouraging

[6] The kittens can't get a grip.

and offering to pull down Pull Ups! The toilet brush is also something that you might consider putting up.

Move things UP! I don't mean all the knickknacks and breakables should be up above three feet, because that not only looks silly but I believe that children should learn 'not for baby' for some things, and be offered an appropriate alternative Believe me, when you're responding to broken glass and a scared, startled child, it is pretty easy to be vigilant on that one. What I mean is move your medications and cleaning supplies UP – the top of your refrigerator is a good place for cleaning supplies instead of under the sink. Put the playable things down low, and to encourage helping, put their dishes (we like the hard melamine plastic ones) in a 'kid drawer' that they can get to so they can help you unload the dishwasher and put things like Rubbermaid and their dishes away.

Get up. Get a basket and move all your cleaning products up, higher than six feet. GO! So, I'm not saying be blasé. I am saying that your house does not need to look like a fortress OR a playpen. It can continue to look like a home, even though there are little people about. In short, your home can continue to be a home, with some basic modifications, rather than all-out refitting. I really do consider most "child-proofing" to be short cuts, rather than something that will keep your child safe in the long term. The only thing that can really keep them safe is your behavior and teaching them the appropriate behavior themselves.

Cleaning products and common household items can be deadly. We have approached this in two ways:

1. There are no cleaning products down below six feet. Period. The ones that must be, are in a locked closet. No bleach, no laundry detergent, nothing down low. Do this now, whether your baby is born or not, stop reading, go move things UP and come back. We had to have shelves built in Third Post, but there was reasonable space in First Post and we used the top of the refrigerator in Second Post. It is a good rule because things are simply too high to be on their radar yet. The dishwashing detergent, we use the ElectroSol tabs, are in a pretty canister on one of those over-the-sink shelf things, and bleach, rinse aid, and dishwasher salt are all on the refrigerator in a little basket.

2. Simple Green or other non-toxic cleaning product: for everything from windows to ovens, I used one non-toxic product. There were Windex wipes and Pledge wipes, but it was in the locked closet, and it is all still UP, in case the closet gets unlocked. Simple Green, and other products like it, is available at Sam's Club or Cosco's. Target has their Method brand that is also non-toxic, biodegradable and they do clean like heck. You can use Simple Green straight on ovens and they are done! I also keep a mini-cleaning kit in each bathroom. In the First Years blue step stool, which opens for storage,[7] I keep a container of Clorox wipes, Pledge wipes, Windex wipes and Swiffers for quick clean ups. They aren't up, but they are wipes only, nothing toxic or potentially destructive.

FIRST AID AND MEDICAL KITS

Just in case something does happen, I have a Kid Kit. It fits right between the dryer and the wall, or on top of the fridge, or under a car seat, anywhere that is close to the playroom or outside, where most incidents that would require it are likely to happen. In it are:

1. The First Aid Guide that came with the store bought Johnson & Johnson Baby Relief Kit, which I bought just for the hard, lockable, easy case!
2. Band-Aid hurt-free cleansing and infection protection foam first aid antiseptic (very nice if you're living somewhere that the water is not potable, and therefore cleaning a wound with it doesn't make sense)
3. Triple-antibiotic ointment plus. The 'plus' is a pain relieving ointment that keeps kids (and animals) from messing with the 'wound'
4. Band-aids, some fun, some practical, some waterproof
5. Hydrocortizone cream, 1% strength (standard)
6. Clotrimazole cream (an antifungal)
7. Diaper rash ointment with zinc oxide
8. A digital thermometer
9. Alcohol wipes (to clean said digital thermometer and other things)
10. Baby Orajel for teething pain or for a cut lip or chapped ones
11. WetOnes travel-pack antibacterial wipes
12. Saline, in this case LittleNoses, non-medicated spray or drops,

[7] They advertise it for tub toys, but I don't think things would dry and we live in mold-prone places.

for rinsing wounds or abrasions
13. Infant/Child Tylenol
14. Nose aspirator; makes a good syringe for sucking or spraying
15. One Beany Baby with a band-aid on his butt for holding while we do the first aid

I don't know if all the cases come with the slide lock and hole to secure it, but since this is your first line of defense, I recommend that you get one that you can slide a D-ring through to 'lock' it. Your child will see you use it, will want to "help" and open it (and surprise you with the accomplishment). This Kid Kit is what I toss in the luggage when we travel, with a few additions of cold meds and Benadryl, just in case. In the summer, this kit also has
16. Insect repellent and
17. Sunscreen

This is such an easy thing to have on hand, and convenient. People substitute things they like, and things they prefer, with ease and so far I've had nothing but compliments, usually from a mother who's child has just taken a tumble in our backyard.

Now, one step beyond the Kid Kit, is a Medical Bin, and our family practitioner helped me put ours together. Keep in mind, I try very very hard not to go to a doctor, ever, and she knows that. She also knows that I have worked with animals (the non-human kind) and could place an IV in my child's vein if required. Work with your doctor and come up with a version of this that works for you if you want one on hand. Most families are admittedly quite comfortable with the kid kit only and don't require an Emergency Medical Bin, let alone one that is so extensive. Items in the Medical Bin would normally be used in consultation with your pediatrician or Med Unit.
1. Thermometer: digital or scanning (on the forehead) or other, but one that remains in this bin
2. Alcohol wipes
3. Poison treatment kit with CharcoAid and Ipecac Syrup
4. Latex gloves in a Ziploc bag
5. Bulb syringe
6. Saline solution (yup, like for contacts, it is a sterile flush for wounds and eyes), replace annually
7. Ziploc bag of cotton balls
8. Ziploc bag of 3" cotton gauze, also available pre-packed and

sterile

9. Children's Benadryl
10. Acetaminophen
11. Kaolectrolyte electrolyte replenisher packets
12. Hand sanitizer
13. KY liquid lubricant, for the thermometer, for getting something stuck on a little finger off
14. Children's Immodium
15. Children's laxative
16. BriteLight flashlight (no batteries required)
17. Saline nasal spray, no preservatives type
18. Adhesive tape, medical type
19. Roll of gauze
20. Small splints
21. Roll of VetRap (bandaging tape that sticks to itself and can keep gauze on or go over an Ace Bandage to keep those little pins safe)
22. Ace Bandage
23. Butterfly closure Band-aids
24. Band-aids, many sizes, particularly the uncommon ones
25. Quick First Aid reference with phone numbers
26. Medical tweezers
27. Hydrogen peroxide
28. Neosporin or other triple-antibiotic cream with pain killer
29. Liquid skin (commonly sold as NuSkin)
30. Hemostat scissors (they lock open or closed and grip better than your fingers ever will)
31. Finally, the odd things that no sane person would have but I did, like suture material and a scalpel and syringes (which did come in handy when I had to sew the dog's ear back on when it was practically ripped off!)

Some of these items expire; replace fluids each time you rotate back to the U.S. or are on Home Leave between posts (approximately every two years).

All of that said, I think I have opened the Emergency kit, instead of the Kid Kit, all of ... three times in six years. Once for Son getting into my vitamins, once for the VetRap to keep a broken foot (mine) wrapped, and once to sew the dog's ear back on. The Emergency Kit is more peace of mind, insurance, rather than something I need or use. If you are a homeopath, keep the homeopathic items in the Medical Kit and UP, because they can be very dangerous, as well as very helpful. The Kid Kit got used fairly regularly in the first few years, usually during playgroups. Other mothers have different tolerances, and they're pretty grateful to see something so handy so close. I do make a point to restock the Kid Kit regularly and ensure that things don't expire and are age appropriate. I had Infant and Children's dosages in it for a few years. Remember, they are different.

THE LITTLE THINGS IN LIFE

Splinters or slivers can be run of the mill or emotional time bombs, depending on the mood and/or temperament of the child. They hurt, and pretty consistently, are mostly invisible. This is dumbfounding to the child. The magic fix is a piece of tape — packing tape works best. You press it gently to the splinter site in general (the whole finger, whole front of the hand, that kind of thing). Step back and tell them to say "abracadabra!" and pull it off in the direction that the splinter needs to come out. Usually the splinter comes out too — saving you the need to try to keep the child still while you excavate it with the needle.

I trim fingernails and toenails as needed, but regularly with no fuss or drama. Like puppies, the more you play with their fingers, toes and ears, the easier things like trims and temperatures are. You don't have to accomplish much, but it teaches them to sit still. While very little, I borrow someone to distract the child while I trim. Sit the child on your lap, facing away from you, and trim the right hand first (if you're right handed, that is), holding each finger between your left thumb and forefinger. Take your time (we use cuticle scissors, since they're slightly curved and very small), and remember, you don't have to do all ten at once.

Teeth are something they don't even have yet! Initially I used Orajel gum cleanser, but frankly it didn't seem to do anything that I could see except tickle. Once there was a tooth or two, we brushed every evening, just a little bit on your finger and quick touch to the tongue and a run around the gums (which helps to check if there is anything else in there yet). Same technique as fingernail trims: you sit on the toilet once the finger or toothbrush is loaded, using so little toothpaste that you're barely scaring the toothbrush with the toothpaste, and in about thirty seconds you're done. They sell 'trainer toothpaste', with no fluoride, for learning, before the children know not to swallow. The point is that they get used to it.

If you're like us, you're living in a place where you have a distiller. Guess what? It takes out the fluoride too, if there was any to start with. So, at about two years old, your child should see a dentist while in the U.S. You will have to speak up so that they hear you when you say you are living in the third world where the water is not only non-potable, but possibly distilled or filtered, and you might need fluoride supplements. Depending on your post, the water tests, and the recommendation of your Med Unit and dentist/pediatrician, you will have to decide whether or not to use fluoride supplements. I've spoken with a number of individuals now, and there are numerous ways that you can get fluoride into your child while their teeth are developing. There is paste, non-chewable pills, water drops, and chewable pills. Believe me, the consensus is to go for the chewable pill. But if there is fluoride in the bottled water, don't supplement! We decided to go for an alternative – we use Concentrace mineral supplements for our water, distilled or filtered. We can safely use this in our filtered or distilled water without OVER-dosing their little teeth and giving them black lines, even though they might drink the local bottled water that reportedly has fluoride. Check with your dentist, as you may have different thresholds or preferences.

The more you play with fingers, toes and ears, the easier nail trims and taking a temp are.

Beginning at about one year old, start 'brushing their teeth before bed', and letting them see you brush yours. You're not really brushing their teeth the same way you brush yours, but you're acclimating them to the experience and giving them something to emulate. I have heard parents talk about having to fight or wrestle with their children to get teeth brushed and have no desire to go there. A minute here, seeing you, two minutes there, is all it takes to get used to the idea. After all, would you want someone to unexpectedly start to shove a stick in your mouth and move it around? At about two years old, they should be brushing themselves, with you doing the "checking". We say, "Let me check!" and take the brush and do a run along the back bottom left, saying each part as we do it, back bottom right, back top left, back top right and smile teeth. Between two and three, they should add 'after breakfast brushing', or before school. Be matter of fact about it and don't add to the drama. This isn't a contest of wills; it is something that everyone has to do. And be very proud of them when you visit the dentist and they have good, strong, clean teeth.

At about two years old, you should talk to your pediatrician about including a vitamin supplement to their diet also (yeah, Flintstones chewables!), and keep all of the pill giving, whether it is fluoride, vitamin and an actual medication like Singulair, to one dosing time per day if possible. We do ours at breakfast so there is no wondering if it was done or who did it — if you feed breakfast, you give the pills. Period.

Finally, it is quite likely that at some point, your child will fall and bite his or her tongue. This causes a whole lot of blood, as they come to you with their hands cupped under their chin and blood literally dripping into it. Tongues heal fast! A rinse with clean water and biting on a washcloth to stop the bleeding and believe it or not, even if they've bitten clean through,[8] it will probably heal on its own and very quickly. If there is pain the next morning, or fever, go on in and get it looked at. Otherwise, prepare to be amazed at the body's ability to heal.

MEDICATIONS

Since we're on the topic of pills and medications, here are a few seemingly simple questions for you: Do you know what is in your purse? Does your spouse carry Tylenol or other meds in his briefcase or coat? Did you take them all out last time you recovered from a cold? My mother has the most terrifying story of a child who got into her grandmother's purse and got into heart medication. There was nothing they could do except watch that child die. Guess what? My dog was on heart medication and it occurred to me that we needed to make sure that all medication is up! We keep meds in three places, the Kid Kits, a set of bins that we call the medicine cabinet that are on a high shelf, and extras in the storeroom in a locked bin. I hang my purse on a high coat hook because I do have Tylenol in there occasionally and visiting friends and family are used to me taking their coats and purses, oh so politely, and hanging them up. UP. Move it up!

So here is a challenge because I'm guessing you're thinking, "good idea" and can also guess the likelihood of it getting done. Right now, set this down, pick up a basket or bin and walk around your house and collect medications — Neosporins and hydrocortizone creams (you wouldn't eat those, but they look like frosting), and animal medication like flea and tick drops or heart worm preventative. Open up drawers and don't be surprised when there is a blister pack of Benadryl in one or a loose Advil in another. It is amazing what you are going to find when you collect things in one go-around. And for a good visual lesson, leave that basket out for your spouse or partner to see when they come

[8] Which Son has done TWICE.

home – we don't think we have lots of that stuff lying around, but we do. Put it UP.

As I said, an additional thing that occurs as a result of this obsession is when guests come – we put their purses up too. I'll offer to hang their purse with their coat and will sometimes go so far as to say, "We have small people in the house, so we keep purses up." Of course, this is a good idea anyway if you don't want purses rifled through regardless. Kids don't think of that as an invasion on privacy, it is more an exploratory action. Son somehow destroyed a retractable tape measure of a friend and I'm pretty sure Daughter absconded with her calculator...

MEDICAL TESTS

I will close on a very sad, but very important note, and the story of Laila Prather. Newborn screening[9] is important and most hospitals do some screening. Appendix 7 lists the website for the National Newborn Screening and Genetic Resource Center. The home page has links to what tests are available state by state, as well as screening programs.It is your choice what screenings are done besides the basic state requirements. However, tell your doctor that you will follow up to get the results, and give them the information to send the results to your Med Unit as well. A screening result is useless if no one has the information itself. Hearing screening is one of the most basic, and is a reassurance to us to know that they tested with normal hearing as an infant, particularly when they're oblivious to us asking them to wash their hands. The rest of the tests are usually blood tests, a small heel stick, tiny sample and quick test, for things like PKU (phenylketonuria, where they can't process protein and must be on a special diet immediately) and cystic fibrosis. The state dictates what is required, but some states, such as Washington and Maryland, do not have mandatory screening yet. You can ask what they are testing for. Most of us are pretty oblivious to the tests and their results, unless there is a problem. If you have family histories, you should discuss screening with your pediatrician, and get recommendations. They do not screen for everything, and if there are genetic diseases in your family history, or believe it or not, a series of unexplained infant deaths, you can request them. Check with your insurance if the results will disqualify you for care, as a pre-existing condition.

Pick up a basket or bin and walk around your house and collect medications from purses, coats, and drawers in every room.

[9] http://kidshealth.org/parent/system/medical/newborn_screening_tests.html

They do not screen for everything. Some things are visited upon us, and we can't figure out why. There might not be a reason, but it is human nature to look for one. Laila's condition could have been detected with a simple test. Whether or not it would have been taken is unknown, because it is not a common test.

Laila's mother and I were pregnant at First Post with Daughters and they were born almost within a month of each other. We all send our hopes and prayers to both of them daily.

Written and reproduced with permission by
Dominique, Laila's mother:

Laila Viktoria Prather was born on January 29, 2004, a healthy baby girl and the second of two for her happy parents. She had perfect Apgar scores at birth and progressed normally, meeting and surpassing all her milestones. She was a happy, healthy baby, and then at four months, she caught a small cold and missed a feeding. The next morning our lives changed forever.

We noticed that something was wrong right away. She kept thrusting her tongue in and out, and it seemed that she had lost all muscle tone. The day before she was sitting up and playing; now she couldn't even hold her head up. She was crying constantly as if in pain and had lost her ability to latch on and suck a bottle. Laila had regressed to a newborn overnight.

As a military family, we were stationed in Ecuador at the time, we had little resource in doctors. We took Laila to the best hospital available. They performed all the right tests, EKG, EEG, spinal tap and MRI to name a few. After a week in the hospital, they had no idea what was causing her symptoms. While they were signing the release papers, Laila had a seizure that lasted 45 minutes. We were terrified and not sure what to do. Our insurance company didn't want to pay for us to return to the U.S. but finally agreed when I told them that the hospital had discharged my daughter to allow her to die at home and they said that they could do nothing further for her. TriCare then arranged for a Medevac and we left within 24 hours.

The plane ride was wonderful, the staff of two nurses and a doctor treated Laila like she was their own. She had a seizure that was so intense that it locked her neck to the left and they rearranged all the equipment so she could see them. I will always be grateful to them.

The first hospital that we were scheduled to land at, Miami Children's Hospital, denied our case saying it sounded like there was nothing that they could do differently. So we ended up going to Lackland Air Base in San Antonio, Texas and thank goodness we did.

Right away Laila got a team of doctors and a room with a bed in it for me. They repeated all the tests done in Ecuador and added a muscle and skin biopsy. Laila was put on IV fluids, medicine to help her relax and antibiotics just to be safe. My mom flew in from Virginia to care for our five year old Serena, and my sister-in-law drove from Louisiana for support.

The doctors systematically ruled out anything viral or bacterial. They ruled out epilepsy and every other regular cause of seizures. For forty-five days they monitored Laila, noting her movements and lack of additional seizures, and inability to regain her prior milestones. One of her neurologists noticed her uncontrolled movements and that she went from hypotonia, no muscle tone, to dystonia, stiffness. The head neurologist tested her for an extremely rare genetic disorder and called us into a private meeting. We were told that Laila has Glutaric Acidemia Type 1, and that there was no cure. This baby, who was so perfect at birth, would now never walk or talk, and would need a special diet given through a gastrostomy tube just to live. Also, we would be lucky if she lived more than a few years. Then, they left us alone to let it sink it. We were crushed, I FELT my heart break and all we could do was cry.

Glutaric Acidemia Type 1 is an extremely rare genetic disorder that prohibits the body from processing protein correctly. The amino acids that the body cannot process are mainly lysine and tryptophan. The unprocessed protein builds up and damages the part of the brain that controls voluntary movement. For instance, Laila knows she wants to pick up a block, but the brain cannot send that message to the muscles in the arm and hand to make it happen. Eventually, the build up of protein will completely poison Laila's brain and everything will shut down, resulting in death.

Laila requires twenty-four hour care, mainly because of her inability to swallow and the risk of suffocation if she gets in a position that she cannot get out of. In the beginning it was hard on us all; everything was thrown at us at once. We had to learn to use a feeding pump, change her g-tube and administer her medications all the while knowing that Laila's life depended on it. It took almost a year to get Laila on a schedule of eating and sleeping, and it is very strict, any upset in her schedule causes major stress on Laila. Her schedule consists of a feeding every three hours starting at 6am. On time feedings are important because of the risk of dehydration. Three medications, three times a day, a nap from noon to three and last feed at 9pm and then bedtime. We are so careful in her care that thankfully she has not had any hospital stays due to illness in the past year and a half. We do a lot of cleaning and hand washing. We are lucky to have home care for Laila eight hours a day and we couldn't ask for a better person to care for her.

Laila also receives early intervention services including speech, occupational and physical therapies. These services have done wonders for Laila in more ways than I can mention. Laila lights up when one of her therapists comes through the door.

Laila has brought our family closer together than we have ever been before. My parents sold their birth home, quit their jobs and moved closer to us for support and to be with Laila as much as possible. Laila has taught us the true meaning of unconditional love. The saddest part of Laila's story is that it could have been prevented with a $25 test at birth. Had we known to ask for extended newborn screening to be added to the PKU test, Laila, besides being on a restricted diet, would have had a chance at a semi-normal life. She would have been able to chase her sister around, tell me she loved me, and lived a normal life span. A few states offer extended newborn screening, but most don't unless you specifically ask for it.

Although we have knowledge of a devastating future for Laila, we have learned not to dwell on it. Instead we put all our energy into giving Laila and her sister the happiest normal life possible. When we see her smile her beautiful smile, we know we are accomplishing our task. We cherish her smiles, but never forget that those smiles will eventually fade away until there is nothing left but a blank stare, leaving us with a hole in our family that can never be repaired.

Log onto: www.caringbridge.org/visit/lailaprather to read
Laila's Daily Journal.

Dominique

8. Travel — welcome to your life

Travel is an essential part of our lives, whether it is our own, with our spouses or our family, we do a lot of it. When I traveled back to the U.S. with Son and Daughter, we checked in at the United desk. Son was 3 and Daughter was 1. The United person was very nice, professional and helpful, made the usual comments about being 'so brave to travel with two children and a dog' and then sort of got distracted and looked up at us a few times and down at the children a few times (who were waiting patiently in their strollers). Finally he said, "Ma'am, I think there has been a mistake. I think someone inadvertently added a zero to your daughter's mileage. Your daughter cannot possibly have 20,000 miles, she's not even two!" I laughed and said, "Son, can you tell the nice man where we used to live?" Son shouted "Kirblackstan" (not really, but it was 'stan) and he said, "Where?" I said, "Exactly. Her miles are correct." He upgraded us for free. Kill them with kindness, folks.

Mostly I will deal with your travel, and the necessities that it entails, short cuts if we know them, and suggestions from ticketing and strollers to what to pack. But one aspect of travel that is rarely touched is that of your family. If they come to visit, and I hope they do, consider using some of your many, many miles to help them do so. There were times when we were just too far away for an actual visit to be possible, but meeting halfway in Istanbul was a treat for us (because we love Istanbul), allowed family to visit, and gave us all a nice break.

TIME

When booking tickets and traveling with children, if possible, plan for two hours minimum for plane transfers. Then add an additional thirty minutes per child to your transfer time. Anything less and you will need to remember to pack a change of clothes because you could miss your flight. It isn't anything planned, but bathroom breaks, getting everything onto the security screening station and then back off and re-distributed, all of these things add time. And I say this with two children who do not go running off on their own in an airport until we are to the next gate and waiting — because just once we stopped en route, and nearly missed the plane as a result. Eating takes a smidgen longer with the small ones.

One of the main reasons for adding an additional thirty minutes is that it is not just you and one carry-on, weaving through people. Now, when you disembark from the plane, it is likely that you will be waiting for a majority of the passengers to depart before you, as you gather your things and get baby ready. You will also be waiting planeside for your gate-checked stroller. Once that arrives, which is not necessarily in a timely manner, you will load it up, put the baby in the carrier on it, and then start on your way to the next gate. So, we're ... fifteen minutes minimum already behind the power curve. Now, you're on your way through the airport, no problem. When you arrive at the next security checkpoint, it is not just letting your carry-on slide off your shoulder onto the conveyor belt and putting your coat in a box with your shoes. Now you have to get all the stuff from under the stroller and anything on either parent's shoulder. You also have to remove the carrier portion of the stroller, collapse the stroller, and put that on the belt too. Then, you must remove the child from the carrier, and put the carrier and any blanket, dolls, etc through with it. Oh, and don't forget any coats and items in your pockets, etc. have to on there too. Then you go through with the child and try to reload, readjust and redistribute, put on your shoes and coat and then depart the screening area. That added another fifteen minutes, which is where the thirty extra comes from! Now, if you have arrived at the gate, you (well, the baby actually) might require a diaper change, and this way you won't miss your plane if Baby does.

> Plan an additional thirty minutes per child for your transfer time in airports; you're not a comic book super-hero.

So, for example, if you, your spouse and a child are traveling, you need three and a half hours transfer time between flights; planned transfer time (none of this "oh, that flight is always late" stuff, thank you). When you have two kids, four hours. Your travel agent might balk, but it is worth insisting on.

When traveling with an infant, use your child's infant seat (up to 20lbs, fits in a base or stroller) on the plane. You generally cannot take the child seat (20-40lbs, single unit, anchored in), mostly because they tend to be too large for the airline seat. And the child's boosters (40lbs plus, uses the car's seatbelt) are not airline approved for travel. All child-seats should be checked and traveled with if possible, unless there is a child-seat on the other end at pick-up. If your child seat or booster doesn't come with a bag, Lands End sells some mighty large, very tough, wheeled duffel bags to do the job.

The next time you are at an office supply store, you can pick up some no-heat laminate for business cards and laminate a bunch of your business cards. With a laminated business card and a zip tie, you can 'label' everything, including strollers, children's bags, (kids) carriers, carry-on and anything else you need. I even tend to make a label on the computer, business card sized, for our destination if it isn't "home" as designated by the business card. Now the children are old enough to tell me what they want on 'their' card and we make a game of it before travel. It's quick, it's easy and they're reusable for a long time. I have a stack of them in the outer pocket of my main carry-on for our return trips and we keep one from each trip for the kids to play with (they pretend to travel sometimes; no idea why).

Carry-on can be a little daunting because we tend to over-think what the children need. We also tend to think that we'll actually have time to need something ourselves! Less is more; and I say that from having hauled around way too much. Your carry-on is basically a diaper bag with a Ziploc bag of your toiletries and one optimistic book. No more than three toys and two books per child. Believe me, the contents of the pocket of the seat in front of you are much more fascinating than that old toy.

A few snapshots of what we looked like when we traveled, at various times in our travels.

1. Extra Small Travel Size: Son 0-6 months old. Infant seat and wheels with carry-on below, manageable by one adult, hands free at all times.

2. Small Travel Size: Son 6 months old to 2 years old. Convertible travel stroller car-seat (very cool), back-pack on adult's back, pushing stroller, manageable by one adult, hands free, even if that adult is heavily pregnant.

3. Medium Travel Size: Son 2 to 4 years old, Daughter infant to 20lbs (for her that was more than two years old!). Infant seat and stroller was still a challenge until we went ahead and got the tandem stroller[1] that the infant seat snapped into. Then we continued to use the tandem stroller when she could actually sit in

[1] One child behind the other, heavy duty version. I've spoken with other mothers that had a very hard time with the tandem/dual strollers, so try it out in the store WITH the kids.

it and not slide out. Carry-on below and well-laden backpack purse on Mom's back. Children had toy bags in the carry-on, and snacks, but carried their blanket and baby themselves. Those all got bungee corded into the stroller when it went through security, and two bags, leaving two free hands to walk kids through. Really challenging, but manageable by one adult. We used that tandem stroller until the wheels literally fell off (um, in Amsterdam).

4. Large Travel Size: Son 4+ years old, Daughter 2+ years old. Umbrella strollers clipped together, backpack on adult's back. Children holding small, light backpacks with their 'stuff' in it and blankets and babies bungeed to their backpacks when going through security. Again, this is still manageable by one adult and still hands-free.

"Gate check". It's a magic word (or two).

5. Extra Large Travel Size: Age 3 years and 5 years. Praise the Lord and pass the chicken! Now it is stroller-free, holding hands, kids managing their own carry-on travel. We all use backpacks or rollies (by the way, a rollie of appropriate strength can hold a small child if they sit with their legs straddling it like a horse, but it gets heavy for the Mama fairly quickly) and go from one gate to the next before we stop. This is still totally manageable by one adult.

Some magic words are "gate check". However, using those words doesn't always guarantee that it will work, depending on where you are. This is a planeside gate check of items too large to go in the overhead. They are taken from you when you get to the end of the jet-way and put into the last hold that is closed, which is the first one opened. Then (in theory) you collect it planeside when you get off the plane. Before you actually board, go to the check-in desk and ask for a Gate Check for your stroller. Request that they put the next city ONLY on the tag (we have had strollers checked through to the final destination, which kind of negates the point). If there is an appropriate box to check for planeside delivery, double-check that it is marked. This means you get to take your stroller right up to the plane door, unload, collapse the stroller, and herd everyone to his or her seats. This is quite manageable because frankly, if they're walking, they can't go in too many directions once they are IN the plane. And if you're managing one and the other one gets away from you, do not feel in any way embarrassed to say to the stewardess at the door, "Do NOT let a child off this plane!"

> *Once we were getting on a plane and I went left with Daughter in her carrier, while Son went right. I knew that they weren't going to let him off the plane, but there is a highly irrational part of you that suddenly panics. I dropped all our stuff on our seats, unsnapped and scooped up Daughter and started down the aisle calling his name. Believe me, my voice was getting increasingly panicked as we went further and further down (how did that plane get so big!) and I didn't hear an answer. I heard someone closer to the front, a passenger, say, "Don't let a child get off this plane!" to the Purser in a very imposing voice. She picked up her little phone and pinged the stewards in the back, so we were covered, but that doesn't reassure me until I hear this small little "Mama?" in the middle of a flock of knees. The feeling of relief is nearly impossible to describe. I said, "Son, go all the way to the back, through the galley and come back towards the front in this aisle please." He said, "Okay." And off he went. The crew was very careful to point him in the right direction, and he nonchalantly strolls by, and we wove back through all those boarding people, against the stream to the chaos I'd left in our seats.*

"Son's Wrong Turn"

STROLLERS

There are a wide variety of strollers out there, but rarely mentioned in the descriptions are the Universal Wheels. This is essentially a stroller frame that any infant carrier can be attached to. It is lightweight and compact and incredibly handy. But it technically isn't a stroller. Infant seats generally come with a base, which remains in the car and secures the infant seat. After the infant is in a car seat, rather than the infant seat, the stroller can still functional through toddler years. They can be very easy to open and close and come with a wide variety of accessories.

Most commonly purchased strollers are the Travel System strollers, which combines a car seat and a stroller, with the infant car seat usually snapping into the stroller. This is very convenient for the parent, since the infant can remain in the car while the stroller is taken out and opened, and then the infant is snapped into the stroller still contained in the seat. Travel systems generally come with a base, which remains in the car and secures the infant seat. After the infant is in a car seat, rather than the infant seat, the stroller is still functional through toddler years, and usually come with snack trays and cup holders and may even have changeable seat positions.

A jogging stroller is a slightly more robust stroller, usually designed for all-terrain travel. They tend to have hard rubber wheels and come in three-wheel designs for maneuverability. This can be useful for a family if they are in the habit of jogging or if they are stationed at a post with particularly challenging terrain. There is usually a basket area in the bottom, just like the travel system. Some jogging strollers are also travel systems!

An umbrella stroller is also called a compact stroller and they are lightweight and usually collapse to the point that they could almost (not quite) be stored in an umbrella stand. They collapse easily and are easy to transport and store. They are also relatively inexpensive (usually under $20). Usually they are metal poles, with fabric seat and back, and security straps, and that is it. Sometimes there is a small storage bag, but these are the no frills, utilitarian strollers and work very well for toddler travel, whether it is internationally or to the local grocery store.

While it isn't necessary until you have multiple children, the tandem or multi-child stroller can come in a variety of styles: lightweight, jogging, travel system, etc. They can be arranged side-by-side, which isn't as easy for airport travel as the tandem, one child seated in front of the other, version. That said, they are long, making a reach for a door in front of the stroller very challenging for the parent pushing the stroller. They also tend to come with cup holders and snack containers, and adjustable seat positions. Compare the different options and consider choosing the most robust, given the amount of travel it will be subjected to. If you have to load the seats up with weight and try pushing it, feel free to do so in the store because it will save you future remorse.

So, now that we know what we are talking about, how about some more information for you to digest?

At our first post, we used the Universal Wheels more than anything else. This was primarily because they were light, convenient, and very portable for a child in an infant carrier, without being a large Travel System stroller. At the second post, the terrain was not conducive for walks – no sidewalks, terrifying drivers, lack of traffic or pedestrian laws (not even suggestions!). The fancy jogging stroller that we had been given was used rarely and briefly. This is one item that you have to know why you are buying a stroller and where you will be using it. Our primary use of strollers is in airports – otherwise, when we go for a walk, we all walk (yes, even the little ones, if they can walk, they go for a walk; they're just shorter walks). If you are buying for convenient transit and travel, take a five-pound bag of flour with you when you go to the stroller store and try to open and close the stroller holding that bag. Have the pregnant mama do it, holding the bag. If it is hard to do with the bag of flour, it will be twice as a hard with the infant. If you are buying for walking, strolling, hiking, check the wheels. Are they solid rubber? Check the axles, will they break if you step on them? How much plastic is the stroller made up of and if you are going to be storing the stroller outside, will it be susceptible to the cold? We had one stroller that we kept on our balcony and one day I went to open it and a plastic piece just snapped off. Unfortunately, it was the brakes! I personally used a stroller for containment and safety while traveling. Know why you are buying the stroller, and where you will be using it.

The Universal Wheels by Kolcraft are fabulous for your infant seat. They aren't just wonderful for airline travel either, but all the time! Getting baby in and out of an infant seat is best done in the house. Therefore, you want an infant seat that makes getting it in and out of the car easier on your arms and shoulders, because no matter how ergonomic they try to make the handles, they're heavy and awkward. If you have other things on your shoulder (like a diaper bag) or your vehicle is large or high, or you're not so tall, the diaper bag slides down your shoulder and you worry about thumping Baby on the face or bouncing on the shade! And it is hard to get the diaper bag off your shoulder first. So, what we did was leave the baby in the infant seat. We used our wheels all the time and kept it in the trunk. Baby was put in the infant carrier in the house, then snapped in the car. While still snapped in, I'd get the wheels out, drop the diaper bag in the bottom, and then unsnap the carrier and click it onto the wheels. We took it when we went to visit people, as if it was a stroller (it is a stroller, only just the frame). I liked the Kolcraft version because it was a true one-hand open or close. The Snap-N-Go version is also very nice, as the infant seat actually locks in with an audible snap. With the Kolcraft you have to use the safety strap to secure the carrier. But the Snap-N-Go doesn't collapse as easily, which can be an issue when trying to get through security screening. Both baskets handle the smallest size rolling carry-on well, and both handles are strong enough to loop your purse or diaper bag onto, leaving your hands free to push and steer and tend to baby without things falling off your shoulder. You can gate check the wheels, but they do actually fit in the overhead. Both of them have the child facing you when in motion.

The Sit-N-Stroll is a car-seat stroller combination, and it is very cool if you're going to travel a lot. We used this from the time Son was six months old to three years. Unfortunately, it didn't take long for him to outgrow it. It is used as a car seat in the car, a stroller in the airport, and a car seat on the airplane (airline approved no less). It was very convenient and easy to steer and it is low enough that when Son was required to get out of it, he could do so without a problem. The handle telescopes down and the wheels fold in and up. I had to have my son get out of it to change it from car seat to stroller. Husband could snap it from stroller to seat without removing Son and lift him into the seat. With the seatbelt extender, it seatbelts in like an infant seat. It does not recline, other than what the car seat itself does, but with a few pillows under the foot for a little more tip, it works fine. However, as neat as this thing was, it did not fit well in bulkhead seats. And airline seats are getting smaller and smaller. Business Class was not problem, but the Cabin class required raising the arm-rests, belting it in and wedging the arm-rests back down.

When we were at the two-umbrella stroller stage, I received these great clips from One Step Ahead, which connect two umbrella strollers. I hooked their carry-ons, ultra-light backpacks, on the back of their strollers, and we were off. Umbrella strollers aren't too expensive, so the loss of one wasn't too painful (one didn't make the gate-check transfer... ever). With two strollers connected like that, one backpack on Sherpa Mama, kids' back-packs on the strollers, well you can breeze through the airports. The key is packing light. We always packed snacks, but I learned early that one 1-gallon Ziploc with graham crackers and dried fruit was all it took, and there was plenty of water on the way. Yes, I had my share of times when I took the whole kitchen and all the accessories, and those were the worst, because it was just too much to manage. I learned from my mistakes.

TICKETING

When you purchase your tickets, if you are financially able to do so, buy your infant or child his own seat. Some airlines have different prices for infants and children. Infant (under two years old) seats are sometimes half the price of an adult one and child (two to twelve) seats sometimes are only two-thirds normal price. That said, a seat is a seat and it might be full price, but it is worth it. It is a staging area and a little extra space if nothing else, and you will need it. If your child is traveling on a Diplomatic Passport, it is necessary to purchase a seat for the child.

As I said earlier, but is worth repeating, my recommendation, and the recommendation of others, is to book the fewest number of connections. Some people prefer the bulkhead section and request the airline have the bassinet/baby bed available for you. Confirm this seating and availability every time you call and particularly 24 hours before departure. If possible, upgrade to Business Class for both of you. My family, when (rarely) traveling together, prefers to sit two and two, preferably in a block of four, like rows 6 and 7 or 51 and 52. This is not only easier for the airline, since finding a group of four in a row can be challenging, but allows me to reduce the impact on other passengers somewhat. Again, it is a containment issue for us: we'll take 5A&B and 6A&B and only have to worry about them getting out past me, on the aisle. Amazingly, at 3 years old and 5 years old, they now want to sit together, usually behind my spouse and I, and that works well too.

Buy your infant his or her own seat when purchasing airline tickets.

Some folks have run into issues where they are not 'allowed' the bulkhead seat with bassinet if their child has a paid seat, and the State Department does require that all travelers on Diplomatic Passports have paid, assigned seats. Again, little honey goes a lot further than vinegar when talking to the Purser (skip the stewards and stewardesses) when trying to work this out. One last note on the bulkhead bassinets, use the security straps – if there is turbulence in flight (your child is not in the bassinet during landing and take off), the baby must be secure. Low and loose, but definitely around that little body so no one has to catch the child (happened, but thankfully, not to me).

You're not having literary *déjà vu*, this was all covered in Chapter 2, but it is worth repeating. The airlines could care less and will occasionally try to pull the 'overbooked' card and say your child must be a lap-baby so another, paying customer, can be assigned the seat. First of all, your child's seat was paid for, by the U.S. Government no less, so bumping him or her is no more acceptable than bumping you. I've discovered that I've lost my embarrassment-gene while traveling with small or infant children. I've gotten further with a smile and understandingly saying, "I understand your difficulties. You may rebook both of us (or all three of us!) and place us in a hotel at your expense, but I need a receipt for all changes since the U.S. government paid for both of our tickets and I will need to document the change." Suddenly it isn't as easy as the child being held by the mama, and they pick a less complicated customer. I've had an American airline move my son from Business to Economy (to sit next to his grandmother), forget to feed him, and never refund the difference in ticket prices. I've had them attempt to turn my children into lap babies. I've even been forced into missing flights and then required to endure a forced layover of four days, because the post we were traveling to had only two flights a week. You are a paying customer; you just happen to pay every time they take taxes out of your paycheck.

Without sacrificing your transit time requirements, book tickets for the fewest connections, versus the fastest travel times.

As I mentioned in Chapter 2, some other things that have come up when it comes to traveling back to your post are a letter of release from the non-present parent (usually Dad) and a Power of Attorney. Believe it or not, some airlines will not allow you to fly, particularly out of the country (and gods help you if you're going to a 'stan), with your child if the other parent doesn't know about it, in writing. I say, how would they know if he knows or not? They don't, so they assume that he doesn't either. A letter from the father, stating that the family really does all live in that foreign place, together even, and that mother is bringing baby HOME, not stealing it, may be necessary. So, if Daddy is going to be departing before mother and child, get that letter written and have it notarized. You may not be asked for it, but then again, you might be! We were asked for it both times. My children have traveled in many instances with their grandmother and not been asked for it (apparently borrowing your grandchildren is not frowned upon). We also had on hand a specific Power of Attorney, a document that basically states that if one parent wasn't present, the other was allowed to travel internationally with the child(ren). It sounds bizarre, but it is a scary world that we live in apparently. An example of the Power of Attorney is in Appendix 2, for your reference.

EATING AND DRINKING

Offer water, pacifier, or nurse your infant during take off and landing. Babies aren't so good at re-pressurizing their ears, but swallowing helps, which is why I recommend nursing them up and down if you are allowed. As they get slightly older, we used a pacifier first, then a sippy cup with water in it to induce the swallowing. It does not have to be a drama, if they know from the beginning that this will help their ears, they're in the habit of it, and like you and I, it is just adjusting to the conditions. The last trip we took, we actually watched our children try to help another child traveling unaccompanied on his first trip, 'pop' his ears, as they unconsciously took sips from their travel bottles themselves.

If only one parent is traveling with a child, some airlines require a Power of Attorney, a notarized letter or both (or neither) from the absent parent.

I made all my baby food when I was home. This was lovely, healthy, easy and convenient ... when I was home. But six weeks prior to planned travel, I ordered Gerber baby food in jars[2] because there wasn't a local alternative that I was comfortable with. Daughter ate two meals a day of fruit/veg, which is four jars a day, plus cereal. So I ordered sixteen total jars of food (eight fruit, eight veg), so I was covered for the day of travel and the day after we arrived, in both directions. This allowed me to avoid having to go out and find someplace that sold baby food immediately upon arrival. If we're going to a place that I am not-so-certain about buying baby food, I'll take more than just the travel days. In that case, I ordered my sixteen jars of food at different times and stored them, rather than try to order them all at once. Cereal, thankfully, comes in a box, and I always take a new and unopened one when traveling. She plowed through one a week, so it was easy to plan. Take two or three bowls. They now make easy, light, portable ones, and take two or three spoons in a large Ziploc bag. You can wash bowls and spoons in hotel and airport bathrooms.

Some airlines still offer a toddler meal, usually overseas carriers, and we're big believers in code-share flights operated by the overseas partner! Make a note if it is available when making your reservation with the travel agent or carrier, and

[2] The Pouch could usually allow small amounts of baby products through and NetGrocer packs it very well. The APOs have no problems with their restrictions.

call 24 hours in advance (usually when confirming flights) and make your special meal requests. For toddlers, if a Toddler Meal is not available, consider getting them the Fruit Plate instead, because it is nowhere near as complex, it tastes good, it doesn't smell odd, and usually has things that they are generally going to eat. We tended to travel with some instant oatmeal, which is healthy and filling and really easy to supplement the Fruit Plate or just to fill time-confused stomachs.

I also pack a GORP bag for Son for snacking en route. We've discovered with him, he will be a great traveler, as long as he can snack or munch the entire time. Literally, the whole time, he's snacking a bit here and a bit there. Who needs to sleep when you can munch? We keep a small plastic container for him to hold and a gallon bag to refill from. GORP is granola, Os (Cheerios), raisins and pieces – pieces of pretzel goldfish or cheddar goldfish, graham cracker pieces, cereal like Kix, and dried fruit of various kinds. No candy, no cookies. They get water in their travel cups (Nalgene bottles) the entire time.

We tried taking the 100 calorie snack packs this last time, and they worked well, but not as well as the GORP bag. They liked the individual "bag of their own" concept, but it wasn't as easy to manage a bunch of bags. I really liked the Playtex bottle and snack pack that they had when younger, which is a sippy cup with a snack container that clicked to the bottom, and we're still looking for an appropriate "bigger kid" version.

PACKING

Sometimes, you're packing as if for an expedition: self-contained, self-sufficient, not relying on anyone or anything else. This can be fun, but complicated. If you are taking a trip like that, for instance an R&R to a place you've never been and it isn't first world, take a little laundry detergent in your luggage for hand washing in the sink. Those bungee cords that I keep recommending work great for clotheslines.

You're a member of the diaper crowd now, or the more elite Pull-Up people. If you're doing the Sorta Schedule method, you know how many diapers they go through per day. This is very cool because you are not guessing. Almost double that amount and pack it in your luggage (it will leave space for souvenirs as you use them and makes for good padding). If you're tight on space, take enough for two days (one of travel, one upon arrival), plus a few extra and purchase there. Pampers are nearly everywhere. I carry a daily diaper allotment in my carry-on plus one extra in the kid carry-ons.

For clothing, this is kind of a personal call (actually, it all is). We pack two pairs of jammies, one in the luggage and one in the carry-on, and one outfit and pair of socks per day. An outfit consists of a top and bottom or playsuit. This seems like a lot, but trust me, you'll still end up washing in the sink. I toss the diapers, clothes, and Kid Kit in the children's suitcase with Boosters (or clip-on high chair when it was appropriate). If there is any room left, two toys. Just two toys is plenty because if you're like anyone else, you'll probably pick up one en route also. Son has a toy plane from every carrier he's ever been on for just this reason. We also try to take not-favorite toys, or rarely played with ones, preferably large enough not to be missed when we're cleaning up. We also bring the bedtime book.

Children like to be like their adults. And adults have carry-on. They're too young for their own rolling ones until they are nearly six (it's hard work), but a small backpack, lightly packed can contain some of their things well and not be too heavy if your toddler 'insists' on helping. Backpacks also are convenient for slinging over the ends of strollers and not making them side- or top-heavy. But before that, there is a kid-carry-on that I pack and haul. The kid-carry-on is the only one I really worry about being in reach. This has diapers and wipes of course, one change of clothes (from above, not in addition to), jammies, snacks, food if appropriate, a few toiletries, board books (one each) and two toys each. This kind of packing means that I don't have to unlock the suitcase or root around for anything before a decent night's sleep, and I admit, it is not for everyone. However, if I want to, I can not unpack and still manage Son or Daughter from one open carry-on, the smallest kind, and not be hunting around for our bedtime routine. This is also useful for forced layovers, which happen.

When they are carrying their own carry-on, keep it light. Imagine that you are going to have to stuff it in your back pack; keep it THAT light. Son now carries in his a MagnaDoodle, crayons and paper, Matchbox cars and a book. Daughter has her Pretty Ponies in hers, MagnaDoodle, etc. Light. Very light.

Children's toiletries are a nice little tin or Ziploc with toothbrushes, toothpaste, Infant or Children's Tylenol and Infant or Children's Tylenol Cold, Orajel for Daughter when she was that age, and hand-sanitizer. Their toys were things beyond their special, touch-stone animal, Son's Apa Eeyore, who goes everywhere, period, and Pink Princess Pony for Daughter (ditto, everywhere), and were usually things like a Fisher Price Little People car and person or pair of animals. By the way, if a toy requires batteries, put it in your luggage, and not it in your carry-on. Tickle-Me Elmo will get you inspected by TSA in person up close and personal.

Your carry-on is going to have literally the basics – and room to shove their carry-on in too, if they're at the toddling and beyond stage. Stuff a change of underwear in a Ziploc on the bottom and forget about it. If you have the chance of a layover, toss in a shirt that complements the pants your traveling in. One small tin or Ziploc will do for some toiletries like lipstick and eyeliner, toothbrush, travel lotion. Toss in your wallet, and a book because we're all optimists and you can dream that you're going to read it, and a 'bathroom kit'. This is another Ziploc with a diaper and travel wipes (the only thing you have to grab when you have to change the diaper). There are plenty of these nice little 'kits' for traveling that are a changing pad that keeps a diaper and wipes, and I liked mine a lot. Don't try to get anything else in there; this is rock bottom travel survival, because at this point, the travel is all about the little ones. Sorry.

EN ROUTE

I am apparently a real witch at heart. I could care less about what my fellow travelers think about my children and me. We work on manners all the time, and they will hold us in good stead or they won't. It isn't that I don't want to leave a good impression, or that I don't work on manners with our two year old (including' inside voice'), but frankly, they're little and the fellow traveler usually is not. Once I was getting huffs and snorts and grumbles from the seat in front of me and I'd had enough. I tapped him on the shoulder and said, "Would you like to try to soothe her? It seems to really be concerning you and I really wouldn't mind the break." I got no more lip from him. Some people think that Business Class is code for Child Free. And airlines are not in the business to make travel convenient for families.

Overseas cabin crews are more willing to assist than any U.S. crew I've ever met. U.S. crews have different liability restrictions. They're not mean, but they're also not likely to try to explain this to you as you struggle with a toddler, an infant seat and a carry-on or two. On Turkish Air we have a hard time getting the kids BACK from the crew because they tend to like kids so much. If you work on proper behavior from the get-go, your child will be as reasonable of a traveler as you are, which the cabin crew will find charming, and you generally get very nice service as a result.

That's not to say that you won't have an experience like our Istanbul to Stockholm leg where Son bawled and was inconsolable the entire time from start to finish and we could not begin to figure out why. Most passengers are not too thrilled by sharing their Trans-Atlantic journey with someone under ten, but keep in mind, you are the one coordinating, schlepping, scheduling, logisticking and managing the entire affair, not them and your responsibility is to your child, not your fellow travelers. In the U.S. it can be a little harder, probably because it is a different pace of life, but don't forget the business man! Ask one if he is a family man; if he says yes, ask him if he minds holding the carrier for a second while you stow the bag, or if he minds stowing the bag while you settle the baby. Sometimes they're thrilled, sometimes not so much, but then you just say "Excuse me for bothering you." And ask someone else. My spouse's step-father travels more than anyone I know, and he is wonderful with children and always volunteers to help when he sees a family traveling. Look for kind eyes, and ask.

Your responsibility is to your child, not your fellow traveler. If you need help, look for kind eyes or empathy and ask.

Please, if you need to change your baby, go to the restroom and do it there at the changing table, not on your seat or tray table. First of all, do you use the facilities at your seat? Second, you might have adapted to the smell, but ick, I say, ick! Third of all, the bathroom is the appropriate place, has disposal and a place to wash your hands. Take a changing blanket and leave your seat. If you're traveling with an infant and a toddler, go to the handicapped accessible bathroom, which is slightly larger, and take the toddler too. If you have to take a toy and an extra changing pad for the toddler to sit on the floor, that's okay, it is still more appropriate than the cabin seat. I admittedly place Son on the sink counter while changing Daughter on the changing table because the floor grossed me out sometimes. If your toddler is sleeping, tap a fellow passenger or better yet, use that People button and call the cabin attendant and say, "I am going to go change the baby and Son is asleep. I will be back in five minutes." They don't have to do a darn thing and there's a good chance that Son will sleep right through. No one wants to smell your infant's diapers and I really do not want to eat off of a tray table, or let my kids color at a tray table, where someone has done that.

SURVIVING TRAVEL

A small supply of toys, books and coloring or drawing things is essential for the actual travel. Keep it all in the carry-on when transiting gates – and transit directly from one gate to the next without more than a bathroom break. Then break out the toys or coloring books.

For a long while we traveled with a portable DVD player. We'd foolishly bought a 'kids' DVD player, brand name, which looked like it might be rugged enough to handle a lot of travel. Unfortunately, it wasn't. Another family we know has one that opens like a small laptop, and it survived much more reliably. DVDs are a traveling friend, but limit it to one small CD wallet of movies. We had special travel movies, but the tried and true favorites were in there, of course.

We also traveled with a laptop, and had downloaded video clips from iTunes, both the Pixar shorts, music videos and Disney shorts like *Chip and Dale* and *Ferdinand the Bull*. We were also able to download *Backyardigans*, although frankly, I found the DVDs to be more convenient and flexible. Again, we didn't open up and power up until we were at our departure gate, but, especially when they were getting particularly tired, this was a brain-minimal, body-minimal activity with their eyes open, and it helped us pass that time until we boarded.

When you are actually on the plane, we chose to reduce stimuli, rather than add to it. When a child gets tired and distracted easily, your initial response is to reach in the toy bag and offer something else, even though they might have six things strewn about. Instead, seriously consider taking things away, one at a time. Sometimes I actually remove all the toys at once, hand them their water and a small snack, and when that is done they are left with their blanket and their baby, and the natural inclination is to go to sleep.

Remember that your children are absorbing more information than you are during travel. I realized this when we went through Istanbul, and Son was less than two years old and he said, "TV airport!" I wasn't sure what he meant, and responded with, "Istanbul airport." He laughed and we went on ... and then I looked around. There are televisions everywhere! Travel, airplanes and transit all are a lot of stimuli for them, and sometimes they just need a little time to process it.

A new toy during travel can be marvelously distracting during a trip. Our travel toy bag is filled with toys bought en route, and they travel with us every time and keep their uniqueness as a result. Regardless, by the end of the trip, they're pretty maxed out. I consider their brains to be off when watching a DVD, and travel is the only time I don't limit their DVDs. It accomplishes two things, it minimizes their bouncing around tendencies and it makes the impact on fellow travelers slightly less intrusive.

ARRIVAL SURVIVAL

I've already given you one of my tips for surviving arrival: I plan my packing so I do not have to do anything on my day of arrival, giving myself one day of grace.

Children thrive on ritual and routine. Theirs is a world of magic, not cause and effect. If you have a bedtime routine at home, do the same routine in the hotel. Keep in mind that 'letting it slide' or 'giving them a treat' of no rules, or major changes in rules, isn't perceived by them as a treat – it is a sudden major shift in how the world works. I am not recommending that you rigidly adhere to all things all the time. Life is flexible and so are kids. They know darn well that certain things are allowed at one house that just are not at another. So a change in dinnertime while on vacation isn't so tough, if the same table rules apply. Believe it or not, changing the rules, even if you think it is because it is nice, or just this once, destabilizes them more than you realize. Imagine if one day you came to work and everyone had on hot pink. Now, this isn't major, it certainly isn't 'wrong', but it is different and can you honestly say that if "just for today" was the only explanation you received, you would continue to work efficiently that day? For this reason, you keep your rules simple and few. Things like manners are forever. What you can and cannot touch may change. Food rules still apply, the when and where might change.

If your children nap during the day, plan your days of vacation to allow for the nap. We tried to get a family suite if we could, or room with a sitting area away from the bed at the least, so that we could nap and Husband and I traded off who was 'on guard' during naps. The one who wasn't got to go to the spa or shop or go downstairs for dessert and an hour of uninterrupted reading. The one upstairs read quietly by the light of one lamp (or also napped) and amazingly, kids slept (after much hushing). If you have a bedtime routine that includes something like bath, book, and prayer, keep it up. It adds stability to their world and allows them to adapt to a new environment because you and your 'rules' are the same. It really makes this strange location safer for exploring, not just overwhelmingly new.

Jet lag is not so hard for infants and can be terribly hard for toddlers. Infants are basically impossible to jet lag because they live on a two-on-two-off or three-on-three-off schedule anyway! If you can manage to sleep when they do,[3] which is hard during travel, both of you will manage fine. Traveling with infants is actually pretty easy. Nurse when you take off, nurse when you land and then by your watch, you keep track of the two or three hour intervals. Once you've landed, you adjust accordingly and go back to the Phase Two process of adjusting feeding and sleeping times for about a week. Even for the toddlers it usually takes three to seven days. We don't fight jet lag, although we will try to minimize it if possible with sleeping en route, or a day room and nap if the layover is more than eight hours. But when we arrive, we're Lagged and we know it. And it is harder with two, and with toddlers, because they don't understand and frankly, don't care. They know that they are either awake or too tired for words.[4]

Immediately upon arrival, we try to get to a local schedule, and time our routines according to local time. We try to stay awake until 8pm if at all possible and allow two hour naps if needed. Their normal nap is 1-3 and if we're really tired, we'll adjust naps the first day for 10-12 or 2-4, but no napping after 5pm. Our evenings are pretty benign with a DVD upon waking up because they're not fit company really. I will comment on two-dimensional media in a later chapter, but while Lagged, DVDs are our friends.

---

[3] That said, I had an eight hour trip where they slept five and a half hours of it and from the time they fell asleep to the time they woke, I tried to sleep, and laid there saying, "Eyes! Close! Close now." And didn't.

[4] I actually watched Daughter FALL asleep. She was walking, and then her eyes closed like a long blink, and when she fell, she hit the floor sound asleep.

When we wake in the middle of the night, we also don't fight it. We get up, go downstairs and play for one hour and then have Jet Lag Cocoa! Jet Lag Cocoa[5] is warm milk with vanilla and cinnamon, or warm milk with just a touch of cocoa. This is enough to mellow them out after an hour of play, which isn't super active play, and settle them down. Then the lactose kicks in and we go back to bed, usually after an hour and a half awake in the middle of the night. I can tell how long de-lagging is going to take by when they wake up. 7am is normal wake-up time in this house. If they wake up at 3am, it will take four nights because we only seem to adjust an hour at a time. And when our day begins at 7am, we keep to a normal routine (usually there is an extra nap only on the first day) and de-lagging doesn't take long. Quiet is enforced in the middle of the night because Husband doesn't have the luxury of a slow de-lagging. He usually has to go right to work the next day, and he goes through his own process to get there sooner rather than later.

The kids know what is going on. We talked about it from before they could actually comprehend. Telling the year old child what is going on isn't a bad thing, never-mind that they cannot actually understand it in the comprehension sense. What they know is we're Lagged and this means we get Jet Lag Cocoa and they're allowed to crawl in our bed in the morning before 7am because we can squeeze another hour or two of sleep out of them that way. Sending them back to their room results in playing and less sleep and longer Lagging.

---

[5] Recipe 1: Per cup, warm milk, drop vanilla and cinnamon.
Recipe 2: 1 ½ C milk, 1 C water, 1/4 C corn meal (really), bring to a boil. Add ¼ C or less of sugar, a dash nutmeg, and cinnamon to taste and simmer 10 mins until thick. Remove from heat, stir in 1 tsp of vanilla.
Recipe 3: 2C milk, 1 egg, 1 tsp vanilla. ¼ C sugar optional or to taste. Continually whisk while simmering on medium, until hot. Do not boil or the eggs will scramble. Add cinnamon and nutmeg and simmer until thick.

When Son was 2 and Daughter was a brand new 2 month old, my mother and I traveled from Wisconsin to our third post, with the children. Unfortunately, things did not go right en route, and we ended up delayed in London for three nights until the next flight. Being stranded in London is not necessarily a bad thing; after all, the signs are in English, which is a bonus! However, we were out by Heathrow, it was our first time ever, and the children were rather small.

Have I mentioned that there were no convenience or grocery stores nearby? Finding diapers was an excursion! The saving grace was that the hotel, a Marriott, had 24 hour room service.

On the first night, my mom and I woke up at midnight and we were wide awake. The kids are snoozing away and adapted far better than we did that trip. We're reading, talking quietly and at some point decided, you know, a cup of tea or cocoa would be really nice right now. We called down to room service and it wasn't just cocoa that they brought up: there were 'biscuits' and that is code for Cookies! We did that every night, for three nights in a row, an hour later each time. I'm sure the kitchen heard the phone ring, saw the extension and just started pulling out the cocoa tin!

When we arrived, finally, in third post, Husband had gotten into our assigned house just days before we had arrived and it was literally filled with boxes. Some things, like bed linens and such, had been unpacked, but he said when he met us at the airport, "I still haven't found the forks."

Mom and I worked so hard, at little kids, at unpacking, at creating a house, it was amazing. And we slept when little people did (fortunately there were a lot of naps in that house at that time, so there was plenty to share) and we woke up in the middle of the night for cocoa and cookies for at least two weeks. Thus, Jet Lag Cocoa was born.

"Jet Lag Cocoa"

9. The Help

This is the section where the non-Foreign Service folks get to roll their eyes and snort a bit – we have a section called "The Help". If you're in Second or Third World countries, you will likely end up with some form of household help. I held out with Son and didn't get a nanny until he was nine months old, but I did have a housekeeper at that time. Help is ... helpful. You're actually doing a small part to employ someone from the local economy and it may be an expectation at your Embassy. It isn't a crime, an entitlement or perk. It is useful. It takes work to manage it and sometimes it is downright frustrating.

I have some very *very* distinct ideas about housekeepers, nannies and drivers and the responsibilities of each. The bottom line for me is that if I have the opportunity to have local help, I will have both a nanny and a housekeeper because I don't want my nanny to be responsible for anything but the kids. This makes it very easy when defining responsibilities; the housekeeper doesn't do anything with the kids. Period. It isn't that I don't trust her, she wouldn't be in my house if I didn't trust her, but because then she is only responsible for one area, and we can train her accordingly. As a result, there isn't the chance that the nanny will do something different from what Husband and I want for the kids. In some cultures giving candy is just an easy habit, and not giving it is a hard thing to learn. Also, an "attention getting swat" on the butt isn't so uncommon, but it is not something we approve of. Once they are in school, I suspect that this separate-employee separate-responsibilities requirement of mine will change.

This brings me to finding a nanny:

First of all, evaluate. Think of why you are hiring someone to help you care for your child? Is this someone who will be the primary care giver (aside from you)? Will they be spending an equal or less quantity of time (per the clock, not qualitative) with your children as you? Will you be around when the child-care provider is, or not? Are their English skills important to you or can you communicate in the local language? Are you willing to communicate in the local language when it comes to your children, or in a language that is not their native language when it comes to your children? What type of person are you looking for: someone that is a mother's helper, a babysitter, or a mother/grandmother themselves with their own child-rearing ideas?

Then prepare. Get a list of available help from the CLO. Most CLO offices have a book of potential help. I don't know of any CLO that offers this book as anything more than a reference; the presence of a person in the book is not a recommendation or endorsement by the CLO unless the office specifically says it is. Additionally, they don't know to take someone out of the book, because they were hired or have a negative recommendation, unless you tell them. Another valuable local resource is International Women's Group or Association. Both of these valuable sources offer word of mouth, on the ground reporting, so to speak, regarding potential employees. The CLO or IWA may have newsletters advertising persons who are available as household help, and you can sometimes be put on their distribution lists.

Public Affairs and the local universities have IREX and FLEX programs for local nationals to study in the U.S. for a year. Their alumni keep in touch with each other and sometimes are looking for work!

Check with Public Affairs and see if they have contacts at the local universities (college seniors have been great for us), especially those that offer classes in English, and consider placing an ad there. If there is an Embassy newsletter, consider an ad there. We have had the best luck with approaching the Public Affairs section and asking for their contacts in the IREX and FLEX programs, which are study abroad in the U.S. for local nationals. As a result, our applicants have been exposed to U.S. culture for a year or more, so we were not entirely foreign to them. Whether you interview from an existing pool or seek applicants, I gathered resumés and applications electronically and went to hotmail.com and opened a free account, which we used for our entire tour (and then ceased using it upon PCS, letting it naturally expire). We named it things like LastNameFirstPost@hotmail.com and LastNameSecondPost @hotmail.com or something similar, and that was where we had replies sent. This allowed me to start looking before we actually arrived, and gave me plenty of time to peruse the applicants. I've done this at every post, also allowing the CLO to contact us prior to arrival easily. I use this address for the CLO's mailing to spouses and any correspondence that I don't want to follow me when we leave. This can be your Internet service provider, or hotmail-like Internet-based. I err on the side of Internet-based, purely because we can begin before we arrive and it is free. Place a deadline on the replies to your ad, and state that interviews will be held the day after the position closes. This not only makes them take you seriously, it makes you take it seriously. Then, choose your six favorite applicants, set aside thirty minutes per applicant and draw up a schedule. Inform those that you are not interviewing that you've reviewed their application, thank them for applying and by all means, let them know that they did not make the first cut. "We are going with a more qualified applicant" is polite and true if they haven't made your first cut. You may soften it by asking if you can keep their resumé or application for future reference if something doesn't work out, or ask them if they've placed their resumé in the CLO's book.

Then you start to interview, and you interview all of them. This will take entirely too long, three hours for six applicants, so ask a friend, colleague, or sponsor to come and watch your child while you and your spouse interview, so you are not distracted.

English skills of the applicants were important to me as my fluency in the country language was not so good that I trusted instructions regarding my children. So, we had two books for them to read to assess their English skills. One was a passage from *The Baby Whisperer*, on H.E.L.P (Hold back, Encourage, Listen and Praise). We asked them to read, and then discuss the passage. This led to very good eye-opening discussions in the good cases, and helped us assess their comprehension as well as their willingness to learn something new. If their English was not that good, there was *Bedtime for Elmo*, because it is possible for someone's spoken English to be lower than their reading English skills. And if we clicked and communicated, I still wanted her to be able to read a bedtime story.

Before interviewing, take the time to clearly define and print a list of duties and responsibilities. To start, you go through the child's day and write it down to define what it is that is done. I gave a copy to applicants to read, while we read their resumé. Yes, I'd read all the resumés before, and written down what questions we wanted. This was to familiarize myself with who they were and what I wanted to ask. But this way, neither of us (interviewers or applicants) was sitting there staring at our feet while the other skimmed. Both parties could read. This also gave them a basis for understanding what we expected; otherwise "childcare" is open to wide interpretation.

Ask them if they smoke. If they do, when do they expect to do it and where, while working for you? Ask them if they drink; is it socially, excessively, moderately? Their answer tells you a lot about how they communicate, more than actually honestly gauging their drinking. Be sure to ask if they've worked for other expat families, and if so, how many, how long with each family, and can you contact them? Hopefully you will have contacted references already. Ask if they keep in touch with those families. Ask how long they have been caring for other people's children and if they have children, what their ages are? If the children are under 15, your childcare provider will need more time to be with their own family and it would be unfair to ask her to be available 24-7 for you.

Give them two or three "what if" situations to gauge how they deal with children and if they think with the same logic as you do. They will want to please you and give the "right" answer, so it is important that you phrase your situation in such a way that there either isn't a right answer or it isn't evident. We went one step further in this respect and actually said that we had a very different approach to child-rearing, more different than a lot of Americans even, and could she allow a child to cry after Child had been laid down to nap? Could she not swoop in and prevent Son from falling, or not make a fuss if he did fall? One woman flat out said she couldn't do that, and that was a better answer than the one that we "wanted" to hear.

Discuss medical and first aid intervention. Let them know if you are going have them take a Med Unit class on food preparation, or CPR or First Aid. Some of your applicants may already be qualified or have taken the courses, in which case, please do ask to see the certificate.

Have applicants that you are possibly interested in meet the child at the end of the interview. Don't even bother introducing those folks who don't meet your basic threshold. By then, you will have a good feel for whom you want to hire. I am an animal behaviorist, so what people DO means quite a bit to me. I immediately react more positively to people who crouch or kneel down to address a child; or to people who address a child, even an infant, directly rather than speaking of or around them. Waiting for the child to answer goes further than talking over them or to me after asking that child a question.

If you have animals, when the applicant meets the child, include an animal or two. An animal can be a good judge of people, and you can also tell if they were truthful when they said they "loved dogs" (as they shriek in terror as a dainty Pomeranian enters the room). Our nannies are told upfront that we will occasionally ask them to house- and pet-sit in our absence, so this is an important aspect for us.

Stand up and face the music and inform all your applicants after you've made a decision. Let all of them know that the position has been filled and thank them for applying and talking to you. Sometimes the jobs with expats are the best paying in the community and very competitive and they will avoid taking other jobs if they think they might get yours. I usually know by the end of that day who I am going to hire, and yes, I usually go with my gut. I know that the person I am hiring is going to be more of a mother's helper and friend for me than primary care giver, so I will be spending plenty of time with them.

The last word on hiring is firing. You're going to have to do it. Someone once told me than it takes three bad ones for every good one (thanks Tom!), and I believe it. In First Post, we had a person who seemed perfect, a pediatrician of all things, who was unfortunately also a bit of a drinker. Our second choice was a younger woman, a fourth year economics major who'd done a year abroad in the U.S., was inexperienced but smart and willing to learn it our way. In Second Post, we had a party-girl, a born-again Christian who couldn't stop preaching and undermined the housekeeper in an effort to get her daughter hired as housekeeper, and then we found another younger, fourth year economics major who'd done a year abroad in the U.S., was inexperienced but smart and willing to learn it our way. Yes, we're going to save ourselves the time next time and just advertise flat out for a younger woman, a fourth year economics major who'd done a year abroad in the U.S., is inexperienced but smart and willing to learn it our way in future.[1] Regardless, set your limits and stick to them. Bite the bullet and say, "Thank you, but it isn't working. Give me my keys. Thanks. Here's your pay." It's hard, and it never really gets easier.

We have three offenses for which one would immediately be fired:

> 1. Opening the door to someone without an Embassy badge or accepting a package and bringing it into the house. Both of these fall into the 'endangering our children or animals' category (one of our posts was a high terror threat post and another one was a critical crime threat post). This also includes giving out personal information on the phone or to others that have no need to know it (like the neighbor), and was included under the catch-all phrase, "Safety and security."

[1] Because three times in a row is something even I can't ignore.

2. Drinking on the job (it happened) and

3. Dishonesty. By this we mean stealing, or lying about something, such as something that is broken. I just want to be told that it was broken (accidents happen) and do not want to find out by discovering it in the trash or having it just go missing.

EMPLOYMENT

Once you've hired someone, if you give them a set of keys to your home, you must inform the RSO who has that extra set of keys. Be sure to stress to your employee that no copies are to be made under any circumstances, and if the keys are lost, you must be informed immediately. Also stress the post-policy regarding the phone list and map if you choose to have one.

Set your limits, make them clear from the beginning and revisit them occasionally.

I put a list of duties, important phone numbers, copies of my children's identification (a copy of their diplomatic passport and diplomatic credentials shrunk to wallet size and laminated) and, in our case, a check-book register because I give her funds to get household things like juice, milk, fruit, etc. and it is kept in a binder.

Of course I had a binder! It isn't exactly always a binder; sometimes it is a folder, sometimes a calendar or a notebook. What matters is that it is one place that you can write things down, they can write responses or journal entries and it is consistently in one place. Keep in mind that it varies from post to post whether or not you can have the phone list at home, let alone a map that tells where people live, so check with your RSO regarding the policy. In the binder, I keep the emergency phone contacts page (from Chapter 3), and include numbers of the Med Unit and Post One, a map of the neighborhood with the neighbors labeled (if allowed), the spouses phone tree or Embassy phone list (if allowed), calendar or blank pages for the days' needs or events to be recorded, and I keep them all together. This is how we communicate between the child-care provider and I, so Husband and I don't miss anything in the kids' lives when we're not physically present. This is not a new idea and there are suggestions at the end of one of the Tracey Hogg *Baby Whisperer* books, as well as others, on the same issue.

The Nanny might write: Son 0800 oatmeal, bananas, OJ; 1030 graham cracker, drinking yogurt; 1200 rice, chicken, beans, apple juice; 1300-1500 nap; 1530 raisins, nuts, drinking yogurt...
... And I added: 1800 spaghetti, garlic bread, water, 2000 bath and bed.

You can also group it by Food, Outside Time, Sleep Time, Diapers (just the poopy ones as you try to figure out if his body has a schedule and how to get him on the potty before a bowel movement) and Misc. There are lots of ideas for this in many places. Find what you are comfortable with, but some form of documentation is recommended. This is particularly useful if the child is receiving medicine (you know whether or not he received it and when) or is on the BRAT diet for tummy troubles.

I include any notes that I want to communicate, such as "No juice today please" or "they need more outside time today and big muscle movement" or "Please buy milk" even. With an appointment calendar, the notation is written at the time of day, allowing us to see patterns.

LASTING IMPRESSIONS

Tom, thank you again for telling us to keep this in mind when working with 'household help': "Treat them fairly, pay them better than average and remember, they are your employees, not your friends." It is very easy to forget this with someone who is around you a lot, who knows about your life in sometimes very intimate (if they do your laundry) detail. Be objective and evaluate what you are expecting and be very clear from the outset. Be kind, fair and always mind your manners (no ordering someone around; ask instead), pay on time and don't take advantage of them. Most of all find a system that works for you and a level of interaction that works for you and stick to it. We define the three things that are grounds for immediate dismissal from the outset, listed in the section on firing, and that doesn't change ever. To us, being a good employer is more important than being a friend, because gods forbid I'm in a situation where they've been taking advantage of us (and therefore aren't really friends anymore, but I'm not aware of the change), and I have to fire a friend. It is hard enough letting someone go, let alone knowing that by doing so life is going to be very difficult for them.

Our parameters are made very clear from the outset – we are not our employee's friends, we don't exchange gifts, we don't know their children, we don't go to their house, we don't accept gifts. I tell them that I will pay them their wage all year round, even if the children are gone or we're on vacation, but not to expect bonuses.[2] On the other end of the spectrum are folks who are very comfortable having a surrogate-family in their household help for the few years they are in this foreign country. For us, our approach has added advantages; they do not impose upon us personally. We are not asked to do things like get visas, broker introductions, sponsor people, write a letter for their neighbor's sister's friend's son or give pay advances. If you are asked to do any of those things, particularly sponsoring someone, you are placing yourself at risk professionally, and should have a very frank conversation with your Consul General about what sponsoring someone means.

Practice patience. They are not your kin and they aren't psychic. You have to tell them what you want, preferably in writing if possible so you can refer back to it, or they can check it off when they've read it. They are in your house, so you have to trust them, however be cautious and remind yourself to make it a guarded trust. I learned that if I am interviewing applicants, sometimes there are ones that I just 'have a better feeling' about, even though their experience might not be the same or they might not have all the answers that we were looking for in the interview. In the end, I am the one who is going to be interacting on a daily basis for at least two months while I train them, and then I will trust them to be alone with my children, so my comfort level is very important.

Plan ahead. If you are going to go back to work in January, start looking for someone in the summer. If you're going to post in May, see if there are any families departing that have people to refer to you. For me, hiring, interviewing and training is a six-week process minimum. We interview hard because we don't want to hire and fire one or two before we find our good fit.

When we're training, I let them watch me, take notes, read the parenting books (sometimes they will pick up on things that I didn't, or cause great discussions!), whatever they want to 'learn', for at least two weeks. Then it is another two weeks of the nanny being primary and me 'shadowing.' This is when I re-read some of the books, because I might think I need to make a correction so something I read is being done right, only to discover that our interpretation has slipped with time. And we end every day with sitting down and discussing for at least ten minutes before they go. Then there is the two weeks of tag-teaming. By the end of that, you know whether you and the person you hired are going to be

[2] Although we do usually give something at the holidays.

a team or if they're literally going to be just someone that does the things you tell them to do.

None of this is required, just information provided so that you can make your own choice. You can hire someone having never met them and have them watch your kids on day one without supervision. It is a question of comfort levels, and since mine are so taut, you can use us as a place to at least begin asking your own questions. It is a long and sometimes frustrating process, and stepping back and just observing can be painfully difficult. In the end they are your children and you have to be comfortable with whom you choose and also with how they raise your children.

Before I knew any of this kind of information about hiring child-care help, I did what most people do anyway. I went to the CLO's office and looked at their book of potential help. Remember, this is a reference only. And they don't know to take someone out of the book, because they were hired or fired, or otherwise, unless you tell them.

So, we went through the book and one lady has several good references, had previously been a pediatrician and said she was available as a nanny. Doesn't that sound like a match made in heaven? So we interviewed her, and just her, and felt fine about it.

Son was about nine months old, and we had some pretty specific ideas about child care, but she had children of her own and was a pediatrician, so she tended to try to teach me her way. I decided that I could work with this because I have what is charitably described as a strong personality.

On day one, she asked us for an advance on her pay. Yes, even though she hadn't worked, she wanted a little up front to make it through to the payday. We declined to do so, so as not to set a precedent. She ended up borrowing some money, not much, from the housekeeper.

On day two, she asked Husband to please bring home the forms for a visa application and asked for a letter of reference since we were her employers. Husband said no, that wasn't appropriate just yet and referred her to the website.

On day three, the housekeeper came and asked if I knew that she, the housekeeper, used a little bit of alcohol when baking (this was before I explained vanilla extract). I said yes I did and she held out one of the bottles and said, "I didn't use this. But the nanny sort of smells like she did." Sure enough, the nanny smelled suspiciously like Jack Daniels.

Needless to say, that was that. Thankfully, we hadn't given her a key to our apartment yet!

"Not Drinking Alcohol"

Part II

In which many tricks, tips, hints and thoughts are presented and an array of choices displayed, all with the end goal of giving small children the skills and tools to flourish, whether in our expatriate lives or otherwise.

10. Sleep! Glorious Sleep

Sleep is one of those incredibly important things and there are oodles of books written about it. The importance of sleep cannot be underestimated. (How many of you just skipped to this chapter?) People who get an appropriate amount of sleep, look younger, live longer and are healthier.[1] Their bodies metabolize better and adapt quicker. If you don't believe me, look up the studies on sleep and health, because they're popping up all over the place. The following mantra of mine goes for you and the baby:

If you are tired, all things are insurmountable; if you are
well-rested, you can handle anything.

Remember, that goes for the baby as well as you! The importance of sleep is starting to find its way into mainstream reporting. It has been recently documented that lack of sleep can contribute to juvenile obesity, and can also contribute to diabetes and its associated weight problems. So this is an important issue for a lifetime of health!

For an infant feeding equals schedule equals sleeping through the night. Once you are getting a straight six hours of sleep, you've reached the 'through the night' threshold. You can catch a catnap in the day with the baby if you need a few hours more than six per twenty-four hour period.[2]

As I said before, I do not mean a rigid, planned schedule of course. Really, I don't. Be flexible around a suggested time, plus or minus ten or fifteen minutes. Yes, I do suggest that if a feeding is scheduled for 3pm, you know when that is approaching and make arrangements for feeding to begin on time. I watch the clock when someone starts crying and I watch those incredibly long two or ten minutes tick by. What I mean is a flexible general schedule, with the goal of introducing the real world's time concepts to these little brains that have no idea that Time even exists.[3] It really is the most major jet-lag we can possibly imagine. This is what you are working at undoing, getting them on a real schedule, in spite of having lived in the dark on their own biological rhythm for nine months (give or take).

---

[1] Notice that it might not be eight hours for you, even though it is nine for me, but eight is the average.
[2] In fact, with baby is some of the most wonderful sleeping ever – lying on the couch with baby on your belly and it will suck you into sleep. Toss in a cat purring nearby it is a sleep black hole and you'll fall right in!
[3] Kronos OR Kairos! Kronos is chronological or sequential time; Kairos is the time between time, anticipation or opportunity.

Don't forget, as I mentioned in the Feeding chapter, you can't really mess them up in the first three months or so. There are plenty of experts out there that talk about the "fourth trimester." Our babies are born when they have gestated in the womb for nine (or ten) months. They could use a few more. The mother's body has adapted to this by birthing early and giving a great amount of care and nurturing in the first year of life because we can't carry the baby more than nine months for emotional, mental and more importantly, physical reasons. But if our bodies (and minds) could handle it, that would be where the babies stayed for another few months – can you imagine, being able to walk within a few hours of birth! I think I'm glad for that "fourth trimester" on the outside, for me to get used to the idea! Even if you start and stop a different method every week, it is sort of like a free pass, they're eating, sleeping and growing for that "fourth trimester." Period. So don't worry if you don't start as you mean to go on or change your mind and change your method. In the Sorta Schedule, feeding is the key, but sleeping is the lock. Truly, the children that I know whose parents kept to this, slept through the night early, and napped well. And you set this up, and slowly turn them into diurnal Homo sapiens.

Weaning from a pacifier can be straight forward or the child can (and will) self-wean. Don't borrow trouble worrying about it too much or too soon.

PACIFIERS

Earlier, pacifiers were mentioned in reference to helping a child with airplane take off and landing. There are many schools of thought when it comes to pacifiers. Sucking is an infant's soothing mechanism, and their mouth is the most sensitive sense organ (which is why everything goes in the mouth). We chose to offer the pacifier rather than have the child begin sucking on a stuffed animal's ear,[4] or his fist or his thumb. I think that perhaps a lot of parents avoid it because of the perceived concerns regarding getting rid of the pacifier in a few years. Many of the pediatricians and parenting forums will address this issue, and suggest a straight-forward approach or self-weaning approach, but it will be your choice.

I knew that I personally did not want my children to "need" the pacifier after they were two years old. At one year old, we simply started leaving the pacifier in the crib. It was available at night or for naps, but that was it. There was no discussion or drama about it, it simply was so. At two years old, Son decided he was "too big", and gave it to the chickens next door. No, I have no idea why he thought the chickens would need it. We magicked the back-up pacifiers away. That night he regretted his generosity, but we said that it was done now. On the

[4] Hairball!

third night he forgot to ask for it, although, on the second night he suggested that Daughter wouldn't mind sharing one of her pacifiers with him. Daughter also self-weaned at two years old, but she had an assist from Son. On her second birthday he told her that the crows needed the pacifier now! She chirped, "Okay." And that was that.

Quite predictably, we had a basket of pacifiers, which we called "the cork" We kept it in the baby's room, and any stray pacifiers were counted and collected before bed each night and went into the basket.[5] When the children were under a year old, we did choose to take a pacifier with us when we traveled, but also chose not to use the pacifier leashes or other pacifier accessories like pocket sanitizers, nipple shields, etc. Husband joked that I had a magic sanitizing pocket for dropped-on-the-floor pacifiers, when actually I had a backup in there. But once we went to the crib-only stage, pacifiers no longer traveled with us unless a nap was in the trip. Try not to borrow trouble on this and worry too much. Some children self-wean, some respond well to the straight forward approach, some need a little more preparation and presentation. On the flip side, some children don't use one, don't like them, or just never seem to get attached to them. As you learn you child's personality, and find your parenting style, you will find the fit that is best for you and your family.

> Learn your child's sleep signs. Do they get grumpy, or cuddly? Do they twirl their hair or go nest? It's your cue!

SLEEP SIGNS

Know your child's Sleep Signs. Do they twirl their hair when they are tired?[6] Does she suddenly become cuddly when normally you can't get her sit down for six straight seconds? Does he start playing with his lip or ears, or chewing on the ends of his cuffs? Do they start staring into space? Or perhaps they start "getting whippy," where they are like a whirlwind flying around the room, sure to upend something and go over on their rear or worse, their head (it looks like energy, but it is faking you out!). Maybe she starts getting mean – biting when teased or trying to scratch when he stands in front of her. Or perhaps he starts to get whiney and annoying and the only reason you finally put two and two together is because you say something like, "I'm tired of hearing that-particular-tone-of-whine" and you mentally smack yourself and say, "Oh, he's tired."

[5] Counted because we didn't want one left on the floor or under the couch where a dog or cat could get to it – not for the sanitary issue, although it was part of it, but because being woken in the middle of the night by the cat whapping it across the floor and down the stairs, or the dog chewing it to oblivion and possibly swallowing some, was worth the price of counting, and sometimes hunting down, six pacifiers.

[6] Son twirled his hair (or tried) in the womb! We have it on ultrasound!

If you notice Sleep Signs and sleep isn't in the next ten minutes, if it is scheduled for within the next thirty minutes or so, *reduce the stimuli* don't add to it.[7] Don't try to distract them with a new toy or new activity. Instead, go ahead and slowly put things away. This is an activity that can take up a good fifteen minutes and reduces the number of objects about. Turn off the television and turn on quiet music, classical or instrumental, quiet. If you have more than thirty or forty minutes to get within the near-schedule time, do the clean-up, slowly and then get a familiar or comfortable book or two and slowly read. You can stretch that forty or fifty minutes, but it will tax your patience, so take a deep breath and just slow down.

Yes, we do Brain Dead things too and turn on a DVD to get ourselves through if it is an hour or so, something like Disney shorts, not the whole hour and a half long, full-length feature DVD. Sitting together with a comfortable cuddly, and me continuing to talk to them, so they are awake, but essentially brain dead to the world. Napping with their eyes open is what I call that pre- and immediately post-sleep DVD watching. Not sleeping, but zoning and then to bed.

> Adding stimuli might perk them up for a few minutes, but you're just giving an already tired brain more to process.

Adding stimuli might perk them up for a few minutes, but you're just giving a brain, which has already signaled that it is tired, more to process. Think of it this way: you're done with work for the day and shutting off the computer, putting away your pens and pencils, closing up your calendar and your boss drops a stack of things to do before you go, in the middle of your desk, some of which are interesting, but mostly none of which can receive your full attention.... This reduction of stimuli also works on planes – when I start seeing sleep signs, I start taking things away one at a time. First those things that could cause damage like markers, go away, then moving toys which are increasingly being caused to crash into each other, and finally they are left with their fleecy blankets and stuffed animals. At that point, I can usually hand them a pillow and they decide that sleeping is a good option. This is not to say that there are not protests over losing the items, but the protests last about as long as the interest in a new object would. They also start to recognize, eventually, that there is winding down occurring.

NOISE

Don't turn the house into a tomb. My house is a naturally quiet place, where there isn't a television on all the time, always a radio or CD playing, barking

[7] For instance, nap is scheduled at 3pm, but at 2pm you are seeing Sleep Signs.

dogs or other loud noises. But the noises of life continue regardless: phones ring, dish-washers wash, vacuums are run, washer and dryer do their thing, doors open and close, and we make no effort to be quiet during a nap. Quiet during a nap is counter-productive. It actually causes them to be disturbed and not nap if there IS noise. It also makes it challenging to nap anywhere else. Just like you, they need to learn to tune out the everyday noises and sleep anyway. That said, we will take days to set up particularly quiet houses for particularly quiet naps — because the sleep is so strong and healthful. It just isn't the norm.

> When Son was ready to be born, I moved in with a best friend who happened to have (no kidding) ten cats and six dogs over sixty-pounds, so the house was not a naturally quiet place. On day four of Son's life, a neighbor with seven children (which house was more chaotic, I ask you) came over to the house. She walked in and said, "What is going on?" My friend and I looked up from our books and said, "What?" She repeated, "What is going on? Why is this house so quiet?!" We said that Son was taking a nap. She said, "Oh no, he isn't!" and walked over and turned on the television and went to get the vacuum. Needless to say, we were floored. She recommended bringing the bassinet downstairs to the living room and putting it in a quiet corner, or at least opening his bedroom door, instead of being isolated. She said, "Make noise! You don't want him to get used to only sleeping in the quiet!" So, we now make no special considerations for napping children or not, and as a result, we can put them to bed when we are having a dinner party and they go to sleep (eventually sometimes) without being distracted by the noise.

"Too Quiet"

A friend of mine brought her six or seven month old infant over. The baby had been put on a Sorta Schedule and had gone to good sleep schedules. However, the baby hadn't ever slept anywhere except her own bed. I had mentioned previously to the mother that it would be a good idea, given our lifestyles, to go ahead and try to let her nap elsewhere, so that it wouldn't be a shock. This sounds like a good idea in principle, but it is harder to put into action, especially when you have never done it before. I told her we'd lay her down in Daughter's bed (with the crib side-rail replaced and no comforter or pillows), in a darkened, comfortable room and simply go downstairs. If the baby fussed, we would both look at our watches and agree to go up after four minutes. Things were relatively quiet initially, I'm sure as the baby visually explored the new things around her. Then it came time to seriously think about sleep. And so she fussed. Down-stairs her mother started to get up. I put a hand on her arm and we both looked at our watches and I said that we would count together. Four long minutes, and we watched our watches. Close to the end of the fourth, the baby settled herself down; she was comfortable, she was safe, she had the familiar cue of her own blanket, a bed, closed curtains, cool room and sure enough, she fell asleep. A few more times, and the baby was napable in other places, in a pack-n-play or bassinet in another home. The mother is also trying it with different locations at home, a pack-n-play in the guest room, just to keep in practice. That said, the mother was surprised at how difficult it was not to just get up and go to the child, and at how long those four minutes seemed. Moral support helps a lot in these situations, so don't be afraid to ask for it. It isn't a bad thing to ask for help, and if that means that you ask a friend to please let you come over on Sunday and bring your pack-n-play so your child can learn how to nap elsewhere ... well, go for it!

WHY SO MUCH SLEEP?

Children do some amazing things when they sleep. They learn and they grow.[8] They do a whole lot of learning and growing, so they need to sleep

Children learn AND grow when they sleep.

a whole lot. You know the children that you see who look pinched and malnourished (well, besides the actually malnourished ones). If you have a chance to observe them, notice if they get naps, how long the naps are, how peaceful they are, and if there is a set bedtime. Lots of people will say that their children nap in the car, but ask yourself how well you sleep in the car. Is it deep, restful, restorative sleep? Do you sleep better in the dark, in your own bed? Are you adaptable enough to rest in other beds? Do you rest better in other beds with your own pillow? Do certain cues tell you that it is time to go to bed (besides the clock of course)? Give your child these things that they may have a decided preference for, but don't have the ability to express. Nap at home, in a darkened room, in their own beds, or at least with a familiar cuddly object or blanket, at familiar times. 3pm at work is a good time for me.

A study was done with kittens on sleep and learning.[9] Their brain patterns were observed when they were introduced to a new skill and it was mapped in various ways. The kittens fell into that deep KEE-rash kitten sleep that little animals do, and dreamed, complete with Rapid Eye Movement, and of course, brain patterns indicating dreams. The amazing thing was that the brain patterns were the same ones observed while they were learning their new skill, but now the kittens were asleep. The new skill was being practiced *in their dreams*. And

---

[8] Think about the sheer physics of going from 6lbs to approximately 24lbs – that is four TIMES the starting weight. We won't ever grow as much as that first year.

[9] http://moninterv.aspetjurnals.org/cgi/content/abstract/3/7/404

when the kittens woke, they were demonstrably better at the new skill – because they had slept and practiced. The neurons were shown to have developed in pathways appropriate to that skill. Kids learn so much every single day. I always liked them to get two or three hours of sleep during the day and a good ten at night. They still get ten hours of sleep at night. When Son was four and Daughter was two, she was still getting a two to three hour nap and he was down to one hour, but they still slept during the day until well into kindergarten, and still a full night. And on the weekends, they sleep hard during their naps, solid two to three hour naps, usually immediately after a solid hour or two outdoors.[10]

That is going to be temperament dependent of course. Some children give up naps earlier than others. Encourage Quiet Time instead of sleeping if that is the case, but all children need some time to slow down and process the information that they have received that day.

Another thing that children do when they sleep is grow. Sometimes I swear that you can see it at the end of a nap; they're bigger. Their bodies are phenomenal little things and they are processing all kinds of things mentally, which they sort and categorize when they sleep. Fortunately they can do that in their unconscious. But physically, when they are awake, all their energy goes into gathering information and dealing with coordination. They'll go on sort of binge eating and then their bodies need to turn that into more muscles and bones. And that happens when they are asleep.

SET THE STAGE

Set the child's room up for sleeping. I have children who can power through their Sleep Signs, so we chose to keep toys to a minimum, in an easily removable basket for a special few toys. I take the basket out when they go to bed, and put it back in when I give them their last kiss before I go to bed, so it is there when they wake in the morning. Go ahead and gate the door to the room or the top of the stairs, at night if you have to, so that they have a safe place to play if they get out of bed. Believe me, you are likely to wake up when they get out of bed and start moving around anyway, but at least they won't be en route to something that they aren't allowed to have (markers in the office come to mind). Get curtains or blinds that darken the room. Unless you are going someplace with floor to ceiling windows, it is likely that the longest length (75" or so) curtains will provide darkness in a number of different window-sizes and the curtains can be moved with you.

[10] A weekend nap begins at 1pm instead of the 3pm weekday nap.

We actually didn't have much other furniture in the children's room since they grew out of crib-size. We chose to avoid temptation after the second or third time of coming in to disassembled drawers or all of the clothes out of the dresser and in the crib. We tried using a long rod through the drawer pulls to prevent it, but it didn't take them long to figure out how to take that out. We tried ... well, lacing the drawers shut with parachute cord (stop snickering), but Son didn't take long unlacing that either. Finally, I decided that I was perfectly happy getting clothes elsewhere, because I wasn't able to catch them in the act of any of these things. So, I moved the dressers out to the hallway. Other mothers chose to take more time, patience and effort to teach the kids not to disembowel their dressers. You'll choose what works best for your family, not to mention your house layout.

If you are allowed, paint the room in a quiet, soothing color.

We decided to always include a shelf in their room, up high, above reach of anything that they might stack on anything else, for a picture of Mama and Daddy, Sister or Brother and a knickknack or two, or a night light or music box. But a child's bedroom doesn't have to be a showpiece for it to be a comfortable place for sleeping. Another family I know has books and those mementos and photographs in a bookshelf in the child's room and it is aesthetically much less sparse. Of course this is going to change as they get older, when their rooms become their sanctuaries, but as toddlers, we've chosen the less is more approach. And the MORE we want is MORE sleeping.

If you are allowed to, paint the room in a soothing, quiet color. Grey-blue is a calm and flexible color, sage-green is a quiet and peaceful color. Yellow is a perky color and pink apparently causes emotional escalation, whichever emotion, but particularly the ones that have elevated heart-rates and blood pressure associated with them. Think, pink as an accent color, not the primary color, or temper it with dark purple or something. From my experience, blue rooms seem to work better — perhaps they just seem darker.

SLEEP ROUTINES

A routine is important to a little person.

Routines are by definition:[11] rou-tine (n)

1. the usual way tasks or activities are arranged

2. something that is unvarying or boringly repetitive

3. a typical pattern of behavior that somebody adopts in particular circumstances, especially insincere or affected behavior (informal)

4. a rehearsed set of movements, actions or speeches that make up a performance

5. a part of a computer program that performs a particular task

rou-tine (adj)

1. regular or standard, nothing out of the ordinary

2. boringly predictable, monotonous and unchanging

Why do I take the time to flesh out that definition? Because for you it is boring; for a little person, it is the structure that all the rest of their life is built upon. Think of your routine as the foundation, or framework, within which all their other learning is going to take place. They get something dependable, normal and the new things (which is everything) do not impact that solid thing. You can begin a routine any time. They can be flexible rather than rigid. In fact, they are stronger if they are flexible. Flexible things bend, while rigid things break!

> For you routine might be boring, but for children it is the structure that all the rest of their life is build upon.

The 'rule' (but of course) for routines is that you can change it up, but if it is different three times in a row, it is now the new routine, and it will take three times as long to reset it. This means that travel does not usually impact routines. But if you 'give in' three nights in a row to the 'I want a drink of water' routine (in the noun, line 4 definition), it is now the new way of doing the bedtime routine. It might take you nine nights to undo it, although they usually catch on after the third night doing it the original way, and they just do an occasional ping to check if you've forgotten.

For instance, our bedtime routine has changed over time, but it started out basically one way and has remained structurally unchanged: warning, clean-up, bath (sometimes), pajamas, teeth, book, bed. Now, the bath didn't happen everything night, but the changing into pajamas was a good cue that this was a

[11] Encarta® World English Dictionary © 1999 Microsoft Corporation. All rights reserved. Developed for Microsoft by Bloomsbury Publishing Plc.

sleep thing. Then came sitting in the Reading Chair (a big comfy leather chair that thankfully fits all of us) and reading a nursery rhyme or, for the nine hundred and sixty seventh time, The *Going to Bed Book* by Sandra Boynton,[12] Eventually it was a story that they picked out, or now, early level chapter books. Then it was into bed while I close curtains, took out the toy-basket, turned down the light and came to do our Godblesses. Some nights I would sing a song instead of read a story. Some nights it was me, or Daddy, or even a grandparent! This routine has been relatively stable all their lives, regardless of where we are, which country, in a house or hotel and they settle down at night fairly reasonably. Oh sure, some nights they talk to each other for what seems like a very long time, but they still sleep in the same room, so that's not unexpected.

While details of the bedtime routine have changed over time, it has remained structurally the same.

I took some time and effort to learn one special song each as well as I could: 'Rainbow Connection' for Son and 'Charlotte's Lullabye' from *Charlotte's Web* for Daughter. We can still calm down either child with a quiet singing of this song, cuddled close, and it is a godsend on a plane when we need it. Believe me, your child does not care that you cannot sing like a pro. When they hear the pro singing it, they say, "That's Mama singing my song!" (I wish). So now you know love is deaf as well as blind.

We use the old prayer, Now I Lay Me Down to Sleep, sung to the tune of Twinkle Twinkle Little Star, but every family is going to have different ideas, traditions and beliefs in this regard. I include it here only because I didn't realize the prayer was so long, and was delighted to find the whole thing.

> Now I lay me down to sleep,
> Pray the Lord my soul to keep.
> If I die before I wake,
> Pray the Lord my soul to take.
> Keep me safe throughout the night,
> Wake me in the morning light.

There are lots of versions of bedtime prayers out there – from ones that don't mention dying to ones that invoke other deities or none at all, to ones that are downright 100% sealed and certified politically correct. This one fits to Twinkle twinkle, which they know and they like doing a long low deep Aaaaa-men like in church at the end. By all means, dredge up your childhood bedtime prayer if you have one, or the one your religious leader recommends. If you don't do a prayer before bed, consider a small wrap up conversation instead, or goodnight moon sort of back and forth. It is more about a small close to the day in some

[12] Which I still can recite from memory!

respects, than a dialog with God.

Our bedtime always ends with kisses on the bean (forehead) and "Love you night night" on the way out the door. The nicest part is that it is easy for anyone to do, keeping it routine, and it fits into an easy thirty-minute time-frame, making planning the evening easy to manage. Husband can do this when we have guests, and only be missing in action for thirty minutes, during which the guests are usually unaware that they are going down for the night.

NAP ROUTINES

We have a nap routine too of course. There is a 'usual time', although that depends on if it is weekdays or a weekend. Depending on if it is the early 'usual', around 1pm, or the later one, around 3pm changes whether it is a snack before or after nap. But if Daughter comes to me in the middle of the day and says, "I want a snack," that is code for "I'm tired." Other children might say, "I'm bored" and even others might go curl up themselves.

Find a small way to bring a close to the day, whether it is prayers, or them telling you the one thing they just loved about the day, or saying good night to family photos.

My children still share a bedroom, and are necessarily separated for their naps. They would just talk and play, and invalidate the whole sleeping or quiet play idea. But, we give them a few minutes warning, "Nap time in five minutes, sweethearts." And then five minutes later we all go upstairs, use the bathroom, get the appropriate blanket and baby and one child goes into the guest room and the other goes into their room. I close curtains and they invariably ask when they can wake up. Now, this is getting tricky as their toddler years come to a close because if I say, "Three o'clock," they'll either know what that looks like on the clock, or ask, "Where's the big hand then, and where's the little one?" and then 3pm rolls around and they're Johnny-on-the-spot with coming out of their rooms — which means, sleep probably didn't happen.

Waking them up varies too of course, but if they don't come down themselves (nearly always surprising me), I go in quietly and open the curtains and leave the door open. Sometimes this is enough. Sometimes, they are far away on their dreamship and hauling them back to earth takes much longer. Daughter is a hard child to wake up, and desperately needs to have fruit juice or something when she first wakes up or God have mercy on everyone around her. Until we figured out that she just needed fuel to the brain, we had a 'Don't Speak to

Daughter' rule for when she first woke up. Son wakes up almost entirely in a snap, like a little light switch, although he is not averse to a few minutes of quiet cuddling afterwards. Learning what their wake up style is can be just as important for your sanity as learning how to get them to go to sleep in the first place! We don't plan to actually leave the house for a good thirty minutes after Daughter wakes up, or it would be high drama.

Delaying a nap is something that may come about simply by virtue of people's schedules. For instance, I worked all day on Friday, which means that our child-care provider has both kids, all day. Daughter was in half-day pre-school and Son was in full-day pre-school. Fridays were days when Daughter didn't get to lay down at 3pm because at 330pm she and the child-care provider had to go get Son from school. They came home, snacked together, and then went up for their nap, hers being delayed about an hour and a half. It is also necessarily shortened because if they sleep past 530pm or 6pm, there is no getting them to bed. This happens once a week and isn't so strange that it throws the whole routine.

Merging a nap happens when they go from two naps as infants to one nap as toddlers. This is the time when you suddenly realize that you liked having two times during the day, which you could count on having to get a few things done and you wish you'd done more! Sorry. Time for you to adjust your routine; they're growing up! This merging happens around two or three years old, but every child is different. Sometimes external situations like enrollment in half-day pre-school dictate that a first nap is dropped. Sometimes you realize that is has been a week or so since they have actually slept during their morning (or afternoon) nap, and are quietly playing instead.[13] If the merging is not dictated by external factors like school, and is a result of the child growing out of more naps, don't forget that some children will drop the morning nap and others will drop the afternoon nap. As a parent, you can look into your crystal ball and see that dropping the afternoon nap and keeping the long morning one might not be terribly convenient in the near future or for the long term and you can ease the merging into a more mid-day option. For example, using the clock, if your child naps at 10am and 3pm, but would naturally drop the afternoon nap, you can see that if they are going to go to preschool soon, it might be best if it was one longer nap at 1pm instead of a long nap at 10am. Napping through noon is not a terrible thing if lunch is at 11am or 1pm.

Double naps are for when my kids are sick. Son calls them Sick Naps, and adults

[13] Nine days is the magical three day, three times. I don't know why this is true, but it certainly seems to be.

can have them too when they are sick. A two-hour nap in the morning 10-12, and a two hour nap in the afternoon, 2-4, because I have said enough times that sleep helps them get better that they believe it. They get a good drink of water before Sick Naps and medicine if necessary (very rarely), and lay down. Toys are out of the room, but if they are not so sick, I might leave a book in, now that I can trust that they won't eviscerate it. If they stay home sick from school, it is a Sick Day, therefore there are Sick Naps involved. The nice thing is, if Husband or I are sick, and we actually call in sick (which means we are really sick), we can call a Sick Nap and the kids understand. They will even remind us to drink more water before a sick nap!

Skipped naps also happen. There are some days when the nap just isn't going to happen. Our only recourse to this situation is to try with all our might to get them to bed on time. We don't try to lay them down early, although it sometimes happens, because their usual 7am wake up time is early enough for me as it is and frankly, I don't think I could handle it if I sent them to bed an hour early and they got up earlier. Other children can skip a nap without any ill effect. You can miss a little sleep and not have it cause ill effects for a few days without incurring too much sleep debt.[14] Don't be surprised if the little one 'makes up' for that missed nap by sleeping in a little or taking an extra long nap one day. Once sleep is lost three days in a row, it can't be made up and apparently our bodies are motivated to keep sleep times normal. And little people are more in tune with that than adults are because adults are tuned to the clock. Little people can also handle the occasional day-without-nap, but don't be surprised if the external stimuli fails to outweigh the internal desire to sleep and a cranky kid is the result. It isn't their fault, they didn't decide not to nap, the events did; and they're not terribly good at expressing frustration, sleepiness or maximum saturation. I am talking about a day at a theme park, airplanes (yes, we hope that they will sleep a lot, but sometimes they don't at all), or timing of something you have no control over scheduling. I'm not talking about just blowing off a nap for fun. Skipped naps, and naps that morph into Quiet or Alone Play are your cues that they are getting ready to drop naps entirely. This can happen literally at all kinds of ages, from two to six! You can mitigate the effects a little bit by helping it become Quiet or Alone Play instead. My children still nap, although sometimes it is a very little nap, and sometimes more Quiet Play than any actual sleeping. They even nap on Christmas Day with the family at someone's house. Of course, on Thanksgiving, so does most of the family!

And then there are the cat-nappers. These little ones snatch a little here and a

[14] http://www.blackwell-synergy.com/links/doi/101046/j.1446-9235.2003.00006.x/abs/

little there. I object to the name cat-napper, because a real cat (any size) sleeps 85% of its day! Keep in mind that napping/sleeping is their growing time, and awake is their learning/assimilating time, so go for the not-picking-up approach and avoid stimulating the child. Let the baby stay in the crib and be alone, and hopefully snooze on and off while there. And do this on some sort of 'routine' that you would want to maintain. In other words, the baby would be able to somewhat anticipate – in the short-term (they aren't into long-term timelines). So if Baby isn't stimulated by being picked up or moved, Baby will be more inclined to learn to sleep. And remember, crying is not a disaster. As long as the baby is clean, dry, safe and not hungry, crying for a few minutes hurts the big people more than the little one.

Overtired is as much of a nap-killer as NOT tired.
That said, there are some babies who just can't quite 'unwind' enough to sleep. Too much is going on, they are too high-strung, or tuned-in or just plain curious. Sometimes what works for them is extra play-time or attention to tire them out. But be sure to watch for the Sleep Signs, because these babies will just keep going and try to power through. Over-tired is just as much of a nap-killer as not-tired.

So, it ends up being an extended dance with a couple days trying it one way (crying) and some more days another way (extra play time) and eventually getting it right and finding your rhythm. It can be really hard to be the parent, especially when it is easier in the short run to just get them to stop fussing. Remind yourself of the long-term goal.

> *If you are tired, all things are insurmountable; if you are well-rested, you can handle anything.*

It is easy to get into a 'habit' of thinking that the little ones will adjust because they are so adaptable. Staying up late occasionally, delaying a nap, skipping a nap, merging naps, double naps; all these are things that can happen. As the parent, the trick is to remember not to let deviations happen twice in a row, or heaven help you, three times in a row. You are the one who has to remember it and enforce it. Enforcing it can be very tricky, especially when visiting family who looks at a nap as reduced visiting time (and the visit as 'no rules' because they are few and far between). Remember, you're doing it to maintain a routine and a maintained routine makes a better visit anyway. And they don't have to agree with you.

11. Clothes

Unfortunately, the saying is not true, because you CAN have too many shoes and clothes! Basically, however you decide to dress your child, you're going to be doing wash at least once a week, regardless. They grow awfully fast, so keep that in mind also when making your clothing choices. I tried not to buy more than ten days worth of clothing. At the under-five years old ages, they don't care about fashion, although you might. And goodness knows they make some awfully neat things out there for little kids!

MATERNITY CLOTHES

Everyone is going to have their own sources for maternity clothes, and friends and relatives are going to be a valuable resource for pointing you in the right direction. Lands' End, Old Navy, Motherhood Maternity, Pea in the Pod … maternity clothes are not that hard to find. However, if you find a site that doesn't put bows, smocking or ruffles on maternity shirts, please let me know! Why they think that women who are going to have a baby want to look like a baby, I don't know. Target has a great maternity selection, at a decent price.

One of the best sites I've found is expressiva.com. In spite of the name, they have some great clothes. They have maternity and nursing clothes that look like real clothes. Their professional clothing really is, and you could wear one to a meeting with the Ambassador and he would never know that it was made with a different purpose planned into it. However, it is also not cheap. But if you can treat yourself, do, because one or two nice things, that you can nurse in and attend a wedding in, is well worthwhile.

APPROPRIATENESS

Infants do not thermo-regulate as well as adults and it is your responsibility to keep the appropriate layers on (or off) them. Cooler is a better option for them because it is easier to warm a body up than it is to cool one down. Both adults and infants function better with a cool face.

A friend was walking from her house to ours, all of six blocks, and had her six-month old infant in a stroller with a onesie, socks and a light blanket since it was 80^F outside. A woman on the street passed her, with her infant in a stroller, Snuggli, socks, hat and heavy blanket. My friend could just see the woman struggling not to ask if her baby wasn't too cold while at the same time, the friend was struggling not to ask if the lady's baby wasn't too hot! It is all matter of perspective.

If you need a sweater, your child needs a sweater and a light blanket. If you need a coat, they need a coat and a hat. If you are hot enough to only wear a tank top, a onesie will be fine with a light blanket nearby. If you touch your child and they feel cool to the touch, put the light blanket over their legs.

When taking a 'touch temperature' of a child, the best place to accurately gauge whether they are too hot or too cold is the back of their neck. The difference between your hand, which may or may not be cool, cold, warm or hot, and the back of their neck, is enough to cue you to either take a layer off or add one.

When taking a touch temperature, place your hand at the back of their neck to decide to add or remove a layer.

Children's clothing is challenging because the months that they put on baby clothes might not match your child's age, and they might or might not put the weight on it also. Then the child turns into a toddler and you discover 2T and 24 months. Aren't they the same size[1]? And sometimes you have a child that doesn't even come close! Daughter was in 2T when she turned three. So, I included the weight in the clothing recommendations because it is so very flexible.

When a child starts walking, they learn best in bare feet, but do need shoes. Every shoe before that is pretty much window dressing. Daughter wasn't even 15 lbs and she was surely a toddler and on the move and finding shoes was a major challenge. Should you find yourself in a similar situation, zappos.com carried Keds in those itty bitty sizes and had functional hard-soled shoes for walking, as opposed to window dressing size 2 shoes.

Since everyone is different, I won't even begin to tell you how many clothes to buy or what to buy. I'll just let you know those things that we, myself and other mothers, found ourselves to be very glad to have or sorry to be without.

What you need, very basically speaking is:

Extra Small Little Clothes (Newborns and Infants): Newborn to 12

[1] Almost!

months or 20 pounds: onesies, footies, blanket sleeper, socks, travel items such as hat and Snugglie.

Small Little Clothes (infant or early toddler):[2] 12 -24 months or 15-20 pounds: onesies, footies, playsuits, sticky socks (socks with grips on the bottom), blanket sleeper, travel items.

Medium Little Clothes (aka Toddlers): 24 months, or 2T, or 20-30 pounds: onesies, footies, playsuits, shirts, pants, socks, shoes,[3] pajamas, coat and weather appropriate outside items.

Large Little Clothes (still toddlers, but almost–gasp!–Kids): 3T-4T, 30-40 pounds: shirts, pants, socks, shoes, pajamas, coat, boots, weather appropriate outside items.

Obviously, that's not a big list. It is also a beginning, not a definitive list. Pretty much everything else is bonus, but these are the basic necessities.

TUFF ENUFF

Consider purchasing less in quantity but of high quality.

The combination of living two feet from the ground and perpetually being washed is hard on clothes. My children were not fashion plates as infants and toddlers. As infants they worn a onsie pretty much 24/7, unless it was a footie (footed pajama) instead. As they reached the larger toddler ages, and until age 5, summer pajamas were underwear and a t-shirt, and winter pajamas were waffle weave cotton pajamas. Pajamas tend to be, somewhat inexplicably, the most worn item in a child's wardrobe, and go through the toughest times. Hanes makes both a tough kid t-shirt in wonderful non-fading colors, and the cotton long johns.

I personally recommend buying less in quantity and more in quality, although there are occasions when it works out better to do otherwise. I know several people who bought locally, and often, not just for the cheap and easy clothes, but to be able to get out there and shop! A good tough pair of jeans or cargo pants from Lands' End is worth six cheap pairs of pants and lasts three times as long. My personal experience has been Lands' End and Oshkosh B'Gosh. Others recommend The Children's Place, Children's Gap, and Old Navy. Their items are tough enough, and for the little girls, they have neutral, very feminine or not at all, depending on your little one. You'll find choices that fit your

[2] B the way, you're not going crazy; it is nearly impossible to find clothes labeled 9-12 months. No idea why.
[3] Your child should have hard sole shoes as soon as they start walking. But when learning to cruise and walk, bare feet or sticky socks are best.

preferences, lifestyle, or brand loyalties.

Some children have clothing preferences relatively young. There are girls that prefer pants and playsuits for being outside in the mud and trees; others that seem genetically predisposed to pink and dresses and tea parties right off the bat; or both, preferably at the same time. There are some wonderful places that make clothes that are adorable, but not going to fall apart. Hannah Anderson is worth the extra expense and Lands' End makes a cotton dress (with a pocket) that is worth its weight in gold. These are good for school dresses or play dresses. Lands' End also has lovely, and comfortable shoes that are pretty, Mary Janes and sandals, and they're tough enough to last until the next size.

Another two 'tough enoughs' in the shoe department are Keenes and Crocs. Crocs make excellent slippers, and lots of places will have the children take off their outside shoes and put on slippers. Crocs are also phenomenally light-weight. Keenes are not as light-weight, but they are easy for children to put on and have a covered toe and they last forever.

Finally, the Lands' End playsuit was a heaven sent item for our family. I am sure there are other places that make them, but these ones withstood repeated washings. They're great for just mucking about, and they're easy to get into and out of by themselves since they're essentially a onesie with longer legs. They snap along the inseam and are great for potty training (because you pull them up and snap them over one shoulder to hold them up).

DRESS CLOTHES AND GIFT CLOTHES

One or two "Sunday Best" types of outfits are plenty. When Son turned three, we got him a nice pair of khaki pants, a blazer and a tie to go with it. We had a few weddings that year, and it worked out very well. Now, there are plenty of choices for lovely clothes, and if you are in a situation that requires that you wear your Sunday Best fairly regularly, you will have to ignore this section. For us, Daughter has a range of school dresses, and only two are the very nice, "Sunday Best" ones.

In fact, I have six dress outfits sitting on top of a wardrobe right now, all of them gifts, that haven't been worn and aren't likely to be worn. It takes a little effort, but if you can, put the clothes that you receive as gifts on your children and take a picture for the giftee. Grandparents and great-grandparents in particular take great comfort in knowing the children are wearing the clothes that they sent. You don't have to put them on again, if they're going directly into the donate pile. I've had ones that I didn't even take the tag off of, took a picture in, and sent it on to a little girl who loved those kinds of dresses.

Keep in mind that as hard as it is for you to keep track of your children's sizes, it is twice as hard for someone else. And those wonderful folks who are gifting more than a few grandchildren will occasionally make a size error.

ADAPTING TO LOCAL CONDITIONS

Remember that it is very likely that you are going to be in a part of the world where there are very differing norms for what is appropriate and what is not. It helps to know what you are going to say ahead of time, when someone 'corrects' you for dressing your child inappropriately for local cultural conditions, especially when you know they are dressed appropriately for the weather. A few suggestions from friends and colleagues include:

> "We're not as adapted to the climate as you are."

> "My home state is also cold/warm."

> "Please don't touch the baby."

> Or just smile and say, "Thank you."

There are so many things that are different depending on the place. Some places have a dread of the cross-breeze and you'll come home to find your house shut up tight and everyone in sweaters in spite of the radiators being on. I've had to literally argue with the nanny that yes, I do want my thermostat set low (comparatively) and even so, I also don't require my children to be in sweaters inside. I try to keep the house at about 70^F or so, usually a little less, and it is comfortable for us. I can't comfortably keep it at 75^F or 80^F in the winter because we're used to it cooler. This is interesting because the same goes for the summer, when I turn the air-conditioning on, to the housekeeper's horror, to keep it in the same 70^F range.

In some cases, shorts are not going to be appropriate, or what Americans call "casual wear" and the rest of the world calls "work out clothes." In some places, having your daughter in pants will be frowned upon, but in other places, it is different but not noticeably so. Take your cue from the locals and those folks who have been there the longest. The information on the internet or in the welcome kits might not be entirely up-to-date. Ask your sponsor if you're concerned that there will be major differences in attire.

When we were at First Post, Husband took Son for a walk with Grandmother. First Post was a little cold, but Grandmother was from a place that could only be described as having a real winter also, so everyone bundled up and went out – winter is no reason to huddle inside and catch cabin fever.

They went through the market with three month old Son in a Baby Bjorn and appropriate winter clothing. Even Grandmother said it was appropriate, and she was our gauge for everything on that point. There was a Snuggli body suit on him, he had a onesie and footie under the Snuggli, a blanket around the edges and a hat, scarf and mittens. He was not cold. A babushka (Russian grandmother) approached Husband and Grandmother started saying that they were going to kill the child by failing to dress him properly and moved to cover the baby's face. Husband ... well, he over- reacted, but the lesson is the same.

You do not have to rap the babushka on the knuckles, but sometimes having your 'line' ready for why it is different is useful for preventing those situations from getting to the rapping knuckles stage.

"The Pushy Babushka"

12. Baths

Your little one doesn't really need a bath terribly often, and certainly not every day. It is more like bathing occurs 'weekly' or so during the first year, about every other day during the second and third year, and then about twice a week or as needed after the third year. I know, that doesn't sound often enough. But that lovely skin protects Baby, and keeping clean while changing diapers by not using too much product of any kind, whether that is Baby Butt (our generic term for diaper cream of any sort), baby powder or lotion, will keep bathing to a reasonable level. The more product you use, the more you'll have to restore that wonderful skin to a more natural state. Baths also are a great bonding mechanism, giving you time to see and feel that little body and them to feel your hands holding them safe.

The more products you use, the more often you will have to bath the baby. A bath adds about thirty minutes to a bedtime routine.

Plan for a bath to take about thirty minute, roughly speaking. If it is part of the bedtime routine and bedtime is 8pm, bath begins at 730pm not 8pm, unless you are deliberately trying to extend bedtime. We have also bathed immediately before dinner (after particularly dirty outside play) or after dinner (after particularly messy meals). After swimming or exceptionally organic play, sometimes a bath is necessary immediately.

SUPPLIES

You don't actually need much for a bath, and you can avoid all the fancy extras for necessities sake, although they are awfully fun. A clean ketchup bottle is much easier and more replaceable than some fancy fountain toy.

Things like stick-on ABCs and 123s, a boat or something that floats, rubber duckies and other animal toys are all wonderful and lots of fun. I recommend a mesh bag that you can hang on the faucet for toys to drip dry.

You need the following items:

      Washcloths or loofah

      Cups

      Baby shampoo/ body wash combo soap

Stool

Towels (hooded or not, just have several)

Toys for when in tub versus sink

Bath Bear sponge or something else to keep them from slipping

You can choose to use or purchase a whole lot more, but you don't need it.

I personally think that the most important tool that you need for tub time is something for you to easily sit on. Your knees work fine for winging it, but in the long run, you want something wide and low (but not too low) and strong. The First Years blue step-stool is great. It is wide enough for me to be comfortable, strong enough for me not to worry that it will break, even if an adult stands on it, high enough that I can see and reach into the tub easily, but low enough for the kids to use it as an actual step stool. And it stores cleaning stuff![1]

TECHNIQUES

This first technique was discovered entirely by accident while on vacation in Rome. The sink in this marble bathroom had schmancy wild fixtures and was slicker than ice. But there was this convenient little thing that looked like ... well, a little tub. But it was at toilet level. Well, it turns out that this ignorant American had seen her first bidet. And no, I still have no idea how to use it properly. However, until about fifteen pounds, it makes a great baby tub! Be sure to bleach it clean the first time if it is in your home. The slope is gentle, it can't get very deep, it is a lovely size and sitting on the little stool, it is the perfect height and there is no strain on your back. The toilet is usually right there, making a perfect staging area for towels, shampoo, etc. At home we cleaned it thoroughly, and later we used it to store tub toys.

Of course, the kitchen sink is a tried and true baby-bathing friend. I'll proceed to describe as if it were in a double kitchen sink, but adapt accordingly of course. Put a few fluffy towels on the side of the sink that is the largest. Fill the large sink about a third of the way, not enough to challenge the baby's buoyancy but enough to feel like they're well in the water. I recommend the bath bear more than the little mini-tub, simply because it is portable and adaptable, it is a sponge approximately the size of your child. If you don't have a bath bear, place a towel on the bottom of the sink. Gently run water into the other side of the sink, the

[1] As I said, it is advertised to hold toys, but they'd have to be bone dry to go in there or they'd mildew in no time flat.

non-bathing side, so that the noise of running water is there and becomes familiar. A third towel goes in front of the sink, a padded place to start and a way to keep the front of the parent reasonably dry. Initially of course, the baby is not going to have much muscle tone and you are going to lower Baby into the sink with a pretty firm grip, usually cradled in a way that gets most of your non-dominant forearm wet too. Start with the toes and talk about the process, keeping the temperature warm but not hot. Put a small bit of baby shampoo on the washcloth or loofah and then gently wipe from toes up, ending with the top of the head, and not doing anything to the face for an infant. You don't need suds. To rinse, lean the baby backwards slightly (this is where your arm gets wet), but not too far backwards or they get nervous, and gently, with the palm of your hand, cup the running water in your palm and slowly ladle the water over the back of their head, avoiding wetting the face if you can, and down over their back and arms and tummy.

To dry, you turn off the water, of course, and pull the plug, rather than lifting them out of the water. I think the suction of the water sort of holds them in, and the little bit of resistance is disconcerting. Through trial and error, I can say for most children I've observed, letting the water run out seems to be a less noticeable method of ending a bath. Later, when they are toddlers, you can allow them to pull the plug and this helps avoid some of the fuss and bother that can crop up when a child doesn't want to end a bath.

Any acknowledgement of bath time drama will prolong it and put it on the next bath's menu.

A necessary variant of the sink bath is the Butt Bath. This is necessary when an entire bath isn't needed but Certain Parts are in desperate need. Place several washcloths on the sink bottom, drip some shampoo/baby wash on them and run warm water into them. Don't fill the sink. With a towel draped over the side of the sink, into the sink and onto the counter, lean your child, tummy side down onto your arm, using your non-dominant forearm to support Baby and leave Baby's bottom on the sink side, your spread palm supporting Baby's chest and/or neck. With your dominant hand, take one washcloth at a time, water still running on low, and wipe that stinky butt! Don't worry about rinsing out washcloths, just use as much of the washcloth as you can to clean up, then shove it aside in the sink and use another. When it is a fresh and lovely baby bottom again, do the gentle rinse with your hand and the running water again. If your baby is not a newborn, a mirror on the counter is distracting enough, but this is a three or four minute process, and does not take long once you get the hang of it. Then, baby goes onto the dry towel, and diaper and done.

The tub of course, is a favorite friend. One of the questions and answers that I can remember hearing is, "What do you do with an upset child?"

"Put them in water!"

We still do this. Now, remember how I'm a little strange when it comes to behaviors? We don't allow things in the tub that we would find inappropriate elsewhere, so no tub crayons for writing on the walls, no finger paints or that kind of thing. I'm selling my kids a little short on this issue because they're not stupid; they can differentiate between where things are allowed and where they aren't. I just choose not to fight that battle. One product that I do like is Tub Tint, because it changes the bathwater color, and it doesn't stain your child. Watch out for the cheap ones that are more paint than tint, or you might have a small blue Pict on your hands, looking like Braveheart!

> We don't allow things in the tub that we would find inappropriate elsewhere, like tub crayons for the wally!

Many of us have come across the problem of mold growth in our squirting toys. The kids have various body-function references to this, but it mostly grosses out the parents who know that this is the opposite of clean. We have tried soaking the toys in bleach and washing them in the dishwasher, but this just results in dead mold being squirted out, and I can't tell the difference between live and dead mold. A cycle of replacement, simple acceptance, or not having these kinds of toys is the best advisable course of action. There is not enough mold, and there is enough dilution with water and soap, that a fungal infection is very unlikely.

Husband is the bath guy in his house; he owns the night time routine. About ten minutes before it is time for bath, Husband tells the kids that he's going to get the bath ready and goes up and starts filling the tub. If it is a hair washing night, he doesn't put in bubbles (baby bath, not Mr. Bubbles), otherwise, sometimes he puts in bubbles, sometimes he doesn't, sometimes it is tub tint, sometimes not. Generally speaking, Husband was just trying to avoid the children interpreting a new treat as something that would ALWAYS happen during a bath. In the time that the tub is filling, he gets the towels in one place, one stack per child, turns on the space heater if the room is chilly, gets pajamas and underwear (or diapers or Pull-ups) on each bed or changing table. In the meantime, the kids have wrapped up their play and tossed toys into baskets, and are ready and unsurprised when he comes down and says that it is time. Then they get stripped, toss clothes in the hamper (we have them do that too), and it is tub time! Supervision required, but not necessary.

Hair washing can traumatize a parent. And believe me, your child will wrest every iota of drama out of hair washing if you let them get away with it. I am not recommending that you man-handle them, disbelieve their discomfort or ignore protests entirely, but if you're using no-tears shampoo, if you're telling them what it is that you are doing or going to do each step of the way, there is no cause for drama (other than the sheer fun of it). Be forthright and then just do it – slowly and with discussion and explanation. We offered a dry washcloth for them to hold on their face while I poured or rinsed. I also gave them the option of doing the rinsing themselves. We encouraged either tipping their heads as far forward as possible or as far back. Heck, we've tried everything. In the end, it was the straight forward, "Yep, you gotta wash your hair" approach that prevailed for my children. You will find your way, but know that any acknowledgment of the drama is fuel for the fire and children will naturally manipulate as far as they can because it is the little teeny bit of power that they have and you can bet that they are going to use it!

It is natural for your child to try to wring every drop of drama out of hair washing. You can avoid it with patience, consistency, and a few well-worded choices.

One surprisingly simple way to get around the hair washing drama is choices. When they're two or so, you can say things like, "Would you like me to rinse with the red cup or spray?" and "Would you like to rise or hold the washcloth?" By now you're going to have a feel for what works best for your child when it comes to hair washing, so you just word their choices accordingly.

Don't start something you don't mean to continue for years when it comes to baths. If you let them dunk instead of pour, don't be surprised when big brother wants to dunk little sister and forgets to warn her. If you let her pour on him, don't be surprised when she pours on the cat standing outside the tub. Be precise in what you say. "Rinse your hair only now, with the cup please." Rather than "Go ahead and pour, honey." There is a big difference to that little bitty lawyer mind!

We allow our son and daughter to bathe together. We haven't experienced anything to discourage us in this decision. I am sure a time will come in their elementary years when it may no longer be appropriate, however as infants and toddlers, it is not an issue for them. You may have other reasons for choosing not to do it, but the child's modesty and mindset is not a determining factor at this age.

Additionally, one of the things my children have grown to love is first baths, and then showers with their big people. We had family baths, family showers, and then boy baths and showers, and girl baths and showers (we got smelly bubbles). Personal choices again will dictate how your family handles this.

When the children were about one and three years old (perhaps slightly more, but not much), the Fourth of July rolled around and we decided to let them paint on the large brown moving paper that was as large as our front gate. I secured one sheet on the gate, and put one sheet on the ground. Then I mixed some of Crayola's non-toxic dry tempra paint (shippable, and mixable in small quantities), gave the kids brushes and turned them loose. Then we paused a moment to strip off clothing and turned them loose again.

We have photos of Daughter with what looks like Indian war-paint slashes on her cheeks and Son with paint in all kinds of interesting locations! And they painted the sheet on the gate in Jackson Pollock fashion, with slashes and dashes, lines and dots, flicks and spots, it was fabulous! The one below got hand prints and then the color mixing began and there were soups and lakes and rivers of combining colors.

All of this resulted in a major mess. I went upstairs to draw a bath, wondering how we were going to get them inside without staining our clothing or getting footprints in the house ... and when I went back outside, I discovered that Daddy had come up with the ideal on-the-spot solution. The diapers came off baby girl, which was the only thing resembling civilization left on either one of them anyway, and while I carefully put paint pots and paint brushes in a bucket to be washed, and folded up the perfect paintings, Daddy found the hose and started chasing them around the yard with the water. We rinsed them off, soaped them up in the driveway, rinsed again and in no time flat they were clean!

And we had collectible art suitable for framing.

"Naked Outside Painting"

13. Siblings — human and otherwise

When we started this adventure, we didn't expect to have any children, let alone two, and we were caught as unprepared as someone with eight month's or so of advance warning can be caught.

The arrival of a little sister likewise caught us by surprise (a bonus miracle; how many people get that), but we were quite lucky that Son had furry siblings long before his human one joined him. Two cats and two dogs lived with us for a decade before we had children. Animals have always been a part of my life, as long as I can remember, and when I was working with them as well as living with them, it was the happiest I'd ever been. Since human children are small mammals that don't speak human, the rules that govern a child's interaction with non-human siblings work equally well for the human ones.

That isn't meant as irreverent. There are four guidelines that we used for teaching our children to interact with our animals:

Do NOT assume others have taught their children animal-appropriate behavior. In fact, assume they haven't, for everyone's safety.

1. Gentle
2. Nice – no hitting, biting, kicking, or pushing
3. Trade or Share
4. Safe place

I will freely admit that Trade doesn't work so well once a human sibling is three or so, and it was slowly changed to Share. There are very few toys that are the sole possession of one child or another, but we respect that ownership, and Son cannot take away Daughter's special toy and visa versa, regardless of sharing or trading rules. They are never allowed to take an animal's toys and are asked to put it back in the basket immediately, particularly given that an animal can express displeasure ... rather sharply.

GENTLE

Gentle is a good rule for pets and siblings. One of our elderly dogs was not about to take pulling, tugging or sometimes even touching or a fast approach. At no time should a child under six, especially one that hasn't been taught how to behave around animals, be left alone with an animal, no matter what the breed.

There is no 'safe breed'[1] and while some breeds are reportedly less safe, I think that is a failure on the humans' part, not the dog's. Do not assume that others have taught their children animal appropriate behavior, or more to the point, your animal rules. Even the sweetest dog will react in the only manner it knows, a growl or a snap, if it is assaulted and a small child does not know that sticking something up the dog's nose is not going to be interpreted as exploring, but as an assault.

This concern about leaving a child and an animal alone with each other will change as the child and the animal become used to each other and what are appropriate behaviors, for both. I say "Gentle" to the dog nearly as much as to the children. So, as the baby, infant or toddler, approaches the animal, insert yourself into the situation and take that tiny hand and say, "Gentle" (or slowly, or whatever careful word you choose) and show them that petting doesn't involve pulling or tugging, but petting or patting. Do this at every opportunity and remember, a grasp is a reflex reaction for an infant, and open palm is not usual or even under their gross motor control for the most part.

To make a careful word like "gentle" click, say it a lot, but keep interactions brief.

This "Gentle" also works for dealing with a new baby. Gentle touching includes slowly as well as not forcefully. If this is reinforced every time, it becomes a habit. If you have animals first, and siblings later, it won't even seem out of character to hear you say that. A way to make this click is to do it often, but briefly. Say it a lot, but keep the interactions brief, so that they don't get burned out on it. Children can't express emotions very well at very young ages, at least not in ways we easily recognize as adults, and pushing something forcibly away from themselves is one way of expressing that they are bored or done. Be brief; we are talking a minute or so.

A four year little boy once told my mother that he had just become a big brother. Much to her concern, he told her that even hugs could be bad. It turned out that he was learning 'gentle hugs' for his new baby sibling, because 'daddy hugs' were 'too hard for babies.' One lovely thing we started was the different kisses and different hugs. Butterfly kisses (eyelashes brushing cheeks) and lamb hugs (soft and fluffy). But beware the puppy dog kiss!

[1] I was bitten by a golden retriever as a child and a brown lab as an adult, two of the 'least aggressive' breeds out there!

NICE

Nice is a great rule. Notice that all the rules are positive? Nice is ... well, nicer than "no hitting" or "no kicking," but it means the same thing. An alternative to nice that we're starting to use now is "Manners," because it encompasses so very much. This is useful later as they get to preschool and are exposed to things that they just aren't exposed to here at home – like spitting. That one just makes me mad.

We don't allow the word 'stupid' in our house, because it is mean. Okay, yes, I know that 'dumb' is the same, but we use synonyms, for instance, by asking, "Why is that foolish?" But stupid is usually used in a mean context, not to mean foolish. When Daughter returned from school one day, all of three years old, spouting "Stupid boys," she did get a time out for it. We also made sure to tell the teachers that this was one word that we don't allow because it is rude (the natural opposite of manners). Teachers generally don't ask why certain rules are certain ways, they just enforce the ones you ask them to. But they aren't psychic, because who could have guessed that stupid would be a 'bad word' in our house?

> "Nice" is just NICER than saying "no hitting" or "no kicking" but means the same thing.

TRADE/SHARE

Trade and sharing are natural partners, and can be interchangeable. Until they are around four years old, depending on the child, sharing isn't a real possibility for them. It is a nice ideal for parents to aspire to, but too often you see children who probably aren't capable of it yet, being reprimanded for something that they just can't do on their own. But they start slowly, and part of the point of suggesting a Trade or to Share is to get them to follow your directions.

Trade means that they can exchange one toy for another. This usually happens after another child snatches a toy that was being played with by one child and you are coming up with an alternative for the screaming first child. You give the snatch-ER the toy to give back to the snatch-EE and say, "Trade please" and direct the snatch-ER's hands to give the snatch-EE back the first toy. Then pick up an alternate toy[2], give it to the snatch-ER and say, "Trade please" again, and direct the snatch-ER's hands to give the snatch-EE the new, preferably more interesting toy. It doesn't always work and now, at three and five, I can say, "Share please" and let them work it out instead.

[2] At this point it is just as likely that the snatch-EE will be distracted by the new toy and render the entire exercise moot, but sometimes it works out as illustrated.

SAFE PLACE

Both children and animals need a place that they can feel safe. Granted, your entire home is supposed to be this place, but within that home, there should be a safe zone that a child or animal can go to and not be bothered.

For an animal the best place for this, particularly a dog, is a kennel. A dog and a kennel are a perfect match, they are den animals and they want a small and enclosed, warm and dry, quiet place that they can escape to. If you haven't kennel trained your dog, please consider it. From the beginning, when the dog went into his or her kennel, we would intercept the children if they were going to either follow or try to get them out and say, "That's her safe place." Again, there were times when the child crawled into the empty kennel first, and the dog went in and joined him, but I didn't consider that a violation of the animal's safe place.

'Safe Place' can be a kennel or a parent's lap.

Cats are easier but will have to be taught to leave rather than smack a child. To do this, if the child is starting to bother the cat, lift the cat up and place her on the windowsill or on top of the back of a chair. Keep doing this consistently, while saying to the child, "Let's put Kitty in a safe place."

We use the parental lap as a safe place. If a child asks to sit on a lap, not only can the other child not eject them from the lap, but they should leave them alone briefly. Yes, we do group laps, but sometimes it is specifically to avoid being bothered. One child's safe place is naturally their bedroom, particularly if you have made it a relatively toy-free zone. I have looked around for Daughter, and not been able to find her, after some volume-intense-sibling-interactions. When I've found her, she was up in her room with a book and a baby, just getting away from the interactions for a minute. I encourage this actually, considering it a part of learning about Alone Play, and will occasionally suggest, "How about some Alone Time?" and take one child to their room with a special toy[3]. This diffuses tensions, encourages them to learn how to play alone, and gives them a safe place.

The most challenging part of this is discouraging the other child, and sometimes other adults, from intruding. The child should know that this is not a punishment or requirement; they can leave the Alone Time at any time and rejoin the chaos. But sometimes children need a little break, and sometimes

---

[3] Sometimes the computer, now that they are older. Computer games are a great way to encourage some Alone Time, but by necessity in this house, is limited to thirty minutes.

152

they can't articulate that. Watch for the child getting pushing, or their sleepy behavior like twirling their hair or chewing on the ends of their hair or sleeves, and if it isn't nap time, try a little Alone Time to decrease the stimuli for a little while.

WHAT ABOUT WHEN AN ANIMAL DIES?!

Sadly, this is the last thing you want to think about when dealing with furry siblings, but we do tend to outlive them. Son was born and we had two dogs and two cats. The dogs were getting on in age and the male dog passed away when Son was less than a year old. The female dog was with us much longer, and they both learned that "grandma-dog" was kind of cranky and a little hard of hearing, and to move slowly around her. When Son was four and Daughter was three, she passed away while we were on R&R in the U.S. We dealt with it in a fairly straight-forward manner, not glossing over the issue, but not providing too much information, or worse, food for imagination.

> "Why did she die?"
>
> "She was very old and it was her time."
>
> "Will she be back tomorrow?"
>
> "No, death is forever."
>
> "Why?"
>
> "Because her body is gone, so now we have to keep her memories so we can have those with us forever too."

And usually that was the end of the conversation, until it came up again, usually with a different lead-in to the 'why.' It keeps you on your toes, let me tell you.

Every family is going to have a different theological basis for what they want their child to believe and process. Your family or church may help you find your approach. Our choice was to just to keep it simple. Don't belabor it and don't belittle it. For them, this is the first time that they are dealing with a power beyond their parent's control. Keeping answers short and simple means you have less to remember when it comes up again. Hopefully you and Husband are giving the same answers, but you can always explain the differences with a simple statement about how everyone imagines it differently and ask them what they imagine.

Oddly, it comes back in strange moments. A year later, literally on the anniversary of the dog's death, although we hadn't mentioned it or discussed that, Son was found sobbing, in his bed, that he missed her. I was dumbfounded. How come? Why now? The best I could do for him was acknowledging his feeling of sorrow and allowing him to cry. It made me choke up too, but we toughed it out and in the end I had to tell him that he could cry, he could be sad, but he had to stop howling and wailing because it was keeping his sister up too. She tried to comfort him, bringing him tissue and patting his hand and giving him hugs, but in the end, she had to come get me because it had reached a point where she didn't understand anymore and her empathy wasn't working.

It turns out, Son needed reassurance that Young Cat, the adoptee that Son had lobbied for, wasn't going to die soon. He understood on a certain level, and certainly it had come up recently, that the two Elder Cats were getting old, and in the end, he was concerned about one of his best friends. Once he understood that Young Cat wasn't old, he was less worried, but still sad.

Sometimes death questions come up at seemingly disconnected times. A child's processing time can be very long.

Tying this back to humans, because our dog died due to complications from old age, for a while, Son was concerned that his grandparents were old. He defined old as having gray hair. We discussed how they were older than he was, but our family approach to death, our theology, and a little biology helped in this case. We acknowledged that people physically die too, and this is different from "going away"[4] and that we will miss them when that happens, and that is usually enough. Since we choose to use a sort of recycle-renew-reuse approach to what happens to our bodies, we focus more on memories, imagination and dreams for 'seeing' someone who has died or remembering things with them.

WORK IT OUT

"Work it out" is another phrase that we use in the human sibling interaction scheme. I will witness (or hear) a toy-centered conflict and one child will come running to me with a complaint. I will say, "Work it out." Either they go back to the situation and do, or at least, play continues without screeching, or I am asked, "How?!" I suggest, "Trading, sharing, playing with something else. Work it out." And then they go back to the situation and work it out somehow, without my actually needing to intervene. The nice part about this is that both Husband and I say it, so the children don't shop for answers and are motivated

---

[4] Please don't say an animal was "put to sleep." If you're afraid of the word "euthanized" keep it simple: "she died". It is honest, but not brutal, and doesn't mention special medicine, because goodness knows you don't want your child afraid to go to sleep or to take medicine.

to work it out. Besides, they know that my solution is going to be to take the offending toy away entirely.

I am sure that "work it out" surprises people upon hearing it for the first time. When there is some drama or screaming or fuss and bother, I go to the stairs and say, "Work it out." And they usually do. By not interfering, sometimes they come up with wonderful solutions. Now, sometimes the solutions are completely inappropriate and some correction is required. Start this slowly, because they will need your examples to draw upon, so don't suddenly start letting them figure it out entirely, alone, all the time. One day when there is a conflict, and you are in the playroom with them reading, instead of getting up and intervening, tell them to work it out. They will look at you like you've lost your mind, which is toddler-ese for, "How!?" You can offer the appropriate possible solutions, just two or three, after a small pause. But stay put, don't intervene and watch.

JUST HOW DAMAGED ARE THEY?

By first telling them to "work it out" and then giving them the means to do so, children learn tools for future use.

"Is there blood or fire?" is a question that I will ask if I hear screams or shrieks from the playroom. At three and five, I am finally comfortable leaving them to play alone. When Son was three, he was offered Alone Play also, but leaving a one and three year old, or two and four year old, can't be maintained for much longer than ten minutes. We worked up to leaving them alone in gradually increasing increments, beginning with Alone Play for each, and then Alone Play together (meaning kids alone, no adults) first for ten minutes, then fifteen, etc.

It is important to keep a child's trust. I witnessed a mother who would come to play, and when her son was engaged in play, would duck out of the room. This meant that the poor child would look up and his mother had vanished without a trace or any warning. This terrified him and it kept happening to him! In spite of first getting suggestions, and then flat out being told not to do it, she continued to do it. She couldn't get a moment to herself, not even to go to the bathroom. She would come into someone's home and say that she was sorry, but she couldn't close the bathroom door because it scared her son. It was as if she just did not understand that it was her actions that were starting the cycle.

Seeing that, we made a concerted effort to always, from the very beginning when they were very young (like so young that they were in an ExerSaucer during a shower!), to tell our children things like, "Mama is going to go to the bathroom, I will be back in two minutes." Remember, they have no concept of time, so don't worry about if it takes you longer than two minutes. But do come back to the child immediately (no distractions or quick chores en route) and announce, "See, Mama is back!" All that results in me now being able to leave them alone in the playroom, because they know where I am – I've told them. They also know when I will be back and now I can use events instead of time limits, and say "Mama is making dinner. I will come back when I am done."

Son was visiting at Grandmother's and my sister, Aunt, was one of this favorites. He was 18 months old and he was on one side of the kitchen door while she went down to the basement. His heartbroken howls and tears just about broke her heart. She had to be taught to just say it, then just do it, and be sure to come back and announce it so that he would know what those sounds meant. And it took nearly three days of howling and heartbreak, before he was able to understand that Aunt was not abandoning him. The point of that is that there are plenty of people who are going to have to learn how to do this, because Baby doesn't just need to trust you, but all the adults in his world.

Teach yourself to SAY it, then just DO it, then come back to your child and TELL them that you are back.

Of course there is thé occasional screaming. So I ask, "Is there blood or fire?" and they usually say no. I've had yes once or twice, and let me tell you that the turbo speed kicks in quick when someone says yes! It takes a good deal of blood in this house to get a band-aid, so it wasn't truly that big of a deal, but we've had our share of bitten tongues and those bleed a lot! Remember that in this house toys get the time out instead of the child. A child gets a time out when the offense is hurting another living thing (sister or animal). Another family I know uses the Two Minute rule. Instead of insisting on Trade or Sharing, the rule is that the first child is allowed to keep the toys for two minutes, then the second child gets the toy for two minutes.

TIME OUT!

Time outs are a delicate thing, and I am pretty sure that I don't do them correctly. However, the version that we have come up with, works well for our family. You might not even choose to do time outs! So don't worry about if it is being done right or not, take what you need and discard the rest. What I have observed in several families that seems to be the two keys to making a time out effective are the duration and the supervision of the time out.

DURATION AND SUPERVISION OF A TIME OUT

First of all, when a time out is required, we do them for just as long as they are old, because frankly, their attention span is pretty darn short. Secondly, an adult needs to sit with them for as long as the time out is. Two minutes is a long time for me too, so believe me, I am watching the clock. During those minutes (two when they are two, three when they are three, or four minutes when they are four), we state why there is a time out and tell the child in a sound bite. Some families discuss feelings during a time out, explain why the behavior was unacceptable, etc., which works very well. You'll choose the appropriate version for your family, but toss that sound bite, "No hurting" (or whatever is relevant) often because that is mostly what they are going to walk away with. The point is, an adult needs to be there. Once they reach five or so, this changes, but for the under-five crowd, the parent should stay.

Be careful not to require an apology as a condition of ending the time out, or you could be sitting there for a VERY long time.

A two and three year old child, even a young four year old, finds apologizing to be excruciatingly difficult, and it will prolong the drama. For these toddlers, we offer the option of apologizing or giving the other person (or animal) a hug instead. That said, if you hear playing, a screech and a child say, "I'm sorry, Sister!" that is an apology from one kid to another. A required apology should include the person's name that they are apologizing to, and the offense. A required apology sounds like, "Sister, I am sorry for hurting." Walking up and muttering, "I'm sorry" isn't an actual apology in this case. They are pretty much parroting the words that they know the parent insists on and might as well be saying, "I'm blue." Be careful not to require an apology as a condition of ending the time out, or you two could be sitting there for a very long time. Instead, at the end of two minutes, sum up the reason for the time out and let them go. Or you can take the child's hand and walk to the child requiring an apology, say something like, "Sister would like to apologize with a hug." You can both go to the child requiring an apology, whisper the formula words to the offending child, and ask them to please say it. Here's the key, don't hang around too long waiting for them to say it, because they're embarrassed. Chances are, they will say it upon your departure.

BREATHERS

Around four or five years old or so, sometimes younger, depending on the temperament of the child, a Time Out might not be necessary, but a moment to pause and regroup might be required. This is the Chill Out. No one is in trouble, no one has hurt someone (the real Time Out crime in this house), manners are getting a little wiggly and rudeness is coming out or, simply, one of them has just had enough. You can work this a number of ways.

A breather can simply be picking up a favorite book or new item and taking the child to a different location, close or far, and sitting down and reading it with them. Or handing the child a drawing board and letting them know they can "take a breather" for five minutes and suggest that perhaps they could draw that. It can also be a special thing, where a never-before-seen toy comes out and they are taken to a different place for a breather. It can also be a nearly-Time-Out, where they are told, "Please find some way to take a breather and come back when you are feeling less grumpy (or rude)." Generally, I either do the first, or take a breather, (although I do articulate that I am suggesting that they chill out) rather than just distract and divert. Or I do the last one and suggest that they find a book and read in their room for five minutes.

As a parent, I've also told the kids that I need a breather, so they can see me use the same tools to cope.

As a parent, I have also taken a breather. I have actually said, "I think I need to go to my room and have a chill out moment." I've set the timer, told them where I am going (my room, upstairs, outside) and go. Usually, this happens when I am at my wits' end and they're driving me nuts. If I didn't go, I'd probably lose my temper and I really hate doing that. As a result of not only practicing what we preach in this area, we've had Daughter quietly take herself upstairs and read for a little bit. Yes, one parent usually follows in a few minutes, but it is something that she recognizes as a combination of Safe Place and Alone Play.

ODDS AND ENDS

Something that is very hard to do as a parent is not label. Even a positive label can have an unexpected side-effect. Daughter hearing that she is 'the brave one' automatically makes Son 'not brave' in a child's interpretation. Of course that isn't our intention, but we're not living our lives as if the whole world revolves around us. Imagine if you truly believed that the entire world was for and because of you. In that case, hearing that someone else is 'better' at something is devastating. A lot of what I have chosen to try was articulated in *Siblings Without Rivalry*. Children are not equal; they are unique and should be respected as such. One does not have to get something because the other one did. While being exactly equal is useful for momentarily diffusing tensions, do you really want to be stuck buying two of everything forever? Why not start as you mean to go along and simply make the distinction between unique children? *Siblings Without Rivalry* also had a lot of useful hints for speaking respectfully to the children, not making comparisons, and positive speech, all of which take a lot of practice.

Another impossibly difficult thing to do is tempering your reactions. Just because Daughter screams at a pitch designed to break glass, does not mean that she wasn't the instigator. For this reason I put the toys in time out more than the children. The toy is not doing well not being shared, so it gets a time out. If Son suddenly starts whining and whimpering, that doesn't mean that he wasn't the one who snatched and got the toy snatched back. Reacting slowly and fairly is very hard. It is so much easier to just make the situation end and snap, "Son! Don't do that!" instead of "Gentle" to Daughter in conjunction with a relocation and "Manners" to Son with a distraction.

Sometimes you just want things to *stop*. A tried and true help is reacting to the situation rather than the person. For instance, Wife opens the back of the truck and a bottle falls to the ground and breaks, spilling liquid all over. Instead of reacting with, "What did you do that for?" Husband takes a breath and looks at Wife and says, "Are you okay?" Immediately, this is a less tense situation. Yes, the liquid is still spilled, and might need to be replaced, but if anyone else was around, Wife is immediately less embarrassed and Husband looks like a million bucks. When child lifts a tray of beads and they go in a million different directions, your immediate reaction is, "Daughter!? I told you to be careful!" Instead, pause, take a breath and look right at Daughter and say, "Wow. That was startling!" You can even add, "What do we do now?" and she will tell you, "We pick them up!" Empathize rather than blame.

When Daughter screams because their brother is stalking her, make a comment like, "Son, that would make me very nervous. What makes you nervous?" Not only does it teach them to articulate what they are feeling, and provides a distraction, but it also shows Daughter that you understand what she is feeling and she might be able to say it next time.

However, that reaction might have been exactly what the first child was going for.

> "Are you scared?" Son asks Sister.
>
> "Yes!" answers Sister.
>
> "What scares you like that, Son?" I interject before he can do it again, because he **was** trying to scare her. If I have to distract him further, I might provide an example of what makes me feel that way. This is usually enough to derail the original intent.

We encourage a great deal of together play, parallel or cooperative. I read in *Third Culture Kids*[5], that expat siblings tend to bond rather closely with each other, because they are the friends that travel with them, no matter where they go. Expat kids tend to either become wanderers themselves or find the smallest town possible and place deep roots. But they don't lose that bond with their siblings. This tendency to allow them unsupervised play can get out of hand quickly, depending on the temperament of the children. Daughter tends to physically strike out when she is tired or frustrated and Son tends to snatch things and get wound up, which of course exacerbates the situation. But unsupervised play works with the occasional check, peek in and keeping an appropriate number of toys available of differing types, and being sure that I've secured all of the things likely to get them in trouble. Things that I would say that they are well-behaved about, occasionally cause some rather surprising problems. Daughter's hair is shorter in one little spot; markers have decorated desks and walls in rooms that I didn't know they went in; crayons found themselves making lovely Dali-like designs on radiators; and stamp pads, that I didn't know the kids even knew existed, were used like sponges. A little prevention goes a long way, but you can't prevent everything and given that there are two, they're going to dream up situations and incredible solutions that will boggle your mind.

Another defusing tool is for you to take a deep breath and put life on pause for five minutes. For a three to five year old, you can kneel down, say, "Deep breath. Okay now. Try words." This is usually used when one of them can't quite articulate the problem and is just screeching or whining. Sometimes words fail them, there is too much going on and words are just too complicated, particularly if they want to use exactly the right one. With an older child, you can give them paper and crayon, or blocks, and sometimes be brought to the right thing!

[5] *Third Culture Kids* (paperback) by David C. Pollack and Ruth E. Van Reken

I'm not sure if I should have been delighted at their intelligence or appalled at my lack of it, but my children managed to plan, execute and conceal the perfect crime (from the point of view of a three and five year old) for a surprisingly long time.

I was given some Lindt chocolates, wafer thin squares that were wonderful, and I kept them on top of the refrigerator. In hindsight, I guess that the children had seen me get one now and again. At some point I noticed that they were not there, but didn't really process it because frankly, I ate them slow enough that I could have finished them and tossed out the box.

Then came the day when I came downstairs and heard what could only be described as evil chuckling. I peeked and the children were both sitting by the box of stuffed animals. One of them heard me and there was a flurry of furtive activity and then they popped up with very cheerful, "hi Mama!" in chorus! The tell-tale smear of chocolate clued me in. Turns out, they had the whole box! And they'd hidden it inside another box and tucked that underneath all the stuffed animals.

It went so far in explaining at least a week or two of very unusual level of activity!

Much later, Son explained that he'd gotten the step stool and handed the box down to Daughter. Daughter immediately tucked it into a second box and, bold as brass, they walked past the nanny with the box, down to the playroom!

"Planned, Executed & Concealed Crime"

14. Family Matters

Family that isn't present is one of the most incredibly important parts, and most challenging part, of having an expatriated baby. Family that isn't in the house is important for these little global nomads because they are the connection to our homeland and culture and sense of self! This isn't to say that your nuclear family of mother, father and child doesn't contribute to that, but family expands upon your values and choices, and eventually will lend context to your life. To give a small child a sense of family, when they see that extended family once a year if they're lucky, is incredibly challenging.

Thankfully, we live in an age of technology. There are so many options, most of which take some effort, but not too much, to help give the little ones the sense of family and friends in the U.S.

VISUAL AIDS

Send around a request for photos if you don't already have them, and buy a series of small frames, 2 inches or so. I got mine at Pottery Barn, in a box of five I think, and purchased three sets. I have pictures of all those people that I want my children to recognize on sight, in those frames. If you choose to do the same, place them somewhere prominent (which is why I recommend the little plain silver ones because those go pretty much anywhere). We had a small area under the steps going upstairs, which you had to pass to go down the steps to the playroom, and I put the pictures there with some silk plants (no sun whatsoever). I've had them placed on a windowsill in the main room. Now, I have them on the windowsill of a large window that is halfway up the stairs to their bedroom. Move the order around occasionally and say, "Good morning, Grandpa!" as you pass by. Let the kids clean them, or help change the picture to a more recent photo, or rearrange the order. But the bottom line is that they see them every day, and they change occasionally, so that they're not just more stuff on the wall.

When they are very little, give them photos of their own to play with. There are commercially available books to do this, "My Family Photos" and that kind of thing that are soft-books. We went with a slightly less expensive, just as changeable, version and just printed and laminated a set of photographs, slightly larger than playing card size and put them on a ring. One holiday, take a face shot of every person, or ask someone to do it for you if you're not back. Print them on regular 3x5 photo size, or business card size, or playing card size, and laminate. Office Depot, Staples, and OfficeMax all have no-heat laminate available in various sizes. The laminate gives the child a chance to hold them, chew on them, drool, spit or urp on them and not ruin the photo. Babies love faces, and faces of people they love is even better. We wrote the name of the individual, what the child would be expected to call them, on the back in big block letters. Not that they can read, but then anyone can hold up the cards and say, "Tia" and "Grandmother" and, yes, "Daddy" and "Mama". This is great if you have family names for folks that are special, Ama instead of Grandmother, or PawPaw instead of Grandfather. Cousins take on a whole new dimension when they can see who this is. They don't really start comprehending the relationship until they are about four, and it only really sets in when they start meeting regularly.

Keep photos of extended family prominent and visible.

AUDITORY CLUES

Chat or VOIP are helpful. Chat doesn't hold much appeal for the under-six crowd (they don't type and don't read well), unless it is video-chat. But a voice chat can mean the world to a grandparent too many miles away, even if all you can wrangle out of the child is "Hello" and "love you bye bye." Skype and IP phones are real options now, although we tend to live in places where bandwidth can have its challenges. For instance, early on in our tour, I could video chat with my family, but the bandwidth has since shrunk due to increasing number of users and now I cannot maintain a video connection.

Vonage is by far my personal favorite because it provides an actual phone (with its own ring), an actual U.S. phone number (you choose the area code) and at this time, if it is Vonage to Vonage, the calls are free. If not, it is currently unlimited calls for $24.99 a month. We use it more and more. We can call vets, doctors, 800 numbers, and family with no problems other than the occasional bandwidth drop-out. When it digitizes, it is easy to reset the connection and try again, or simply try later (or earlier) in the day. The nicest part about it is that it gives folks in the U.S. a U.S. phone number and area code to call, and doesn't rely on the computer being on. The kids hear the Vonage phone ring and come running.

THE ELECTRONIC ASSIST

E-mail doesn't seem like a very kid-thing, but they love getting their own e-mail. Someone once wrote my Son, who was just learning his alphabet, an e-mail and used clip-art pictures for most of the words, just like some kid books. So he could read his own e-mail and asked me to print it. With enough time and planning, printing a certain number of clip art images and cutting them out, you can have them arrange them into a story and fill in a few words (by themselves or with help) and send the same.

An audio-visual tool that is just lovely is Elmo Mail. These are thirty-second videos that you can take on the digital camera. Your family can do the same; and if they don't have one, consider gifting a Kodak, which makes some of the most user-friendly cameras out there with limited video options. Thirty seconds, at the right camera settings, rarely exceeds anyone's limitation for down-loading or up-loading, about 1MB. As the children get older, they know that they are talking to Grandmother or saying hi to Cousin So-and-so. It will allow you to capture the playing in the sprinkler moments, opening gifts of Christmas Day moments, and even the 'just saying hi' moments.

> Elmo Mail is a thirty-second video sent via e-mail to family and friends.

If you have a technologically savvy family, or a family willing to give it a shot, you can ask them to please read stories to DVD or video. An advantage to this is that you can get certain things from certain relatives. If you have relatives who practice your family's religion, or an alternative one that you want to expose your kids to, ask them to include some traditional stories. If you have a bilingual family, you can get those stories in the other language, read in a voice familiar to the child. It makes the reading of that story in person just magical too. It is pretty easy to record to a video-tape and send the set of book(s) and video (whether it is DVD or VHS), sitting like at story time so they can see the pages turn. Even more wonderful is when Grandfather reads their new favorite book.

Among others, Shutterfly.com[1] and mac.com have the some of the easiest custom calendars that you can put the children's photos on, pictures of where you live, you name it. You can also send direct from the website with no hassle and very quickly. If you send them to yourself and reship, you can clip those address labels and stamps to each month. Both sites will allow you to personalize the calendar, adding birthdays and anniversaries, moves if you know them and other tidbits.

---

[1] I have also used Shutterfly for change-of-address cards and special thank you cards.

Kids also like getting their own snail mail, even if it is just a card from the grocery store. For them it is a fun thing to carry around and tell people, "My Uncle sent me a card!" Give a sheet of address labels and a book of stamps to those who you want your child to hear from – this isn't rude, its just an assist. There is now a fun option of photostamps.com, which allows you to put a picture on a legitimate U.S. postage stamp! A picture of the child being written to, a sheet of address labels and a few envelopes and even the most recalcitrant relative will pick up on that. The trick is remembering to do it. I've done it and given it with a nice stationery box, as a gift. Okay, it is a broadsided hint and as well as a gift.

Subscribe to a 'local' newspaper. We don't read the entire newspaper with the kids, but we look at certain stories, certainly the pictorial pages for the fairs and various other events like parades. They go back, to their Grandmother's home, every summer for a few weeks and they remember things like the County Fair and Fourth of July Parade, so seeing it only reinforces 'what is happening at home.' We used to stutter when people asked us where we are from, and only now finally just answer, "Wisconsin." It used to be a long, drawn out, "I was born in Wisconsin and Husband was born in Northern California and we settled Colorado... Pick one." Now we say Wisconsin, and the kids say Wisconsin, and after a few summers being there for a few weeks, they even know what that means.

FREQUENT FLYING FAMILY

As hard as travel is on you, consider that it might be twice as terrifying for your family. I'm not entirely sure that my mother even had a passport before we moved to First Post, but she has one now and has come to every post that we have been assigned to at least once per year. For not having had a passport for a long time, hers has some very interesting places in it now!

Transferring frequent flyer miles is an exercise in frustration, but worth it if it means that your child gets to spend two or three weeks with a grandparent (or two). If they're worried about imposing on your hospitality, consider transferring some hotel points instead.

Letting your child go, with or without you, to the U.S. for a month is the longest and loneliest month that you can imagine spending.[2] However, in the long run, it is worth it because they will connect with the places as well as the people. I know families who make a point to return to the U.S. with their children every single year, come hell or high water. That willingness to "go to Grandmother's" might not last past the age of ten or twelve, but we will take every opportunity that we can to get them there in the meantime to build those bonds, not just with family, but with the places.

Sometimes you are just too far away to get back every year. In that case, meeting somewhere halfway is a worthwhile way to spend an R&R or visit. If you are meeting in a mid-way point, like Istanbul was for us, it is still a visit, not a vacation. Plan for a comfortable hotel because this is where you will spend most of your time with little ones that need to nap.[3] Boutique hotels, apartment hotels (ones that let apartments or small houses, rather than multi-guest establishments) are a true blessing. Choose a place that is easy walking distance to places of interest and the adult that remains behind with napping children can rotate, allowing the parents and visiting adults to get out and see things without children as well as with them. Remember that your child will be zoo-friendly relatively young, but museum-friendly doesn't start to take until closer to four years old. Get separate rooms or suites so that everyone has a place to retreat to, nap without interruption or go to chat when the other room is quietly napping. Bed and breakfasts are particularly wonderful for these kinds of visits. Consider inviting someone on a visit as an alternative to your R&R in Rome. It's still in Rome, but it is a visit with family.

Be prepared for some incredulity – only 14% of Americans actually have passports, let alone travel outside of the U.S. It isn't much different than traveling from New York to L.A. (okay, a little longer) and you can ease them into the idea of visiting you in the back of beyond by meeting somewhere mid-way. The percentage of passport bearing Americans will change soon, thanks to some new security measures, but you are giving them a chance to use it!

You can advise them to find a good travel agent, one who is practiced at finding less expensive alternatives, like empty group fares and such. You can also find that person for them, and put them in touch with each other. Then do what you can to facilitate their travel. Family is worth it.

---

[2] I'm a big proponent of the WITH me version of going somewhere for a few weeks in the summer. I MISS them.

[3] Maintain routine. If it is normally 12noon lunch and 1300 nap, try do the same while on vacation. You will have much better travelers as a result.

VISITS VERSUS VACATIONS

Oh, remember that visits are entirely and totally different than vacations. There are different stresses, different benefits and very different dynamics. Seeing your family is not a vacation, and tends not to be wholly relaxing sometimes. Set your standards and rules for a visit early, when the child is an infant and the entire dynamic is new; your family is most open to adapting at this time. Blame naps and say that a large picnic or barbecue would be better than trying to visit each and every relative at their home. Check your guilt with your luggage and consider it lost en route! You just traveled a gazillion miles with an infant or child or both; they can try to come across the town or state. It is hard-core, but if you have to, early on set up the two sides of the family for visits every other year. Blame the stress of travel on the little one as just not being able to do four cities and two states in three weeks, and promise that next year you will come there instead. Believe me, it takes only three years to set that pattern and have it be normal. You'll still get, "Oh, I wish you could come" and there will still be times and events where you will actually break that pattern (weddings and baptisms come to mind), but in the meantime, you are looking out for your immediate family's needs during the travel.

Family gives your child a foundation from which to work; roots. These little wanderers grow up so quickly, are so self-sufficient so soon and so self-reliant so suddenly that we forget that they need a *place to be from*. Expand their horizons beyond geography.

My story here is not so easy, and I hope you are not ever in a situation where you have a similar one. There might come a time, either before or after your child is born, where you are going to have to clearly define some parameters ... for adult family members, not for the children.

Husband and I had a falling out with a very important person in our lives soon after Son was born. It broke both of our hearts and left us with a void in not only our life, but in Son's. Not having contact with this VIP was not an option for us, even though sometimes we thought that it might be wisest since there are battles and wars that cannot be won, particularly on emotional issues.

Instead, we tried to find a way to make the contact we had cordial and work towards friendly. This was terribly hard because, being family, of course other people were affected by the falling out. We decided that our children's behavior was the most important issue and for the first few visits, didn't go to their home, or have them come to ours, but met in a third location. Part of this was so we were all on neutral ground, but also because we recognized that our family needed a place to maintain our routine, retreat to at the end of the day, and the city would offer opportunities to go do things together without the pressures of having a guest in our home. It worked out well and frankly, was an important step in maintaining the relationship.

It has taken a while, but now we are at the point where we've been visited at our assigned post. We asked, as gently and kindly as we could, if VIP would be offended by not staying in our home, but in a hotel instead. We did this for the same reasons, and explained that we felt we would all need our space, and a place to decompress at the end of the day, as well as making it easier to put the children down for the night and maintaining their routines.

It is a slow road towards healing the relationship, and we're five years down that path and have no intention of stepping off it – VIP is too important to us, too important not to have in our children's lives and selfishly, we don't want to give up. If you find yourself in a similar situation, put your nuclear family first. Make kind but firm decisions on just a few points and be ruthless in their enforcement. You're planning for a long-term relationship, not visit by visit. By placing your family first, you cannot be faulted (as if there were a record-keeper) and you will also demonstrate to your children that they also can handle challenging relationships with grace and patience.

"Handle With Care"

15. Animal Behavior

This is the part where I don't even attempt to sum up the parts of parenting books that worked for us – there are just too many books and too many parts! Seriously, at least one thing from every book I have read has helped us. We are all winging it! I have had the incredibly great fortune to have a great role model – if I have been half the mother that mine was, I will be content and it is a beautiful thing to aspire towards for me. But that didn't stop me from reading about a dozen different parenting books. Now, they're few and further between and have to come really highly recommended for me to pick it up. I tried to keep this one short, because you will find your own way, but I am verbose if nothing else, and there is just so much to share. So this is my odds and ends chapter.

> Let the Daddies do their thing, even if it is different than how you do it. If you agree on the overall goals, it will work our.

Mamas, here's food for thought, "Let go." Let the Daddies do their thing, make their mistakes, do it different from you ... if you agree on the overall goals, it will work out. Daddies that I have run into have this line, the "I'm sure you know what you are doing" or "I think you can handle this better than I can" theme. WHY?! No, I don't know better or have a better handle on it! I'm just as new at this as HE is! Being in the house with an elephant doesn't make me an elephant expert. But Mama spends so much more time with Baby than Daddy does that it seems like a logical conclusion. If you don't know, please tell him.

On the flip side of the coin, if you catch yourself correcting your spouse or partner more than you correct your child, get a babysitter, go out in public and have a serious discussion about how to find a middle ground. So, when I blithely say, "let go" that doesn't begin to touch on how impossibly hard that is ....

Of course, there are a few things that have been particularly helpful, and being me, I can't help but talk about them....

CONSISTENCY IS THE KEY TO EVERYTHING

Children watch and listen to everything. Consistency is the key to everything (just like puppies). Scary but true: a toddler does not see a deviation from a rule as "special" or cool, they see the rule going out the window and starting over from the new rule. It will take at least three reinforcements of that original rule or limit to make it stick again.

Consistency does not mean rigid adhesion to a party line. For instance, Husband and I had a major disagreement because he interpreted a rule without flexibility, while I interpreted it with flexibility and we were enforcing it differently. The children, knowing that every law has a loophole, were not slow in figuring it out. The parents, being slower on the up-take, finally figured out that there was variation in the interpretation when we realized that the kids always asked me to do one particular thing. So, we talked and came back with a middle ground that both of us were comfortable with, and could consistently uphold. We had this discussion in front of the children, much to their chagrin. The result was neither as rigid as the one interpretation, nor as flexible as the other. Oddly, when we were done discussing, we told them what the 'new' interpretation was, summing it up for ourselves as well, and that both of us would respond the same way and they never pushed it.[1]

> A game plan is a quick outline of the events to come, and no more than three expectations for the child.

GAME PLANNIT

I love this trick! For my cautious little son, he can handle most situations, as long as he is warned ahead of time. The Game Plan or Pre-Game Briefing works for big things like moving or airline travel, but it also works for the little things in life, like grocery stores and play dates! To Game Plannit, you simply outline, very briefly and with short and sweet comments, what is going to happen with no more than three expectations. I tend to go with two expectations and a result, but the result does not always have to be a reward.

For instance, before going into a grocery store in the U.S., which is overwhelming for me, I will say that we are going to go in the store and shop for food on this list (showing them the list). If Daughter sits in the cart and Son walks and holds the list, and we get right through the list, we can each buy one thing not on the list. I will offer those things at the end (gathering them as we go), to avoid them pointing things out left and right as things that they 'want.' So, one point is going in and getting things on the list, the second point is their responsibilities and the third point is my offering a choice of item as reward.

This also works by including a reward for successfully meeting all the

172

[1] Granted, they could be holding a trump card of some sort for a later date, when we're least expecting it.

expectations. Once we went to Toys R Us[2] and I told them that they could get one thing each in addition to the few things that we were there for, which were gifts for other children. I took a page from my great-aunt's book and if they said they wanted something, I just put it in the cart (within reason; the electric powered car did not go in the cart). We ended up with three different things apiece at the end, in addition to the things on our list. At the check-out counter I had them pick one out of those three items and asked the checker to put away the other two. This worked really well because there wasn't a bunch of discussion, drama or anything except a choice!

It also works for non-shopping things. I give them one goal (mine is always that they have manners) per trip, or playgroup or representational affair. If they are pre-warned, and told respectfully about the situation, they might surprise you at how well they assimilate the information and adapt. That said, by speaking respectfully, I do not mean as an equal, because they're not. They're little and you are the parent. I mean speaking to them kindly and patiently and not dictating or ordering them about. I might speak 'hard' as Son says, when they are not listening in particular. This is when I say, "Son, cars, away." But when Game Planning, I go down to their altitude, speak quietly and tell them what we are doing, what we expect and if appropriate, what the result will be. Sometimes, the third point is, "and if you are able to be good through dinner, we will only stay for conversation for thirty minutes and then we can go home." And that is reward enough.

Finally, since moving is such a large part of our lives, a pre-game briefing needs to begin before the move. *Third Culture Kids* addresses this somewhat, but the basics are that you give them two or three chances to process the information. For a two year old, two months before the move, you mention it. Then you drop it, unless specifically asked, something that is very difficult for adults to do. Then two weeks before the move, you mention it again and ask if they have any questions. Then two days before the move, you mention it twice a day until the actual move, in the form of the Game Plan. For a three year old, better able to process the information, you do the same: mention it and drop it three months before the move, mention and ask for questions three weeks before the move, and mention it three times a day for three days before the move in the form of a Game Plan. Under two years old, they're not processing that kind of larger picture. Over five years old and the level of interaction is quite a bit different and mentioning it more than six months out can actually be confusing. Unfortunately, a younger sibling will be grandfathered into the older siblings

[2] I must have been drinking.

time frame. Three year old Daughter hears about it at five months and five weeks, rather than three months and three weeks, because Son is older.

THREE DAY RULE

It seems like no matter what the situation is, this rule applies. If you have a new behavior, it usually takes three days for the baby to adapt to it. If you want to instill a new habit, like sleep, it is going to take three days for it to take. This 'rule' is something that you will find yourself repeating like a mantra to help you survive those three days.

On the plus side, you only have to be very careful to not deviate for three days.

If there is a new behavior, it usually takes three days for little people to adapt.
After that, the flex factor kicks in and you can remain consistent, but if it is bedtime, you have a little bit of wiggle room on either side. If it is picking up toys, you can put away more or less. If it is feeding however, don't flex too much. Three days of flexing means a new rule, and you've got three days of the adapting to go through again.

SOUND BITES

Repeat the order back to them. Or, have them repeat it back to you. He says, "I want to ride my bike." You clarify, knowing full well that there are two different bikes. "You want to ride your tricycle or your bike?"

These are one word sound-bites, "Son. Shoes." is much more effective than, "Son, love, we have to go or we will be late, honey, and we can't go until you put your shoes on, so please put them on for us." Unfortunately, he wasn't listening at all after the words 'have to'.

RINSE AND REPEAT

Repeat, reiterate and repeat again. Should I say that again? This is just a different way of reminding you that consistency is the key. Pow-wow with your spouse and come up with catch-phrases that you can use to remind each other (like the three below) and stay consistent to them with each other. So this is more about being consistent with the other parent than with the child. Don't have too many catch-phrases or you will confuse yourself (that's pretty easy for me) and a parenting pow-wow doesn't have to be a major event. It can be a nightly thing, a weekly date or only as needed.

In our house it tends to go something like this. Someone recommends a book. I read the book. I tell Husband to read the book too. Husband doesn't read the book. A month later, I sum up in one line sentences the things from the book that I liked. We agree to try it for a month.

From the *Baby Whisperer*, Tracey Hogg, come these three sound bites:

> SLOW: Stop, Listen, Observe, Wonder (infants)
>
> HELP: Hold back, Encourage, Limit, Praise (toddlers)
>
> TLC: Talk, Listen, Clarify (everyone, including adults)

Notice the emphasis on not immediately reacting? Study this little wonder, and learn from what you observe. They are talking to you long before they are talking.

Sometimes one word sound bites like, "Son. Shoes." works better than a long explanation about why he should put them on.

Sometimes, it is an odd thing that turns out to be helpful. Sometimes it is seeing something on a show somewhere that triggers your interest. Believe it or not, it is almost always worth following up on something that catches your interest when it comes to parenting books. Trust your instinct, something in your mind is telling you that this is worth a second look. If you can afford it, go ahead and order the book. I can almost guarantee that there are other parents that will be interested in reading it or a CLO bookshelf that it can be donated to, if it doesn't work out for you.

I was given the *How to Talk So Kids Will Listen* book on the recommendation of a work colleague in reference to communicating with your manager and/or supervisor. In these two republished books, I found some very helpful things for my children and for our nanny as well. The books have not been updated very much, some of their examples are out of date, and some are just plain strange! But remember, take what you need and discard the rest. Remember how our parents safely and legally left us alone in the car, drove without us in seatbelts, let alone child seats or boosters? Those kinds of things are in there and a little odd to read. So read them for content and see if you can also take one or two useful bits out of these books. These books have helpful summary pages for each chapter and that is a good thing. These are two books that I copied pages from for the nanny's binder, to give her tools to deal with the kids' interactions as siblings.

ANIMAL BEHAVIOR

Okay, I admit it. This is a bonus chapter where I can wax poetic about animal behavior. My attitude towards infants and toddlers is that they are small mammals. For me, school, socialization, and all of that is whittling away at the wondrous little animal that they are, "civilizing" them. It is a fascinating process, enculturation, and the anthropologist in me is amazed at how well it works. But the zoologist in me wants to see more of the primitive little beasts that they are, *au natural*.

Your choices are based on so many pieces of information, you CAN trust your instincts.

An animal behaviorist has to spend most of their time watching. I admit, there were times when I would watch rather than interact, much to my spouse's impatience and frustration. But honestly, I want to see how they work things out, and how that working out changes over time with their ages and experiences. I am not a proponent of letting them go wild (I guess you probably figured that out by now), but I will wait a little while before I step in, and see how things are progressing. Of course there are times and situations when immediate intervention is necessary. If someone or something is being injured, I'm not going to sit on the stairs and watch it happen.

That said humans are incredibly social creatures. There is both competition and cooperation at work on a vast scale – from the cells in the brain competing to be neurons, and then working together to cause action and reaction, right up to the siblings planning, executing and concealing their first major crime of stealing, hiding and eating Mama's expensive Swiss chocolates. If they can do that, they do not need me to be micromanaging who has the red crayon for how long.

I think part of our challenge as parents in this day and age is that we are not taught to trust our instincts. Everyone has intuitions, thoughts and ideas that are not in the mainstream. Why is it that only women are allowed to have intuition, but it is commonly laughed at? Why not take a moment and listen to that thought? We had a foster dog for a while and Son told us that she couldn't live with us. I asked him why, and he said he didn't know. Not too long after that he came up to me and said, "She doesn't smell like us." Okay ... well, after deciding to ignore the small concern that we might have an odor, I decided that if he could articulate such a subtle cue that she didn't fit in, I could respect that thought, and there was no more talk about adopting the foster-dog. Intuition is probably a combination of subtle cues, barely remembered experiences and subconscious processing; go ahead and listen. You don't have to do what you intuit, but you certainly can process the information with the same value as a doctor's advice.

Your child is going to tell you, long before they are talking, if they are sensitive to stimuli, but it is up to you to limit the stimuli and simultaneously give your child the tools to be able to process them. My son was barely two and we returned to the U.S. for the first time. Much to my concern, whenever we went outside, he wouldn't play. He would stand with his hands on his ears and just sort of fail to interact. He was pretty little, so I of course wondered about earaches and things like that. It turned out that he thought that the U.S. was loud. Close your eyes and listen – cars, horns, trains, planes, ambulances, fire engines, radios, televisions .... We had been living in a place that was so dark and so quiet that you could read by starlight. Our means of helping him deal with this was something that the rest of us learn unconsciously: identify the sound and ignore. You'd be surprised at how hard it is for you to sort through those sounds.

Your child is going to tell you long before they are talking whether or not they need to feed their brain before they can be dealt with. My daughter, like my sister, needs to have food immediately after waking. Daughter can be downright mean when she wakes up, but two sips of apple juice later, her brain starts to kick in and she's the normal toddler we know and love. However, it took a good few years of watching her to figure this out. We had a "don't talk to Daughter" policy at the breakfast table, until we could figure it out.

When my son was born, I was very curious about this new little creature that had come into my life. I did all the usual new Mom things, keeping a first year calendar with his milestones and a baby book for memories and keepsakes.

And every month on the 23rd, I would sit him in front of a mirror and place a sticker on his forehead and watch his reactions. He was fascinated with the baby in the mirror and would usually eventually reach for the sticker on the baby in the mirror.

This went on, until the seventh time that I sat him in front of the mirror. He watched the baby in the mirror and played. I'd gotten pretty good at getting the sticker on there without him seeing me do it. The next time he looked up, he frowned at the baby in the mirror and then, oh so deliberately, reached up to his own forehead and took the sticker off.

"He's sentient! He has self-awareness!" I exclaimed, in that VICTORY sort of voice, to my husband.

"NO more anthropological experiments on your own offspring," he answered from the other room.

"Sentience!"

16. Two-dimensional Media

I count two things (so far) as two-dimensional media; television and computers. Both can be useful tools, but we have chosen to use both with a lot of interaction. Parking a child in front of a television, whether it is Baby Einstein or SpongeBob, is not the best use of these tools. Sitting with the child, watching and talking about it (whatever it is) is the only way for our children to watch television. And if you can't stand to sit there and watch it through, well then, why are you programming your child to? Keep in mind, I love my computer and use it incessantly, but I'm not comfortable enough with that piece of technology interacting with my child to walk away from the child on the computer.

TELEVISIONS & MOVIES

Kids are pretty oblivious to television content through age one but *they are hypnotized by the TV from the very beginning.* Don't imagine that they are getting anything out of it besides two-dimensional stimulation; and that is not what a developing brain (which lives in a three (or more)-dimensional world) needs. Studies have stated that two-dimensional stimulation actually impedes neuron development, and that whole 'zoned' thing is not what a healthy, active, thriving child needs.[1] BIG muscle movement cannot be accomplished in front of a television.[2] Again, moderation is the key. I'm not a proponent of getting rid of it entirely, because goodness knows I enjoy it too. We have personally chosen not to leave the children unsupervised for more than fifteen minutes, unless we know the program well, like Sesame Street. However, even Sesame Street can cause some interesting conversations and discussions that are answered easier if I've seen the program also.

> Kids are hypnotized by the TV — regardless of content. Don't mistake the TV Zone as interest.

The BBC did a study that said that *if* you let your children watch television, up to age 8 to 10, the one thing that you should not let them see is the news.[3] They are okay with things that they can say are pretend, but news is real, and they get that. Unfortunately, they cannot conceptualize that it isn't happening to them or where they live. Remember their entire world started with Mama and Baby, and the small circle of stimulation that revolved around that, family and home.

---

[1] http://www.jneurosci.org
[2] Okay, unless they are 'doing' Tae-Bo with you, in which case both you and they are spending more time laughing than actually watching the television.
[3] http://news.bbc.co.uk/2/hi/entertainment/3128990.stm

Slowly it expanded to include friends and neighbors, so of course they are going to think that the news about the real world is about them. They don't learn about Other for quite some time. The television shows them a wider world, but they don't know that the hurricane isn't coming here, or that the buildings that are rubble aren't the ones that are rather shabby and run down in this town that they see from the car. And no amount of reassurance or explanation can make them think otherwise.

For the most part, our television remains off about 75% of the time. Yes, sometimes we watch the news after they go to bed, but frankly with access to the Internet and the pre-packaged programming options on AFN,[4] we are not really missing it. The second child got 'grandfathered' into the first child's rules about television, so she was younger for the following guidelines.

Movie ratings have their place and can be useful to control exposure to things.

Remember, the guidelines are what our choices were, and are illustrated to give you one spot on a wide and varied spectrum of choices. You will take this information, and a lot of information from a lot of other places, and make choices for your own family.

Through age two, we only allowed two benign children's programming shows. Our choices were Sesame Street and Fisher Price Little People. Then, between age two and three we added Disney (and Pixar and DreamWorks) animated movies. As they got older, one of the Nick Junior (Nickelodian) programs that we liked a lot was *Backyardigans*, because the kids in the show are polite and have manners, they're clever and they use music and dance very creatively. The kids love them. Except for some special occasions, they are limited to one DVD per day, from beginning to end, which means that they have to pick it up where they paused if they don't watch it entirely. This is good because it isn't so much an hour limit, as much as it is a stimuli limit. This worked out well for us because the television is on from 8am to 9am for Sesame Street on AFN, which gives us the number and letter of the day. Finding the letter of the day in real life is fun. Just go ahead and try to hide a giant cardboard W somewhere and have them come across it in the yard, and see how much fun it is when they discover that WATER is a W word! Then the television doesn't come back on again until a DVD after dinner, from 7pm to 830pm, usually the whole DVD. Initially Daughter missed the ends of movies because she went upstairs at 8pm. One day, Son was having a hard day and he went up early and Daughter was thrilled to be the bigger kid that night.

Movie ratings have their place, and they can be useful, but you have to choose

[4] AFN programming is admittedly getting more varied and expansive. I remember when it was ONE channel!

to use the rating system. You can leave a room during a G movie and not come back to some major misinterpretations. PG means Parental Guidance; be there, guide their perceptions and interpretations. We went one further, and it may have caused us more challenges in the end. We only allowed animated movies. We did this because we were able to then say, "Nope, that's for big people," when something non-animated came on. Unfortunately, that meant that the first time we watched a "live action" movie, *101 Dalmatians* to be exact, they were very concerned that this was real. Glenn Close plays Cruella DeVille really well.

Movies will still require interpretations. The rating system might give you a guideline about whether or not they're going to see something inappropriate, but it doesn't necessarily mean that *The Fox and The Hound* isn't going to cause questions about hunting and trapping. You will be in a better position for interpreting the child's associations if you are there to give them the party line.

Remember the Disney movie Bambi? How many of you are weeping already? I remember Bambi as being very sad.

However, Son and Daughter watched it with Husband for the first time. The scene comes where Bambi's mother is urgently telling him to run, and for a kid this is scary. Both kids are glued to Husband's side. They hear a gunshot and she's just gone, he's alone and can you imagine anything scarier to a little kid? Then Bambi's father comes. Son looks up at Husband, "Is that Bambi's daddy?"

"Yes"

"What happened to his mama?"

Husband, who comes from a hunting family, receives "Field and Stream" magazine, and for whom hunting and guns have been part of his make up since he was about six, said, "A very irresponsible hunter shot her, which is against the law."

Son said, "Oh. But he has his daddy too, so he'll be okay."

I was floored. Here I am anticipating tears and nightmares and goodness knows what else and with one participatory interpretation, my son doesn't have the same weepy sad connections to Bambi that I do.

The power of words — not just words, a parent's words.

"Parental Guidance"

Another of our silly parameters is that they get as many choices as they are years old. This means I offer them a choice of two movies, not the whole rack, when they are two years old, and of four movies when they are four years old. As they got to be school-age, five or so, it wasn't so difficult to discuss the choices and moderate their choice. One way of doing this was saying, "Pick something you both agree on." They look at me with annoyance, "Both of us?!" But when they are younger, this allows us to keep the choices varied and prevents us from sitting through *The Incredibles* for the 700th time.[5]

COMPUTERS & VIDEO GAMES

Another insidious fact of life, slowing moving in on the television territory, is the computer. And somewhere between the two are video games! I love my computer. Son is not fooled at all that a LeapPad is a computer. To him it is a toy, not a computer. When he was young, a two-ish small toddler, he was given a JumpStart program for the computer. He loved it. But it was addictive – he'd give up anything to get to play on his JumpStart program. Anything that seems to compel that much attention has got to be suspicious in my eyes – color me cynical. So, we kept it to fifteen minute intervals, and unlike the television, we used it as a reward for good behavior. Then, during the next move, the JumpStart programs (several of them now, all gifts) never really got unpacked and weren't ever really missed. Beginning with late-pre-school and early kindergarten, we found a rebuilt, inexpensive computer with an operating system that JumpStart and Reader Rabbit can handle and it is the kids' computer. This is partially in self-defense because kids are smart and I don't want them on my computer at all. Again, we use it as a reward tool. Another family I know used the computer on a daily basis as a teaching tool. Their child loved this time, but his mother devoted an uninterrupted thirty minutes to monitoring and interacting with it, she didn't just "park" him. Later, she was confident that he could do some of the things without her direct supervision and commented that this freed her up quite a bit. Since her son liked it so much, as a penalty for infraction of a rule (such as receiving a time-out in pre-school) he would lose that day's computer privileges.

Son figured out pointing and clicking faster than some adults I know. One of the JumpStart CDs has a commercial on it, a QuickTime movie for a video set. Son said, "Look Mama, I found dinosaurs!" and click, open folder, drag the icon, drop, double-click and go, and he's showing me the video! I was floored. He also likes to send 'e-mail' and Elmo Mail, which is a thirty second video taken on the camera and e-mailed as an attachment. He knows that the names go in the first line and the subject is the one before you write your letter. It is pretty

[5] By the way, DVDs wear out. We went through THREE DVDs of *The Incredibles*!

astonishing how fast they pick it up. To my three year old and five year old video chat is as casual as picking up the telephone is to my spouse and me. Talk about changing times! I'm fairly computer literate and they made me feel behind the power curve! Like television, until they're using the computer as a tool, I'm choosing to practice participatory supervision.

There is a difference between video games and children's computer programs, although there are educational programs for both. Some provide necessary skills for today's world, like problem solving and risk assessment, or simple mouse and keyboard skills, which they will encounter in the educational world. Violence is beginning to be described as a viral process. Unfortunately, exposure won't provide immunity. It just seems to make the escalation to violence less difficult. This is why fist-fights have turned into knife fights, or why instead of a knife, a child brings a gun to school. I am not suggesting that video games cause violence; but the exposure to the pretend violence may make true violence less difficult. Both video games and computer programs are practice for actual physical activities, so keep that in mind when you decide between golf and a first-person-shooter game. And none of that takes into consideration the effect of a parent moderating the exposure, providing context, or limiting the access.

Because you are going to encounter both video games and computer programs, either in schools or other homes, consider what your choices will be. Will you limit it? Why will you limit it? Will you allow certain types, character games only, educational games only, or all games? These questions will guide you to your "answer" when someone asks, "Why not?" In writing this I was forced to not only articulate what it was we didn't like, but why, and my opinions were altered as a result of those discussions. Your choice doesn't have to be set in stone, and goodness knows technology is changing, so why can't your opinion?

When we finally decided to incorporate the video games into our family, we decided to get Nintendo Gameboys and rated E for Everyone games. Since our primary reason for purchasing was to provide some controllable (of course) entertainment on airplanes, the lack of headphone jack was an issue. In hindsight, I would have rather that we'd gotten the Leapster L-Max, for pre-school aged children. The Leapster L-Max has a headphone jack, which the Nintendo doesn't. We didn't get any video games until Son was five, and then only after we'd seen another family's use of them. And we chose to remain with the specifically educational, school skill type, games, both on the hand-held video games and on the actual computer.

TRICKS TO MAINTAIN CONTROL

Seriously consider removing the television from the centerpiece of the house. Tuck it in a room that is just for watching television; you will be surprised at how much less it is on. As the children get older, we intend to keep the computer (when it is a desktop versus a laptop) in the same room as the television simply to be able to be there while they use the computer and I watch television or video, or visa versa, while they watch television or a DVD, I can computer. This is a way of at least being in the same room. Although you're not actually doing something together, it maintains all the right illusions: they feel like they're getting to do their thing on the computer, but you're right there so it is unlikely that they will go into unapproved Internet areas. And if you're on the computer and they're watching the television, it is unlikely they will watch something that they are not allowed, if you're in the room. Since I am not a cheerleader for televisions, I wouldn't ever recommend a television in a child's room or a computer for that matter. I think that there is too much there that is just too accessible and while I know that it is going to happen eventually, I would rather not be the one who facilitates that access.

Remember, one of the easiest means of maintaining control is keeping the bedrooms for sleep. By not having a television or computer in the bedroom, you don't have a place where they can watch unsupervised. Not only that, as they get older, the computer won't be turned on at intervals that you have not chosen to be present to supervise. So, that one mechanism, a room for sleeping, provides a safe and quiet sleep environment, keeps toys from taking over, and keeps the two-dimensional stimulation under control.

17. Controlling the Chaos

Children are chaos; glorious, wondrous, essence of the universe in its most primordial form of chaos![1] If you had a nice, orderly, quiet existence before you discovered that there was an impending stranger coming into your life, you're in for a major change. It's not a bad thing. Change happens and we adapt. But there is just so much *stuff* to deal with that we weren't dealing with before. There are new things we have to do and new routines to make up and then learn. Then we unmake up, change and relearn! This chapter is about how to maintain a little bit of control in the center of pure energy. And we start with *stuff*.

Changing tables are not necessary. They're nice, but a Changing Basket makes the changing table a flexible thing. A Changing Basket has about a dozen diapers, a box of wipes, a rolled up changing pad (thin), and what we call Baby Butt (Aveeno diaper cream, A&D ointment or other diaper rash cream). This gets restocked regularly and we had one in each bathroom and in the baby's room, a restocking area where the extra diapers were and any other supplies, like burp clothes and an actual changing cushion. If we weren't in the baby's room, I simply plunked the baby down on the floor of the nearest bathroom, or on the top of the washer and dryer, or on a bed and changed the baby. I recommend that you do this in the bathroom; the bathmat adds cushioning. And as they get closer to 2 years old or so, this helps ingrain the idea of where elimination should take place, if only by inference.

Another convenient chaos-control mechanism was already mentioned in the Medical chapter. Kid Kits are great things. I originally had one per child, but it worked better to have one per floor. They are a briefcase size carrier with things like Motrin, Tylenol, Band-aids, etc. in it. Some of the stuff is kind of useless, or in some cases, redundant. But there are always folks looking for something, and it isn't always easy to find, let alone describe where to find it. Mine came into existence when a mother at playgroup at my house was in a panic because I did not have antiseptic rinse. I've added Neosporin Plus with the topical pain numbing factor to it, Band-aids (fun, waterproof and flexible), antifungal cream, hydrocortisone cream, First Aid foam, and various other things, including Children's Benadryl in case someone's child is stung by a bee and is allergic. Hardly any of it gets used, but it is all in once place and believe it or not, this is where the adults go too now if we need something.

---

[1] In Greek mythology one of the Fates, Clotho, would travel through the Void to the center to gather pure chaos to spin into the threads of Life. Don't you feel lucky, handling chaos daily!

Believe it or not, you can help control the chaos by keeping bedrooms for sleeping. Other than some stuffed animals, there are no toys in my children's bedrooms. Because our family has chosen to keep bedrooms for sleeping, Quiet Play (which resembles napping) happens here, and maybe the occasional time out now. But bedrooms are not for playing; the bedroom is a quiet place. I had the luxury of a playroom in Second Post, but in First Post, we didn't and the guest room did double-duty as playroom and guest room. At Third Post we had both a playroom and a yard (heaven!). All of our toys are in the playroom. When they were toddlers, we also had three toy baskets; one in the library/office (where we spend a good deal of time), one in the living/dining room and one upstairs in the hall by the bedrooms. The guest rooms make a reasonable playroom, you simply let the little person know where the playroom is moving too, or when access isn't allowed, when you have a guest because chances are it is a grandparent or other individual with whom most rules are generally flexed anyway.

TOY BASKETS

There are many advantages to a small, easily portable toy basket. If it is very small, the child can move it, which is nice. But first and foremost, it controls the chaos. If you make it a habit from the beginning to "put the toys away" before you 1) leave the room, or 2) go to bed, or 3) leave the house (or any or all of the above), you teach the child to be neat, as well as prevent the safety hazard of walking into a room and not knowing whether toys are up or down. Believe me, you can break a foot by stepping on a toy wrong, and that is no fun. I know from experience.

Second of all, your house doesn't look like it was taken over by Lilliputians. They (and sometimes you) play with the toys, or they play with them while you cook, or work on the computer, or whatever, and then they get tossed in the basket and put it in a corner. You will do 99% of the tossing, but if they toss 1%, they're helping. When someone shows up, the house looks real, lived in and everything, but not like it has been hit by a tornado.

Finally, there is a sense of newness. If you have several toys in a basket and rotate them in and out of the playroom once a month or so, toys don't get so boring quite so fast. We usually have one toy that always stays in the basket (in each room, one permanent resident, so to speak), but the rest rotate. It takes a little effort, but if you have animals, the likelihood of pieces being lost or eaten by resident animals is minimized.

Toy baskets do die a natural death. As the children get older, the living room has become more of a place that we go to watch Sesame Street in the morning, or a DVD before bed, and less a playing place. Upstairs, bookshelves and one large MagnaDoodle each replaced the toy baskets, for Quiet Play. The upstairs toy baskets sort of migrated into the bedroom and became an Eeyore/Piglet repository, because on the weekends they were allowed to take more than one 'baby' to bed and wanted them close. So, only five years from their inception, toy baskets have turned back into kitty baskets.

If a toy has crossed over to being a 'very boring' toy, it can go in the donate pile during regular rotation. When you sort out for donating, keep one bin of infant/toddler toys for visiting babies and sponsorees who don't have their UAB yet.

Keeping several toys in a basket and rotating baskets or toys once a month creates a sense of newness.

I have recently seen another wonderful adaptation of the Toy Basket. The Book Basket is a lovely thing because children must see you read, and know that they are allowed to read also, and a basket of books is conveniently at their level. You can change what is available, as well as upgrade as needed or rotate.

ANIMAL TOYS

Regarding furry siblings, believe it or not, you can train a dog to take his toys to his basket too, and teach the children to respect that difference. An animal can be told, "Not for Puppy" and taught eventually not to bother things, no matter how tempting, if the item is in or from the child's basket. And a child can be taught, "Not for Baby" regarding Puppy's basket of toys just as easily. They can also be told, "No touching, this is Puppy's safe place" as you gently move them away from the kennel (kennels are safe places). But then, you also might be looking high and low for your child only to find child and dog curled up in Puppy's safe place.

You can take time during pregnancy to train or re-train animals to expect their toys to be in one place. Oddly, it makes for very good (and relevant) practice because dogs require the consistency in a manner we humans understand. We have a hard time extrapolating that same consistency to our little humans, but a habit is a habit. A little time each day (fifteen minute intervals) of play followed by 'putting away' in the basket will show how quickly this can be accomplished — with consistency.

RUBBERMAID TO THE RESCUE

Another means of keeping some semblance of control, especially when you move as often as we all do, is the twenty-gallon Rubbermaid bin. Don't get a knock-off, they crack or warp with weight or temperature changes. But the Rubbermaid Roughneck can take what we dish out. I have three bins per family member. These bins are currently sorted about once a season as I rotate out clothes that are too small or wrong season and rotate in the new size. We don't have much shelf space, so this is a necessity for us. It also happens before each move, because I have a very systematic thinning routine.

Some toys are out all the time: a bin of Matchbox cars or ponies; things that are too large. But mostly it is containment we go for.

More big bins are found in the playroom and almost all our toys fit in bins of various sizes. If I keep the quantity of toys to these bins, it isn't ever unmanageable or grossly conspicuously consumptive.

The kitchen has its share of big bins for things that don't come out often like blenders or the picnic plates. I don't have to find shelf space, which is usually quite limited, and I know where to look for something. I have a whole bin of kitchen linens, napkins, placemats, tablecloths and such, that I literally forgot to open one tour entirely!

Even more bins are found acting as our medicine cabinet. Four shoebox size bins are labeled for colds, bandages, kids and guts. And shoebox size bins are in each closet for belts, ties (kid ties, not man ties) and miscellaneous.

There's a bin for swim and summer stuff, and another bin for bathroom things like extra shower curtains and rings and the extra washcloths and linens.

I even have trunks. The trunks are packed with my own personal welcome kit – coffee pot, spices, pots and pans, the whole nine yards. Just two trunks save my sanity until arrival of my UAB. It is admittedly overboard but worth it to me.

THE TOWER OF TOYS

We had a steel restaurant shelving rack (from Sam's Club) shipped last time around. The playroom bins all fit on the rack and this is the Tower of Toys. As a result of the limited space, we had to go through occasionally and set aside some toys. Son didn't realize that this was to make room for new toys, he thought that it was just because we were helping Santa and picking toys for the orphans. Not surprisingly, we rotate these toys too. When they were toddlers, the kids did not take things off the rack, the adults did. I would have the Legos out for a while, but not the MegaBlocks, and then would switch them occasionally. There are toys, like the children's sized kitchen, like his Matchbox cars and the multitude of stuffed animals that are out all the time. As an added bonus, the top of the toy tower was high enough for toys to go into time out. In our house, if a toy is causing a problem, the toy goes in time out, and is visible up there, out of reach, in its time-out-ed-ness.

ELECTRONICS

Now, this doesn't sound like me at all, since I believe in teaching the child what is appropriate and what is not. But my one major exception is electronics. Put them up high, on top of the entertainment cabinet instead of in it. We did teach our children, "Not for Son" and "Not for Daughter" but electronics have a hypnotic hum and you still say it about a million times a day anyway. By being up, they just never touch them, and won't and don't. These are things that are just too expensive for me to shrug off – mostly everything else is just stuff, so I can be patient about the teaching and touching. But electronics aren't so easy to replace. By the way, the remote controls are electronics too, and part of the entire entertainment systems package, so put them up too. I cannot tell you how bad baby drool is for remotes and yes, they can get a small shock.

We bought this clear plastic shield for the television buttons, which was being sold as a "child-proofing" thing.[2] The television sat on it and the plastic came up and covered the buttons, also available in VCR/DVD player size. The remote signal worked through the plastic and it looked like a relatively benign, not too expensive, and easy way to protect the electronics. Well, it does not stop the kids from just taking the plastic thing out, and playing with it. And when it breaks, it is hard, melamine-type plastic, so it shatters into sharp pieces. The television wasn't quite large enough, and the lip didn't go under the television far enough, to prevent the children from getting to it. I would have had

---

[2] And now you know that I am not immune to the various 'tricks' that the child product industry throws at us.

to double-side tape it down or something for it to be effective.

When my children were small, and got close to the television, we would ask them to step back, ask again, and then just get up and physically move the child back to a reasonable distance. Children are very visual, so we set the living room rug edge at the distance away from the television that we thought was appropriate, and said things like, "Please come back from the television onto the rug, Son."

These are not children who pop in their own DVD or play on the computer from powering up to double-clicking the program open (heavens no), and they're tickled when we allow them to run up to the television after something is done and turn the television off. This will change with time of course, as they get older, but as toddlers to age five, my attitude is that electronics are not something they can afford to replace, so they shouldn't be playing with them.

Cell phones are also not toys and should be kept away from children. We finally bought a fake cell phone, that looks very real because a toy was not something Son was interested in. And I personally tried not to just take things away from my children, but to trade, his phone for mine. I am not sure if allowing him to play with his a good idea, because it is still a phone and leaves him with the idea that cell phones are okay for play, but it was the compromise that we came up with. I am not allowing him to play with my cell phone, which is being taken away regardless, and it results in a great deal less fuss overall.

We let family and friends know that we did not want battery-operated toys please. Getting batteries at Second Post was ... challenging. This mandate was only mostly understood and partially followed. We simply let the batteries run out and don't perform the Batteriectomy required to turn the toy into a noisemaker again. Secondly, we decided that we would only have a limited number of toys. One family we know requested, or purchased at an Embassy auction, two additional wardrobes and only had two wardrobes' worth of toys. I did two things to keep the toy stuff under control. First of all, I bought a bunch of Rubbermaid bins: in the under-the-bed size, in a portable size with a handle and in the extra large 25-gallon size. We only kept the number of toys that fit in those bins with one exception – Fisher Price Little People were allowed to overflow the bins. This was our family's choice for an easy answer to the what kind of 'what toys do they like' question and they are durable, offer long-term and different types of play. So we are willing to haul them around (that said, all the loose parts besides the buildings did go in the bins).

SHARING VERSUS TRADING

We didn't even try to instill a concept of sharing until age two or so. We are, however, heavily into trading. It works for orangutans and gorillas, so why not the human primate? Instead of insisting that your, say, two year old child share, insist that they trade. At that age, they don't even understand the idea of two people doing something together at the same time. They do grasp "if I want that I have to give something else in trade" remarkably fast. Yes, the exchange is still going to be to snatch the toy that they want and toss one that they don't want at the other child, but it does get gentler as you say, "Gently" each and every time, *ad nauseum*. Remember that the small ones, to age three or so, are usually parallel-playing children, not interactive-playing children. They play in the same area, not necessarily together.

They get that two kids are playing at the same time, but that isn't playing 'together'.

Slowly but surely, you begin to introduce the idea of asking, "May I have that, Sister?" who, being one, is instantly enamored of the whatever-new-toy (or old favorite) thing that Brother has brought over to trade for and willingly trades. This reinforces the idea of respecting each other and having manners and starting young makes it status quo, rather than a chore to be learned. Beginning at around age three, depending on your child's temperament, we began to tell our children that there are things that have to be shared. For instance, he wasn't playing with a particular toy but Friend was, and so now he wants it. We say, "When she is done, you can have it. For now, share." This can be interpreted several ways, and usually is, but he eventually picks up on the concept. Another family we know uses the Two Minute Rule to keep the sharing concept alive. This works well because Child One gets to keep it for two more minutes, then Child Two gets it. By the end of Child Two's two minutes, Child One has usually moved on.

Once, Daughter was teething and had been given some Infant Tylenol. When I was done, she liked to hold the bottle (she cuddled it to her face, like she was saying thank you for making me not hurt). Son, three years old, saw this and wanted the bottle. He went to take the bottle and she pulled away. Without prompting, he went and got the box that the bottle came in and offered it to her in trade. She took it and he took the bottle. She screeched, like no one on the block could have missed hearing it. Son was stunned, stopped dead in his track and looked at her incredulously. I told him to share please because she really wanted the bottle. He did, but was upset. "I traded!" he howled. I told him that he'd done a good job, but part of sharing was when the other person didn't want to give it up. He said, "I really want it." So I told him that I'd put the bottle away now since it was causing tension. He asked if he could do it and I told him to get a toy. While he was getting the toy, I told Daughter that it was going away, and she gave it to me as Son handed her a MagnaDoodle to distract her. I handed him the bottle, lifted him up, and he put it away. He picked right up on the no one gets it angle, and was happy to assist to make it so.

"Not Fair Trade Agreement"

18. The Chaos

Ah, everyone else's little monsters! My favorite. I can say, with deep and heartfelt honesty, that I hope you are blessed as we were once, in finding a family that had the same approach to child raising. House rules were the same, in both houses. No parent, *any* of the four, felt any concern over intervening or stepping in, and as a result, all of us, adults and children could have a more relaxing time and amazingly, at ages three and five (two three year olds and two five year olds) we could leave all four children in a child-safe area like a playroom and not worry. Oh sure, there was always the occasional need to go unstuck someone, or dig a child out from under a dog-pile of other children, or time a toy out, but no one wondered about the rules or parameters, because they were almost the same. It was comfortable to have the village raise the children.

That doesn't happen often. In fact, the most challenging thing for me with toddlers was maintaining my rules and standards in the presence of other families, children and homes. I am still asked why I am so strict, can't I just let kids be kids, and even what my problem is with kids having fun. I used to take offense, but I'm quite comfortable with the outcome, so I just smile and say, "Oh, it takes all kinds," usually as I watch their child pulling all the Scotch tape from the roll to hear the click or something equally harmless and inexpensive, but not allowed in our home.

> I used to feel hurt when someone would ask why I am so strict or why I can't let kids be kids. Now I smile and say, "Oh, it takes all kinds."

So, how do you deal with maintaining your standards, whether they're as, um, shall we say, controlled as mine are or not?

PLAYGROUPS

While I don't necessarily recommend playgroups until the child is walking, it is a great social, networking and resource function for the mothers. I'm willing to be antisocial, and keep the playgroups few and far between, and I preferred not to have my children learn some of the things that they learned at playgroups, let alone have unrestricted access to sweets and such. As tiny people (to age three or so), it isn't as much of a playgroup as it is new toys to play with, because they still enjoy solitary play so much. It wasn't until the children started to recognize and look for other children that I started to see any value in it. My compromise was to make sure our child-care provider knew our parameters (no sweets, the sharing rules, and manners) and let *her* go with the kids! That's cheating, and I fully admit it, but I was torn. I didn't want to go because maintaining our standards was difficult initially, but I did want the kids to get some playtime around other children.

That said, I know mothers who look forward to playgroup on an entirely adult-relationship level. This is a chance to have conversation that you lack all week, with another adult. You discover resources of someone finding one thing in this place, or knowing where to go to find this other thing. It can be challenging to keep in mind reinforcing positive behaviors in your child, or discouraging negative ones.

Before a plyagroup, be specific with your nanny about what they are responsible for — your children, and a few ground rules to keep it simple. There are a few different kinds of playgroups, each having an entirely different purpose and make-up. There is a social, or unstructured playgroup, an educational playgroup and an organized playgroup. Some of these groups occur in homes, some are at the schools, some are even in the Embassy. Each will have different expectations and different parameters, and might not be as clearly defined as below. You may have to go to the group itself, evaluate if it meets your needs or expectations and make your decision at that point. You may have to establish the playgroup yourself.

A social, or unstructured playgroup, is one where there is no organization beyond a time and date. This is the kind where mothers and children go and all bets are off. It is usually a social event for the mothers more than the children and children are usually not even in the same rooms as the mothers, as the mothers migrate to where the tea and coffee are and the children migrate to where the toys are. This kind of group can result in some incredibly bad learned behavior. Sadly, if there is a nanny or two present, they are usually left with too many children, not their charges, to watch well. If you do go to one of these to socialize, take your nanny and explain quietly and carefully that they are responsible for your child only and do not have to take care of anyone else's child (they will, for things that are dangerous, but this will relieve their pressure a little). If you don't, you may spend all week undoing things that were learned while you were having tea one afternoon – such as jumping on the bed or pulling all the cushions off of the couch and jumping into them or climbing bookcases like ladders.

If you host one of these playgroups, which will be expected most times as a rotating host type of thing, I recommend that you also have your nanny there. Before hand, be specific with your child-care provider about whether or not they are responsible for other people's children or just yours, and be sure to tell the other mothers the same thing. I would recommend not being responsible for children other than yours. That said, I have had to say, "If you want my nanny to watch your children, we pay her $5 and hour...." and that usually takes care of that. Granted, that was in response to a woman very nonchalantly saying, "Oh, your nanny can watch them." I might have offered, but I sure wasn't going to have it be presumed.

This would be a good time to remind you that this is a book of experiences, personal ones. Everything you read is opinion, backed by practice, animal behavior observations, other mothers and observation. But it is all opinion, and there are so many different interpretations that can be arrived at. My intention is to offer Informed Choices. If I let you know what I know, added to what you know and observe, you can make informed choices for you and your family. And children can be the most rewarding and entertaining experience out there.

If you ask me, educational playgroups are pretty much nonsense unless they are age-appropriate, and they generally aren't. On the up side, play is educational for children under five! An educational playgroup usually seems to be an attempt to 'improve' children, usually without an assessment first. They also are not grouped according to age, and there is a vast behavioral difference between a three year old and three and a half year old. Trying to make a two year old play like a four year old is hard on the two year old, too much stimuli and frustration at not being able to do it well. Brazelton has good definitions of what they're doing and why, and what is next, and it will help you assess whether or not the playgroup is age appropriate. There is also a group of books by Louise Bates Ames entitled *Your Two Year Old*, and *Your Three Year Old* and such that is a good assessment tool.

That said, there are educational playgroups that are actually arts and crafts playgroups. At about age three, depending on the temperament of your child, these can be loads of fun. They like making things. You're going to have so many created things you won't know what to do with them all! I've seen this done very well, from simple construction paper, glitter and glue[1] to making and

---

[1] Theoretically simple anyway. Getting these kinds of arts and crafts supplies requires careful planning ahead of time, long trips to craft stores and bins of supplies. They're just not things that one finds in most local markets.

decorating cookies or pizza.

An organized playgroup is one with rules, more organized and interactive. Of course this would be my kind of thing, because one of my most favorite things is to create order out of chaos. These playgroups have defined limits, and any parent or nanny can enforce them, and sometimes there are games or activities for the kids. In her *Toddler Whisperer* book, Tracey Hogg (the author of the *Baby Whisperer* books) has some wonderful things to say about playgroups and being involved, and tools to manage yourself and the group.

When a playgroup is hosted at my house, it is of the organized variety and I am very clear ahead of time about the parameters. But gracefully! For instance, I have a cute little framed picture on the way down to the playroom, with a silhouette of a kid at a table that says, "Food upstairs" and then there is another of a child on a hobby horse, "Toys downstairs". People get it. It is particularly effective when a child walks upstairs with a toy, and I point at the picture and say, "Oops, toys downstairs!" and help them take it back down. There might be whining, but I can point to the sign and say, "Sorry, it says so right there!" as if it wasn't my idea! This is especially helpful with food and frankly, I host several times in the spring and fall simply so I can do it in the yard, and can keep all the food and chaos outside.

No matter how much you, the parent, are looking forward to it, if your child is not feeling well, don't go to playgroup!

A lovely variation on the organized playgroup is to theme the playgroup. For instance, make it a fish playgroup. Sit down with the little ones and read a book about fish. Then they can make little fish from construction paper and glitter. Move them on to making paper plate fish masks, while you attach paperclips to the glitter fish and then let them go fishing for the glitter fish with a magnet on a string. Having planned ahead by ordering gummie fruit snacks from NetGrocer, finish up with blue Jello snacks with gummie fruit fish swimming in them and leave *Finding Nemo* on the DVD player the whole time (which gives you a convenient timing mechanism which to base the whole event on). With four activities, that is thirty minutes each, which is about their maximum attention span, it works out very well. You can do all sorts of variations that make it both interesting and not so unstructured. I got this idea from a children's book club called Read On Wisconsin. The Governor's wife would choose the books and questions, for a number of age groups, and you theme your playgroup accordingly and read the book and use the questions!

GERMS

No matter how bored you are and no matter how much you were looking forward to it, if your child is not feeling well, please don't go to playgroup. You don't do the other children (or their parents) any favors by exposing them more than they already are especially when you already know your child is sick. The other half of staying healthy that I love and live by is hand sanitizer. I kid you not, there is some in every diaper bag,[2] purse, car and even coat sometimes (if we're sick and sneezing). Another thing is washing hands! The best thing you can do to limit sickness is to practice good hygiene with hand washing before meals, after bathroom, or after coming in from outside. You should just see me with the Clorox wipes after playgroup at my house – I wipe down light switches, banisters, door handles, and if we're sick, I also wipe telephones, remote controls and keyboards. I know it sounds ridiculous, and I know it could be purely coincidental, but I've got the healthiest kids that I know – and I attribute it to lots of outside play and washing hands!

On the other side of that coin, *don't go anti-bacterially crazy*. Kids do need to be exposed to germs and stuff, but in the outside-playing exposed to life, washing hands afterwards way; not the sneezy-snorky-sick germs. So, maybe I am only half a hypocrite. That said there is some basis in fact for this attitude. An immune system is like a learning house alarm. To take this metaphor a little further, imagine that this alarm system only works when it is exposed to crimes. An immune system learns to defend against diseases after it is exposed to them, which is why vaccines work. If your child lives in a sterile environment, that system had no chance to learn to defend itself.

Remember, life happens. It is messy and it is full of people. This is just life, not an excess of stimulation or germs.

OVER-STIMULATION & TOYS

The expat and Embassy community can have a lot to offer in terms of activities and opportunities, although you might have to seek them out. If you are concerned about over-scheduling your child, or limiting your child's stimuli, whether it is social or sensory, sometimes having an answer ready can help you deal with limiting their activities. For instance, we chose to limit their outings to no more times per week and no more hours per time, than they are years old, particularly for the child under five. Your ready answer might be, "It's none of

---

[2] I didn't actually have diaper bags, but diaper Ziploc sounds funny.

your business." Life is stimulating enough for these little people, playgroup each and every day is over-stimulating for me, what in the world can it be like for them?! For a baby, they are busy learning how their own world (home, you, them) is defined, let alone categorizing and sorting, which is what a toddler is doing. You will expand their circles of stimulation slowly enough. They are not going to be interested in socialization until they are closer to three years old. Under that age, and it is parallel play; same room, different stuff. Sharing ... not so much. Until they are about four, this is an alien concept, like headless goat polo is to an American in Kyrgyzstan.

At two years old, Son went to two playgroups a week, each being two hours long. Then, when he was going to be three, we added one hour of gymnastics, which is also big muscle exercise, which boys desperately need. If you practice that line, "I keep it in ratio to his age" no one will hassle you because you sound like you know what you're talking about! "Oh, I keep his external stimulation to as many times per week that he is old." Sounds good! Keep in mind, I am talking about playgroup, children's activities, classes and organized activities.

Consider limiting socialization to no more times per week, or hours per time, than the child is years old.

There are a bunch of things that are in our Not For Children category (which is different than not-toy toys): electronics, cell phones, digital cameras, computers, televisions and associated peripherals, appliances, transformers, phones, space heaters, animal bowls, and filing cabinets. All of these things get an AAAAAAAAAAAAAAAccckckkkkk! Noise (that makes Husband, kids, dog and cats all stop whatever they are doing), and then "Not for...." But you have to hand them something that is for... or it isn't fair. But they think that they are having all kinds of fun with something special when they pull the Nalgene bottles off of the shelf to play with.

Another not-toy that is very easy to blur the edges on is the computer. Son and Daughter receive Elmo Mail (you'll see) from my mother; these thirty-second e-mail movie clips just make their day. They also send it, which grandparents adore. Son inferred how to make them go: the <play> button on the keyboard. Well, Mama's computer is not a toy; in fact he is not allowed to touch the keyboard or mouse at all. So, when it is time to hit that play button, it is a treat. He did play JumpStart Baby, which is a mouse-only program in fifteen-minute increments, but heavily supervised. Once we start with other computer programs, it will be harder to keep him away from our computers. To fight this, at about four years old, we bought a cheap, refurbished computer, no Internet connection, and use it for JumpStart programs, which we don't do on school-nights. Again, that is a comfort level thing, because I know other parents who regularly use the playing of computer games as a reward, and even others who don't consider it anything other than another toy.

Don't forget the fun that Not Toys offer. These are items that become toys and are played with like toys. These are things like boxes (paint or wrap some shipping boxes for the best blocks ever!), toilet paper or paper towel tubes, shoe-horns, and mouse-pads. We regularly sort out the Not Toys from the actual toys, just to keep them from taking over. My current attitude towards not-toys is to let them play with them, but to send them away sooner rather than later. I used to have all manners of odds and ends in the playroom where he could play with them – lanyards, broken timer, shoe-horns, pouches, airline socks, etc. About quarterly when we do a major clean, I go ahead and get rid of all of them because it was becoming a little difficult to differentiate and was turning into a mess.

> When you tell your child that an item is NOT FOR, you do need to hand them something that IS FOR, or it is not fair and you will get conflict.

ALONE PLAY

Alone play is not a bad thing. It is a hard thing for parents and nannies to do, but it is not bad. And it provides an incredibly wonderful opportunity for you to come back quietly and watch when they don't know you are watching.

When Son was about two years old, we purchased a kitchen timer and set it for fifteen or twenty minutes when we wanted to give Son some "Alone time." The trick here is to set it up high, or on the stairs beyond the closed baby gate, because kids are no dummies. In fact, they are born lawyers and loophole finders! If you set the timer for fifteen minutes, and he's bored, he'll turn it until the bell rings! But we tell him, "Son, I'm going to go upstairs and (insert task here), and when the timer rings, I will come back down and play." And keep your promise, because every word you utter to your child is a promise. Come back down and play when you hear the timer. Don't give yourself an extra second or just finish up. Go back when you hear the timer. Short of changing another child's diaper, there is very little that you must finish immediately or can't have company when doing it. Stoves can be turned off (or timers set there). Laundry can be sorted together. It takes longer, but it is more fun.

If you have been in the habit of speaking with respect to your child, when you say that you are leaving and coming back, they believe you. So, to leave them alone somewhere safe is not abandonment, and they do not react as if it is.

Imagination blossoms when they are left alone for free play. Sometimes they do the most amazing and wonderful thing. Sometimes the connections are mind-boggling and you just have to stifle a giggle and hope that they don't see you so they will continue. Sometimes is it downright upsetting, and you have to bite your tongue and try to keep watching quietly at all. Sometimes you come back in fifteen minutes only to discover that they have pushed the chair next to the table next to the mantle to get to the dry-erase markers that you put safely up and now you, and they, will have a good half hour of cleaning to make things right.

There are words for sure. "Oh no! How did this marker get here? Why isn't it on the board where it belongs? We will have to clean it up!" Sometimes as you stand in the door, you hear strange and wonderful connections being made. Sometimes they are somewhat worrisome and you need to make minor corrections in their perceptions.

Keep your promise, because every word you utter to your child is a promise.

Do find out how you can be comfortable with alone play. Keep it safe of course, and preferably non-destructive (we had to make markers for supervised playtime for a while), but try to make it happen on a regular basis to get your children used to it.

Also remember that the practice of alone-play will serve a useful purpose in the future. If you can teach your child to accept being alone and entertaining his or her self, if they should have siblings in the future, they will be able to accept the ideas of privacy from older siblings, who will want to be with their friends rather than their younger siblings, even if the siblings are very peer-oriented towards each other. Setting it up, and practicing it, will be an investment towards future peace, not some intellectual exercise.

MY ANTI-SOCIAL TENDENCIES

I think that play, other children and a little chaos is important for my children. I also know that I am not the person best equipped for dealing with it. To be honest, I do not want my socialization failures to be the only example that they are absorbing. I go to playgroup and sit, on a chair usually on the edge of the group, and frankly focus on managing my child. I don't let them eat outside of our home parameters – no cake because it is just there – we don't do sugar to excess (some of course, because moderation is a good thing) – and I bring a healthy snack from home in case there are no fruit or non-sugar options, which happens a lot. If you were to listen to me, I'm not interacting much with the other mothers or children. Mostly you'd hear,

> "Son, please trade."
>
> "Daughter, gently."
>
> "Son, trading."
>
> "Daughter, no throwing."
>
> "Son, slowly please."
>
> "Daughter, please give that back, no snatching. One ...two[3] ... thank you."

I know we have a lot of rules, and I know it isn't easy to be consistent. That is why we devote such time and effort in our hiring process for a nanny. I flat out tell them that I don't do playgroups well and they will be expected to go with me the first three times and then take over and keep our standards while at playgroup. Then I don't go.

We devote a lot of time to our hiring process so I can trust that manners are being enforced at playgroups.

This makes me a hypocrite, because when I first had Son, and first went to baby group,[4] I came home and said, "I don't want to hang out with a bunch of nannies!" So what do I do ... send my child with the nanny. But then again, some of the other mothers must feel the same way, so at least I am not a lonely hypocrite! These groups make me miserable. I feel like I am too strict when I go to these things, because I am always correcting. But I also feel that this is right for my children, these rules[5] and the socialization both. I hate second guessing myself and avoid it all costs.

However, I do know that it is important for the kids to be exposed to other children, other germs, other houses. So I host at appropriate intervals, dependent upon the size of the playgroup circle, and ensure that the children go to them also.

Some of the playgroup chaos changed when they went to school. It turned into

---

[3] Always get up and make the correction on three, or it is an empty threat and they know it.

[4] (there were two, one for babes and one for toddlers; babies until they were walking and toddlers afterwards, which was nice because the babies were, well, safe)

[5] ...or suggestions and guidelines that must be adhered to and have consequences if they are not.

school chaos instead! My kids like to have fair warning about something, so we started with half-day pre-school only the first year. I consider half a day of school to be an activity. Daughter had playgroup and "Tiny Toes" — a kind of move-to-music sort of class. Son had full-day preschool eventually, and one additional activity, which turned out to be horseback riding for a while. Fortunately, finding things like ballet, horseback riding and gymnastics is very affordable in places that we have lived.

For years now, we had been supervising our children entirely and completely, in the same room and participating ... in other words, missing all the adult conversation and usually the food too ...

We were lucky enough to meet a family with similar styles, and similar values. We all got along and the kids clicked and played very well together. We'd had a few play-dates and things were working out fine. The thing was, it was usually me who went with the children to them, due to timing, and not Husband. Once Husband was out of town and the two moms decided that we could possibly imagine trying to have a sleep-over. I give her full credit for not batting an eye when I came with my pajamas too! I couldn't imagine just dropping them off! We had a really nice evening and while the kids didn't sleep very much at first, it all worked out well.

So I'd gotten used to the idea and practice of going over, kids all going to the playroom and staying downstairs in the lovely kitchen for tea and conversation and occasionally one adult or another going up, checking on children, sometimes mediating and sometimes attending to a minor injury or major drama. The kids all very quickly learned to listen to whichever adult came. But the first time that Husband was able to join us for one of these kinds of things was really kind of interesting. Keep in mind, he was used to one or the other of us being with the children at all times. The kids knew by our presence that our house rules applied, even if we weren't in our house. So when I took off the kids' shoes and they all pounded up the stairs like a herd of elephants, he went to follow, thinking he had the first shift. I asked if he'd like to stay and talk and said, "The kids will be fine."

He looked at me like I had lost my mind. Is this the same woman who has now managed to write hundreds of pages about rules and limits, parameters and guidelines for children? Is this the same woman who would leave a function rather than upset a routine? I said, "It's okay, they have the same house rules."

I don't think he believed me. At each bang from above (barely discernable pause while all four parents tilt their head slightly to determine the cause of the crash, okay, just cars, and resume conversation) he'd partially stand up. At each rise in volume, he'd make it about a third of the way off of his seat. For a screech or yell, he probably managed half way off his chair each time. Unbeknownst to the other three parents, we'd sort of developed a routine. First crash and one mother went. Second crash, the other one went. If the other husband was around, he'd go up for the third. Without ever articulating it, we had a pattern, allowing all the adults to continue to participate in the non-child activities and the kids to have what they perceived to be as unsupervised play! And for these kids, all four of them, it was grand.

That my friends, is what is meant when they say it takes a village. Meals are on the table, or cleared, or washed on time and with minimal fuss. Kids are cleaned or dressed or undressed by whichever adult is there. No one worries about offending someone else because well, first of all house rules apply and second of all, they're the same rules! And most of all, parents get to relax and not worry about undoing too much (a head full of glitter perhaps, or Play-doh in the pockets), when we get home.

"It Takes a Village"

19. Potty Training

Oh dear, I can honestly say that this issue is such a ... quagmire. I will reassure you first - everyone is wading through the quagmire, just like you. You will, like the rest of us, find a method, use it, change it and adapt as you choose or need.

SUPPLIES

It is a surprisingly short list for what you need to potty train:
> Child-size, floor level, training toilet
> Pull-Ups
> TWO waterproof mattress pads
> TWO sets of bed-sheets

There are other things of course, books, dolls that 'do it' and videos and all kinds of things, but they are bonus items, not necessities.

DEFINITIONS

I should point out that I consider a child to be potty trained when these three criteria are met:
> 1. They physically know that they have to eliminate.
> 2. They can communicate this fact to an adult.
> 3. They can prevent themselves from going in order to get to an appropriate bathroom.

I do not consider a child potty-trained if the parent observes a behavior and drops everything and whisks the child to a toilet, tearing off clothes en route practically and holds them over the toilet. This is certainly clean in the sense that you're not soiling diapers or underwear, but it doesn't mean that the child knows a darn thing about the social requirements of elimination. For me, that demonstrates an admirable set of trained skills learned by the parents.

I should point out that in all of the countries that we have lived in, the above paragraph was the preferred method of potty training. Keep in mind that diapers are expensive! Washing clothes is hard on them and if they don't even have disposable diapers, they're using cloth ones and doing the laundry is a little more labor intensive than we're used to. This required me to think about and define, for explanation to someone else, just how we were going to go about doing things.

THE BASICS OF TRAINING[1]

1. Sit down and stay awhile – this means you have your child sit on the potty chair, with or without clothes, as practice, whether they're using their own potty chair or the big person toilet. We used the little one mostly to get them used to it and sat them on it when we sat on ours.

2. Show and tell – monkey see, monkey do. Wash your hands, and let them practice washing theirs. Let them see you use the toilet. Teach them to wipe appropriately (front to back, especially girls)

3. Clean up – let them watch (and help to a very limited extent) of how their chair is cleaned, and flush the waste, rinse and flush again. The toilet is where our waste goes to 'get cleaned up'.

4. Be on the lookout – watch for the signs that show that the child needs to go. Say the signs out loud so the child learns what they are, how to recognize them, and act on them.

A parent whisking a child away is a trained PARENT — not a potty trained child.

Not included in the website's recommendation is teaching the children to get in the habit of emptying their bladder before bed every single night. Other recommendations include not having a drink within an hour of bedtime, or leaving a nightlight on in the bathroom so that the child see the destination and get there. The parenting books almost all have a chapter on potty training. And they say, "Praise success" and "Don't draw attention to lack of success."

THE BEST INTENTIONS

For starters, we decided not to do anything on our own personal timeline. We decided to watch the child for signs of readiness and willingness, rather than just begin at age two or whatnot. It wasn't until Son was three years old that he began to show any interest. Daughter was also three before she started to show any signs of readiness. Before that, while diaper changing happened in the

---

[1] paraphrased from Pampers' LetsTalkPottyTraining.com website, which is admittedly also interested in selling its various products like Pull-Ups, KanDoo hand sanitizer, soap and flushable wipes (same stuff, different packaging as yours) etc.

bathroom, and they knew what we did, it wasn't even on their radar. This will depend on the child - I've met children who definitely showed interest at age two, and some who were pushed at four. When they began to show interest, we immediately went from diapers to Pull Ups, making a big deal of ordering the Pull Ups and potty seats for them and waiting, checking the mail to see if Son's boxes had come in yet. The change was both a physical and mental reminder for him, "this is different." Only babies wear diapers, and since he was learning a little kid thing, he got Pull-Ups. When he got it, and was a bigger kid, he'd wear big boy underwear. Remember, kids need cues.

It started out with the usual, getting a potty chair. We chose one that was simple, a white outer housing, red receptacle and removable seat that could be put on an adult toilet. Closed, it could be used as a stool. No bells, no whistles and certainly no music for us, but there are all kinds out there! Then we got a few potty books, to read on the potty chair and changed from diapers to Pull-Ups (remember, they were three years old). Then we would simply make a point to place the child on the potty whenever Mama or Daddy went in to use it, and immediately upon waking, and before bed. Praise for any success and no comment for accidents.

And we had messy Pull-Ups for a long time, and no means to motivate him to tell us when he was ready. We tried bribery, a cookie every time he pooped in the potty, and that worked for a little while. Eventually, in about three or four months, we were finally running out of Pull-Ups and I told him that he had to wear big boy underwear because we were running out of Pull-Ups and since everyone cleans up after themselves when they use the toilet, if he made a mess, he'd have to clean himself up (but we'd help).

Amazingly, for both children, on approximately the same timeline, that worked. It took one time with Son standing stinky in the tub with me handing him washcloths as I used the shower head to rinse off this clothes, for him to decide that was awful. Unfortunately, Daughter could have cared less.

I was assured that it would be different with Daughter, being a girl and being second. I was told she'd be ready sooner, and she'd train faster. Yeah, well, not so much, thanks. She was three before we noticed her signs of being ready and it took the three to six months that it took him. She would actually wet (or worse, poop) in her big girl underwear, and clean it up! Sometimes you didn't even know that she'd done it – she would quietly take off her panties, get a washcloth and wipe up the floor, start upstairs to take the panties and washcloth to the laundry and get new underwear and you'd figure this out next time you went to help her and she was wearing different underwear!

Son was three and a few months and figured it out. Husband and I were a little slower on recognizing it and realized a good week or two later that we'd been, well, a week or two, with no accidents and he'd 'gotten it.' By three and a half, he was in big boy underwear day and night. Daughter was the same timeline exactly.

Once your child is consistently (you choose how many days equals consistent) having dry days, they can wear big kid underwear during the day. We stayed with Pull-Ups until there were dry nights as well, which took another month or two. By three and a half both children were day and night accident free. There is still the occasional odd accident, usually precipitated by something very unusual, like sickness. Good habits, such as going potty before bed, and immediately upon waking, help them maintain the dry spells.

CHALLENGES

The occasional night accidents occur of course, after they are having dry days. This is inevitable and we made as minimal amount of fuss as possible, frankly, because you just want to get back in bed. I kept a full set of sheets, waterproof mattress pad and change of pajamas staged at the ready for what felt like an unusually long time.[2]

More blankets on the bed is good because the colder they are at night, the more likely they are to need to pee. We keep the bedrooms cool at night, so it was important for me to put a hand on his neck when I went in for his last night kiss before I went to sleep and if he was cool, add another blanket.

Our lifestyle doesn't necessarily help. With all the travel that we have, I suggest that you if you start a "regimen" of some sort, or an actual method or plan with timeline, consider starting when you will have six months in one place with no travel. Six months is what it is going to take to really "set" the behavior, three months of practice and three to have it take.

The travel part really threw us with Daughter – she was on the road towards potty training, earlier than we'd expected, when we were returning to our Third

[2] Granted, I could have simply forgotten to put them all away once we had consistent dry nights.

Post. Three weeks later, with jet lag both ways, we were back at square one. She was willing to tell us, but she was unwilling to use public toilets. One month our efforts were set back due to automatically flushing toilets!

RESOURCES AND RESEARCH

When Son was three years old, we (um, that would be me) went online and tried to find articles about potty training. I went to parenting.ivillage.com, babycenter.com, parentsplace.com, and parents.com and you will be glad to know that they all have essentially the same information and advice.

Since Son was older than three, I started to read articles on Reluctant Trainees and tried incorporating some methods from various sources. But I swear that we did nothing consistent except for not making a big deal of it. Husband and I thought it was the longest three months (both times) ever.

So, one day Husband and I are downstairs discussing something and I see Daughter come down stairs out of the corner of my eye. She's very serious and careful and I think, "Hmm, I wonder what is going on here?" A few seconds later I say, "Good napping, Peanut! Let's go in and go potty. She said, "Nope!" and patted her bottom. Sure enough, that bottom doesn't look particularly well padded. I go and pat the bottom and it is Pull-Up free! I say, "Oh oh! Is there a poopy Pull-Up upstairs?" thinking that she is naked underneath. She says in this chirpy little voice, "Nope!" I pat again and realize that there is underwear on under there! I ask if I can peek and she grins like all get out and I peek and, oh my goodness, big girl underwear! Husband says, "Did you poop in the potty?", which is what was required for her to do before she could wear big girl underwear and she grins even bigger, if that is possible. So we all troop upstairs and there is a Pull-Up, dry, in the garbage can. The Hand sanitizer is down off of the back of the sink, so I suspect it was used. And while all other steps had been remembered, the flushing had not (or she forgot on purpose), so there was the evidence too!

Sure enough, she had woken up, gone into the bathroom, taken off the Pull-Ups and disposed of it properly, pooped in the potty, wiped, washed hands, went out in the other room and opened the dresser, got the big girl underwear, put it on and came downstairs.

Just once.

"One Success Story"

PERSONALITY DRIVEN

One suggestion was to offer little boys little paper targets (hole punch stars and such). One suggestion was to sink Cheerios, but for Son this was a bad idea because for him that was food and one did not abuse food. For Son, food was just too important to pee on!

We encouraged the children to start using the little seat on the big potty as soon as we could, mostly so I could get rid of that little potty chair. We did encourage Son to sit and point his penis down to pee if he was pooping and that was fine, but being a little ham, he discovered that he'd get a lot of reaction if he 'forgot'.

Daughter provided other challenges. She would wake up dry and then pee almost immediately - in her Pull-Ups. Nothing would motivate her, not big girl underwear, not a cookie, not a deterrent like cleaning up after herself, not even sitting and just waiting. She had to determine the when; she will do it on her own time and if we suggest it, she says, "NO!" (and two minutes later goes in and does it herself). She could also pee on demand, but also would go with no warning, saying, "Mama, gotta pee ... oh. Peeing." (which is funny, but not helpful). She is also StealthBaby and can vanish off anyone's radar in no time flat. She can be standing in front of you one second, you turn away, turn back and she's gone. And when you look for her, and she finally giggles, she's right there, practically in front of you.

> Potty training is personality driven. You can't just plunk a cautious child on the toilet or convince a spirited one to sit still for too long.

All of that said, she knew what it was that we wanted. She is too much like me in this respect; the more you push one direction, the more she pulls in the other. Seriously, we could talk about it, mention it, remind, hint and everything else we could think of, but she'd pee or poop in her Pull-Up without a second thought. Finally we simply had to say that she had to learn because we were running out of Pull-Ups!

I have no idea why that worked, twice, but since it did, it is worth mentioning.

LAST THOUGHTS

Patience. It isn't taking as long as you think. They're processing a whole new way of doing something. Consider if you had the basics of a new language, but weren't acknowledged when you didn't speak the new language, and were praised to high heaven when you did. You'd try, but it might take a little while for you to figure out that those were the new rules. I think that one of the reasons that kids don't show the interest in earnest until around age three is because up until age three, they're doing amazing developmental things like learning to eat, learning to walk, learning to talk, getting teeth, that kind of thing. Patience. It is the very rare child that doesn't go to kindergarten potty trained. If you are approaching four or five, please do seek assistance from your pediatrician, especially to determine if there is a physical reason why it is delayed.

Our "method", if you can call it that, was to watch the children's habits carefully, put them on the potty regularly, praise them when they succeeded and not fuss when they didn't.

Hysterical, but I didn't show it when it happened.

Daughter had been being stubborn about potty training. She knows exactly what to do, and has, in fact done it without prompting or pushing. The more we push one way, the more she pushes back the other (hmm, sounds like me).

So one day she's running around post-nap with no Pull-Ups or underwear on (no underwear unless she poops in the potty – something she knows) We chose to do this because she's a little red down under from wetting in her Pull Ups. So, I go get cookies out of the oven, and she gets up off of the couch and I hear her walking in the bathroom vicinity. I put down the cookie tray, go follow and there she is, naked bottom, one foot on each side of the litter box, peeing.

I immediately turned around and went back to cookies before she could look up. I did have to change cat boxes but what does one say to THAT!? Besides, we had told her, "You are not a kitty!" since it had come up before for sleeping in baskets or under beds and 'clawing the furniture' (she just wants us to shoot her with the squirt bottle then). Her usual response to that admonition is, "Mew."

"Right Idea; Wrong Species"

20. Manners

I cannot tell you how proud I was when my not-yet-three-year old said, "Done, please?" And my not-yet-five year old says the full, "Excuse me, may I be done?" when they were finished with their meals. Even more fun is that they do it anyway, not just in front of people! They have been please and thank you consistent, and I can honestly tell you why. We do it and we do it with them. Every time. All the time. This is the one time where I can actually see that they learn by example. And they see and hear everything.

Now my little miss gets a lllooooooong pause and look from me when she says, "Milk!" ... and she follows up with, "Please?" because she knows that is the correct formula. And we prompt and remind all day long. Even now.

Manners are more than just a social nicety, they are also tools for coping. As I mentioned before, my son is cautious, and we are working on teaching him that while he gathers information about the people or situation, he can rely on manners to keep the situation from being awkward and that manners usually deflect the talking part away from him.[1] It also prevents people from saying, well meaning or just ignorantly, "Oh, he's shy." Then we have to try to explain to him why he doesn't have to be shy, or why it is okay to be shy.

> Manners are more than just nice; they are tools that can help your child cope with new situations.

I am as guilty as the next person of automatically 'labeling', but when your son comes to you and asks if shy is bad, it makes you not want other people to do it to your children! Conversely, our leap-before-she-looks daughter, the bravest little thing I have ever met, is gradually being taught to slow down because she has to take the time to go through the manners requirements.[2] For her it is an inadvertent counting to ten pause; for him it is a shield. Either way, you want to avoid labels because kids want to please their parents and will live up to the label you provide, whether it is, "My son is always a little wild." Or "Isn't she cute?" It is better to get in the habit of describing an action or item instead, "My son loves playing with fast cars." Or "Isn't her dress nice?" since it doesn't place pre-existing expectations on personality.

---

[1] He could care less if it is awkward, but we care and our guests sometimes do too,

[2] She was watching *Beauty and the Beast*, and when they are storming the castle she STALKED up to the screen and when Gaston came on, she LEAPT at it, growling. And yes, that is a label and so we try not to say it in front of her so she won't live up to the expectation. We've also banned the c-u-t-e word around her entirely.

Additionally, manners are going to hold you in good stead when you are traveling. A child who asks please and says thank you or excuse me will always receive a little more consideration than one who doesn't. This can be helpful in these travel-challenging days. After recent changes that disallowed carrying bottles of water on board, something we always have plenty of on hand, we travel with empty Nalgene water bottles. Son wanted some water. Now, remember, lots of people label him as "shy." But travel is a familiar situation for him, and he took his water bottle, went to the back of the plane alone, to the galley and asked, "May I have some water please?" They were happy to fill it. Then he held up Daughter's bottle and said, "May my sister have some too?" They were charmed and one walked back with him. The stewardess said that they didn't have extra water on board so she was sorry that she couldn't just give us a liter bottle, but if he needed a refill, she'd be happy to fill it again.

It is better to get in the habit of describing an action or item, since it doesn't place pre-existing expectations on a child's personality.

That said, manners are hard. Listen to a group of adults some time. So few say please or thank you. 'Excuse me' is more common, but certainly not standard. Like puppies, children need routine and consistency and consistent manners goes further than all the lectures in the world (which are way over their head and irrelevant to them anyway). Practice what you preach when it comes to those things that you want your child to do – manners included. You don't have to be Emily Post and an etiquette maven to get basic manners. Remember that most dogs are not police-dog trained, but any dog that can sit-stay-come makes a better impression. Children are quite the same. I'm an animal behaviorist who treated my children like small mammals that couldn't speak human for a while, so I don't consider saying that kids are like puppies to be an insult. A child who says please and excuse me, but slouches at the table will be tolerated much more than the grabby child who does the same.

This child is more welcome at the dinner table:

"Please pass the bread, Son."

Son does, and receives a "Thank you" in response.

"You're welcome, Daddy."

And believe me, planning a meal where you seat everyone, regardless of age, is much easier than trying to figure out who will be where to watch the children and eat with them in the kitchen.

Your children learning manners can be disconcerting at times. We had to institute a new 'rule' in the house, and that is "Children cannot correct adults." This came about because Son, and Daughter, would consistently tell guests, "Chew, swallow, then talk." And one should not embarrass your guests, even if the child is correct, particularly if they are representatives of a foreign government.

And that brings me to one of the most important reasons, for us, to practice and preach good manners. You are representing the U.S. government, by default. Others should see well-behaved children (and therefore conclude that this is just how all our kids are!) if possible. You can practice this by taking them, even as infants and toddlers, to restaurants and low-key events. As first tour officers, we weren't required to do anything representational at all, given the size of our first post. However, we were advised by a couple that had been living the expatriated diplomat life for a much longer time than we had to "practice." So we hosted dinner parties on occasion, giving me a clue as to just how complicated and confusing that can be, and we sat our children at the table and expected them to participate, even if it was just for a little bit. As they got older, we would answer their, "excuse me may I be done" question at the kitchen table (as opposed to the long formal dining room table), with, "Not yet, we're having a conversation." They got used to having dinner guests, and having to have manners for the duration.

Recently, we've even started having dinners where they are not included, which is a significant deviation from the norm for them. But before hand we gave them the briefing, three points to remember for the evening, and their baby-sitter came even though both Husband and I were present. We rewarded their exceptionally good behavior one evening by allowing them to 'help' us play a few rounds of cards, and they happily went up to bed. They were a little disappointed that the guests didn't come kiss them good night also though. Combining the techniques of a sort of pre-game brief, reminding them that manners were required this evening, and letting them know they'd be eating separately, gave them enough information to adapt to the slightly different evening.

Don't forget your first "function." You know, on some levels what to expect, but you still sort of watch out of the corner of your eye to make sure you're not doing something terrifically inappropriate. After the third or fourth one, you settle into a pattern of behavior for yourself and they become much easier. The same is true for your children, but you're giving them the tools to handle it, regardless of setting. Not all children can go to a Georgian supra or Turkish dinner — but then, not all adults can handle it either.

Not all children, even the children of diplomats or Embassy employees, will need to put on their best manners and participate in a representational event. But if they do, it is a source of great pride and joy when they perform well! Yes, it is a performance; truly the world is a stage and you're showing the rest of the world what little American kids are like, whether it is your intention or not.

One such event was an invitation from a Chinese diplomat for our family to join his family for lunch at a Chinese restaurant. The children were expected to come, the time having been planned specifically to include them. Occasionally the invitation is for family, but you can sort of slide and get around it if you choose. Not this time. So, the children got a bonus day off of school and we put them to work on popsicle stick and construction paper flowers that morning, which they thoroughly enjoyed. Of their own choosing, they decided that they were going to give the host flowers, having seen Husband and I give flowers to the hostesses often enough.

We arrived at the restaurant and immediately were shown to the private dining room. No menus, no English, food just started appearing and dishes and utensils appeared and disappeared like magic. The kids asked to be shown how to use the chopsticks, complete with "please", and sat at the table without fidgeting or fussing. We didn't force any of the dishes on them (all delicious!), and they enjoyed the ones they tried and politely asked for more.

During a lull in the parade of food (did I mention that it was all delicious?), Daughter brings out her bag of craft flowers and Son and Daughter went around handing out flowers to the great appreciation of the hosts, and (believe it or not) entirely unprompted! Dinner continued and we were complimented on our children's manners (positive reinforcement for us).

We'd come prepared with a coloring bag and a few discreet toys for them to play with in the corner or otherwise out of the way, but they weren't initially necessary. However, when the food portion of the meal was done, and the adults began to talk over after-lunch cordial, they asked to be excused, and went to play and color until we departed. And when we left, we left a good impression of an American family. Now, this isn't to say that I wasn't waiting for the other shoe to drop the entire time, thinking, "Aliens have taken over my children, what are they up to?" But no one else needed to know that!

While an event like this isn't always so ... smooth (and we've had our share of early departures, or partial departures where I slink off with the children and leave Husband to smooth it over before the children break something), it is worth mentioning because the key to that whole scene was manners — both table manners, introductions, and in this case, the local good manners of giving your host flowers. The fact that they were handmade just cemented the good impression.

"East Meets West"

21. ... finally ...

I deliberately kept this book for infants and toddlers, through about age five because, well, school overwhelms me. And I've survived those first five years in this odd expatriate existence. I also tried very hard to let you know what went into our choices, particularly the ones we made for our family. I think that little children are probably the smartest, most intuitive and amazing little creatures on the planet and then we send them to school to dumb them down, bring them to our way of thinking, so we can actually cope with them. I don't believe in UNschooling at all. I personally love education and the pursuit of knowledge, but crunching those little minds into preset ideals, someone else's ideals, is painful for me. But I want them to succeed....

I had intended to Home School Son here in Third Post, since I was to work part-time and school is not covered by the State Department until kindergarten. I researched and discovered The Calvert Program and purchased it. Then, to my never-ending relief, an International Preschool opened, using the Calvert Program! This was wonderful for us because Son wanted to be in a different location entirely to learn. He knew I was the Mama and not the Teacher and no amount of costuming or props, locations or tools ,was going to convince him otherwise. We couldn't afford the mainstream preschool and we needed a curriculum that would challenge him to learn and not let him choose how to complete a task. Other mothers, or their children, are very good at making that transition. Not only that, but other mothers will have the patience to home school or supplement the schooling, even pre-schooling, at home, either a little or a lot.

There are pluses and minuses. You've spent three, four or five years teaching a certain set of things and I swear, it feels like they go out there and forget it all the instant they step across that threshold. If you are overseas and sending them to a school that has an English-language curriculum, you are also dealing with the language skills of the teachers and administrators, and that can be frustrating. So many things happen once they are out of your immediate control and I don't know where to start, what to say or even what to think myself yet.

So, I will content myself with hundreds more pages written than I ever anticipated, all covering things that you as an expat American might encounter with your new little baby, while living overseas and ideas on how to adapt to this life in the first five years of theirs. I can even wrap some things up, just to put a little bow on it and call it done.

Consistency

Consistency is key because if you are consistent, whatever you are doing or trying to do, will take eventually. Routines are consistent by nature. They lend a structure to life that gives the child somewhere safe to grow from and something to return to when needed. Little rituals can become fun traditions. Bedtime routines can have variations, making them flexible tools that make travel easier, hotels survivable and families livable. You wouldn't believe how much easier it is to say to family, "Nope, they nap at 1" and how well they go along with it. New homes or countries are just new places to explore; same routine, different setting.

Respect

If you respect their personalities as being theirs, not some wish or dream or hope of yours, and give them choices that you can live with and respecting that choice when they make it, they will learn that they are people who should be respected. And we all know that there is more hoopla about self-esteem than you can shake a stick at. It starts with you and how you treat them and others. Be careful to offer choices that you are okay following through with, because if they choose the hot pink and sherbet orange shirt, even though they are wearing the lime green pants, you did offer the choice. And if you veto the choice, well ... why did you offer it in the first place? They feel empowered without giving them control *per se*. Give them a vote, not the power to rule their world. I know I wouldn't want to give that power up if I had it for a little while!

Patience

Patience is for you; but it is something worth teaching to your children too. Asking them to wait, and then rewarding them when they do it, with a simple hug even, can turn out to be a good thing. Can you say wait and trust that your child will not leap from the edge of the pool into the water until you say so? Patience is not natural to a child. It must be taught. It is also not natural to some of us! And we must practice it as well.

CHOICES

The entire book was about choices. I tried to show choices that we made, and illustrate alternative choices that you can make. Mostly, this book is to offer you, in your unique situation, some resources for making your choices be informed ones. I hope I've pointed you towards the right people to ask. Mostly, I hope I have given you some small bit of confidence in trusting your intuition and instincts, and permission to say (or just think) some things too. I hope that there was one tidbit in here that made you laugh, smile or, better yet, helped you and your family.

Dare to live and dare to know, children are the greatest adventure in both.

EPILOGUE

ALL MY BABIES ARE GONE NOW

By Anna Quindlen, Newsweek Columnist and Author

Reprinted with permission from the author, 7 May 2007

(I asked if I could use the article because it is the perfect thought to leave you with ....)

All my babies are gone now. I say this not in sorrow, but in disbelief. I take great satisfaction in what I have today: three almost-adults, two taller than I am, one closing in fast. Three people who read the same books I do and have learned not to be afraid of disagreeing with me in their opinion of them, who sometimes tell vulgar jokes that make me laugh until I choke and cry, who need razor blades and shower gel and privacy, who want to keep their doors closed more than I like. Who, miraculously, go to the bathroom, zip up their jackets and move food from plate to mouth all by themselves. Like the trick soap I bought for the bathroom with a rubber ducky at its center, the baby is buried deep within each, barely discernible except through the unreliable haze of the past.

Everything in all the books I once pored over is finished for me now. Penelope Leach, T. Berry Brazelton, Dr. Spock. The ones on sibling rivalry and sleeping through the night and early-childhood education – all grown obsolete. Along with *Goodnight Moon* and *Where the Wild Things Are*, they are battered, spotted, well used. But I suspect that if you flipped the pages dust would rise like memories. What those books taught me, finally, and what the women on the playground taught me, and the well-meaning relations -- what they taught me, was that they couldn't really teach me very much at all.

Raising children is presented at first as a true-false test, then becomes multiple choice, until finally, far along, you realize that it is an endless essay. No one knows anything. One child responds well to positive reinforcement, another can be managed only with a stern voice and a timeout. One child is toilet trained at 3, his sibling at 2.

When my first child was born, parents were told to put baby to bed on his belly so that he would not choke on his own spit-up. By the time my last arrived, babies were put down on their backs because of research on sudden infant death syndrome. To a new parent this ever-shifting certainty is terrifying, and then soothing. Eventually you must learn to trust yourself. Eventually the research will follow. I remember 15 years ago poring over one of Dr. Brazelton's wonderful books on child development, in which he describes three different sorts of infants: average, quiet, and active. I was looking for a sub-quiet codicil for an 18-month old who did not walk. Was there something wrong with his fat little legs? Was there something wrong with his tiny little mind? Was he developmentally delayed, physically challenged? Was I insane? Last year he went to China. Next year he goes to college. He can talk just fine. He can walk, too.

Every part of raising children is humbling. Believe me, mistakes were made. They have all been enshrined in the "Remember-When-Mom-Did" Hall of Fame. The outbursts, the temper tantrums, the bad language – mine, not theirs. The times the baby fell off the bed. The times I arrived late for preschool pickup. The nightmare sleepover. The horrible summer camp. The day when the youngest came barreling out of the classroom with a 98 on her geography test, and I responded, "What did you get wrong?" (She insisted I include that here.) The time I ordered food at the McDonald's drive-through speaker and then drove away without picking it up from the window. (They all insisted I include that.) I did not allow them to watch the Simpsons for the first two seasons. What was I thinking?

But the biggest mistake I made is the one that most of us make while doing this. I did not live in the moment enough. This is particularly clear now that the moment is gone, captured only in photographs. There is one picture of the three of them, sitting in the grass on a quilt in the shadow of the swing set on a summer day, ages 6, 4 and 1. And I wish I could remember what we ate, and what we talked about, and how they sounded, and how they looked when they slept that night.

I wish I had not been in such a hurry to get on to the next thing: dinner, bath, book, bed. I wish I had treasured the doing a little more and the getting it done a little less.

Even today I'm not sure what worked and what didn't, what was me and what was simply life. When they were very small, I suppose I thought someday they would become who they were because of what I'd done. Now I suspect they simply grew into their true selves because they demanded in a thousand ways that I back off and let them be. The books said to be relaxed and I was often tense, matter-of-fact and I was sometimes over the top. And look how it all turned out. I wound up with the three people I like best in the world, who have done more than anyone to excavate my essential humanity. That's what the books never told me. I was bound and determined to learn from the experts. It just took me a while to figure out who the experts were.

THE END

(You are now an elephant expert – SSVB!)

∝

APPENDIX 1

DEPARTMENT OF STATE REGULATIONS

I believe that the Comprehensive Guide below is re-published annually with any changes, but your Med Unit can provide the most current. MOST Government agencies have the same or very similar regulations, but it is your responsibility to ensure that you are adhering to the appropriate one.

UNCLASSIFIED STATE 00000002
R 271956Z MAR 07
SUBJECT: UPDATE – A COMPREHENSIVE GUIDE ON PREGNANCY AND RELATED ISSUES

1. SUMMARY: For families assigned abroad, pregnancy and childbirth are reasons for both joy and confusion. To help our Foreign Service employees and family members who have questions about leave, medical evacuation to the U.S. and to locations abroad, and other pregnancy-related issues, the Bureau of Human Resources has updated its comprehensive guide, last issued in July, 2005. END

SUMMARY
2. We ask that management and human resources officers distribute this guide widely among their missions and keep a copy on file at post. References to the Foreign Affairs Manual are included so that management and human resources officers and employees may access complete details of regulations. Employees interested in adoption should consult the Foreign Affairs Handbook, 3 FAH-1 H-3423, regarding the use of sick leave for adoption, and the Intercountry Adoption Guidelines for the Foreign Service Family found on the website for the Bureau of Human Resources, Family Liaison Office.

Subjects Included:
Item 3   Coverage
Item 4   Non-Coverage
Item 5   Prohibition Against Pregnancy Discrimination
Item 6   Leave Options
Item 7   Medical Travel
Item 8   Travel Reservations
Item 9   Per Diem
Item 10 Layette Shipment/UAB Shipment
Item 11 Information/Documents To Take With You
Item 12 M/MED Contact
Item 13 Health Insurance
Item 14 Working in the Department Before/After Baby is Born
Item 15 Child Care for Siblings
Item 16 Birth Certificate
Item 17 Adding the New Baby as a Dependent
Item 18 Passport
Item 19 Medical Clearances
Item 20 Medical Records
Item 21 Return Travel
Item 22 Travel Vouchers

3.   Coverage: This guidance applies to all American Citizen Department of State Foreign Service employees, Eligible Family Members (EFM), and other agency employees who are covered under the Department of State's Medical Program (reference 16 FAM 110).

4.   Non-Coverage: This guidance does not apply to Foreign Service National employees (FSNs) (ref. 5 USC 6301) and other locally employed staff (LE Staff) including Rockefeller hires, Personal Services Contract/Agreement personnel (PSC) (3 FAM 8100 Appendix A section 171.1), non-FMA employees on Temporary Appointments (Note: FMA employees on intermittent non-work schedules (INWS) are eligible for applicable benefits as an EFM only), or any other individuals not participating in the Department of State's Medical Program.

5.   Prohibition Against Pregnancy Discrimination: The
Pregnancy Discrimination Act is an amendment to Title VII of the Civil Rights Act of 1964. Discrimination on the basis of pregnancy, childbirth or related medical conditions constitutes unlawful sex discrimination under Title VII. Women affected by pregnancy or related conditions must be treated in the same manner as other applicants or employees with similar disabilities or limitations. See http://www.eeoc.gov/facts/fs-preg.html http://www.eeoc.gov/facts/fs-preg.htmlFor>

For more details.

6.   Leave Options: For leave purposes, the definition of a serious health condition includes pregnancy, childbirth, and recuperation from childbirth (5 CFR 630.201). Birth mothers and fathers may use leave as described below.

Appropriate medical documentation determines the amount of sick leave that can be used by both birth mother and father and is required except when an employee is on home leave, annual leave, or staying home with a well baby. A medical certificate is a written statement signed by a registered practicing physician or other practitioner, certifying the incapacitation, examination or treatment, or to the period of disability while the patient was receiving professional treatment. For family care, employees may provide a written statement from the health care provider concerning the family member's need for psychological comfort and/or physical care. Home leave may be used only if home leave orders coincide with the birth and recuperation, and it may not be used when invoking the Family and Medical Leave Act.

For additional information, refer to 3 FAM 3530 and 3 FAH-1 H-3530 on the Family and Medical Leave Act (FMLA), 3 FAM 3420 and 3 FAH-1 H-3420 on sick leave, 3 FAM 3410 and 3 FAH-1 3410 on annual leave, 3 FAM 3340 on the Voluntary Leave Transfer Program, and 3 FAM 3510 and 3 FAH-1 H-3510 on leave without pay. The Office of Personnel Management (OPM) regulations implementing the FMLA for Federal government employees can be found in 5 C.F.R.   Part   630   and   online   at   http://www.opm.gov/oca/leave/HTML/fmlafac2.asp

Leave Used by the Birth Mother

-Accrued Sick Leave - Employee is entitled to use accrued sick leave for the period of incapacitation for pregnancy, childbirth, and recuperation from childbirth.

–Advance Sick Leave - When there is insufficient accrued sick leave, up to 240 hours of advance sick leave may be requested.

–Accrued Annual Leave - May be requested, but approval is at the discretion of the leave approving official unless the employee is invoking FMLA.

–Advance Annual Leave - May be requested and approved at discretion of the supervisor for an amount that does not exceed the number of hours the employee would earn through the end of the current leave year.

–Leave Without Pay - Employee is entitled to LWOP for

period of incapacitation and/or for bonding with baby when invoking the FMLA.

–Voluntary Leave Transfer Program - May be requested for the birth mother's period of medical incapacitation if all annual and sick leave have been exhausted. Medical documentation determines duration in program.

Family and Medical Leave Act - The FMLA, and OPM's implementing regulations pertaining to federal employees, entitle employees up to a maximum of 12 weeks of unpaid absence in a 12-month period for the following purposes:

(1) the birth of a son or daughter of the employee and the care of such son or daughter (bonding with the baby); (2) the placement of a son or daughter with the employee for adoption or foster care; (3) the care of a spouse, son, daughter, or parent of the employee who has a serious health condition; or (4) a serious health condition of the employee that makes the employee unable to perform the essential functions of his or her position. Supervisors should ensure that expectant parents are fully aware of their rights and responsibilities under the FMLA.

Employees (both full-time and part-time) with 12 months of government service are eligible to invoke the FMLA. Annual leave may be substituted for LWOP. FMLA does not have to be invoked until entitlement to applicable accrued sick leave has been exhausted. Advance notice of 30 days must be given when possible, and if FMLA is invoked because of a serious health condition, appropriate medical certification must be submitted.

Under FMLA, if appropriate medical certification demonstrates that the employee or an immediate family member has a serious health condition requiring the employee to take intermittent leave or LWOP, the> intermittent time off must be granted. If the employee would prefer to take intermittent leave or LWOP to bond with the baby, the request may be granted at the discretion of the supervisor. If granted, the employee can be temporarily placed in an available alternative position for which the employee is qualified and that can better accommodate recurring periods of time off, as long as the employee is eventually returned to his or her position or an equivalent position.

The FMLA may be invoked to bond with the baby at any time during the 12-month period following the baby's birth. Leave or LWOP must be concluded one year from the birth of the baby. Sick leave may not be substituted for LWOP to bond with a well baby.

Leave Used by the Father

–Accrued Sick Leave - Employee is entitled to use up to 104 hours per leave year to accompany the birth mother to doctor's appointments and to provide general family care, and up to 480 hours during her period of incapacitation for pregnancy, childbirth, and recuperation from childbirth. Sick leave used to care for a family member for general family care and for a serious health condition may not exceed a total of 480 hours per leave year.

–Advance Sick Leave - When there is insufficient accrued sick leave, employee may request an advance of up to 104 hours to accompany the birth mother to medical appointments and to provide general family care, and up to 240 hours when required for the birth mother's incapacitation due to pregnancy, childbirth, and recuperation from childbirth. Advance sick leave for all purposes related to the pregnancy/childbirth may not exceed 240 hours.

–Annual Leave - May be used to care for the birth mother during her incapacitation, but approval is at the discretion of the supervisor unless the FMLA is invoked.

–Advance Annual Leave - May be requested and approved at the discretion of the supervisor for a period of hours not to exceed the number of hours to be earned by the employee through the end of the current leave year.

–Leave Without Pay - Employee is entitled to up to 12 weeks of LWOP to care for the birth mother during her incapacitation or for the new baby with a medical condition, and/or to bond with the baby, if the FMLA is invoked.

–Voluntary Leave Transfer Program - May be requested for the period of the birth mother's incapacitation if the father has exhausted all annual leave and all accrued sick leave permitted when caring for a family member. Medical documentation determines duration in the program.

Family Medical Leave Act - For eligibility, see Leave Used by the Birth Mother. The Act entitles employees up to a maximum of 12 weeks of unpaid absence under the FMLA to care for the birth mother during her period of incapacitation (duration determined by medical documentation), to care for a new baby with a medical condition, and/or to bond with the baby. Annual leave may be substituted for LWOP, but sick leave may not be substituted for LWOP to bond with a well baby. FMLA may be invoked to bond with the baby at any time in the 12- month period following the baby's birth, but the employee's absence must be completed no later than one-year from the date of the birth of the baby. Thirty days notice must be given whenever possible when invoking the FMLA. FMLA does not have to be invoked until the employee exhausts his entitlement to use his accrued sick leave to care for the birth mother.

The mother and father may use accrued sick leave to care for a baby with a medical condition and for any doctor's appointments, subject to the limits on use of accrued sick leave to care for a family member.

Leave Without Pay - An approving official at post may approve LWOP not exceeding 90 calendar days. Requests for LWOP of more than 90 calendar days must be submitted to the employee's Career Development Officer in HR/CDA for approval. For all LWOP requests in excess of 80 hours, Form SF-50, "Notice of

Personnel Action" must be completed.

Employees who take LWOP for more than 14 days at one time (whether at post or away from post) will not receive any allowances while they are in LWOP status. Post Differential and Danger Pay are suspended the day the employee enters a non-pay status regardless of the length of the LWOP.

(Note: The following paragraphs (7-22) apply to employees and EFMs covered by the Department of State Medical Program. Employees of other agencies, and their EFMs, must also check with their agencies for assistance with infant passports, health insurance, travel orders, travel vouchers, and return travel.) Please consult checklist at post before departure for delivery in the United States.

7. Medical Travel
A. To the United States
The Office of Medical Services (MED) recommends a pregnant employee or EFM member return to the United States for delivery. Medical travel will be authorized, unless such travel is superseded by other U.S. Government-funded travel, such as Home Leave or Permanent Change of Station (PCS).

Medical travel funding for expectant mothers will be authorized to any location in the continental United States, Alaska or Hawaii rather than just to the first point of entry into the U.S. (Reference 3 FAM 3715.2-2).

Per diem funding will be at the rate of the specified U.S. location. The patient should depart from post no later than six weeks prior to the expected date of delivery and is expected to return to post six weeks after delivery, if it is medically appropriate for her to travel at that time.

Post should alert the Regional Medical Officer (RMO) or the Foreign Service Health Practitioner (FSHP) of the planned medical evacuation. Post is required to send a telegram to M/MED/FP requesting authorization for the medical evacuation (MEDEVAC). M/MED will reply with:

1) a MED CHANNEL telegram authorizing the MEDEVAC; and 2) an OPEN CHANNEL telegram providing a fund cite for medical travel for STATE employees or their family members (other agency employees must request fiscal data from their sponsoring agency).

MEDEVAC authorization telegrams contain other important instructions on administrative matters such as a letter of authorization for hospitalization (Form DS-3067) issued by M/MED, medical insurance, processing and reimbursement of medical claims, and medical clearances for the mother and newborn (ref 3 FAM 3713.5-3). Employees are urged to review these cables carefully and to seek clarification promptly of any questions.

B. Travel and Per Diem to a Location Abroad Away from Post
If the expectant mother elects to deliver abroad and away from post, travel will be cost constructed based on travel costs to Washington, D.C. This means, transportation costs and per diem are paid at either Washington, D.C. based rates or those of the chosen MEDEVAC locality, whichever cost is lower. MED will authorize a MEDEVAC abroad only from a post with inadequate obstetrical and neonatal care to a location with suitable and adequate obstetrical and

neonatal care. This suitability determination will be made by MED/Foreign Programs. Women planning an obstetrical MEDEVAC abroad are advised to contact MED/Foreign Programs through their Health Unit early in their pregnancy to determine suitability/adequacy of obstetrical and neonatal care at the proposed MEDEVAC location.

The expectant mother must have a local physician willing to assume her prenatal and obstetrical care upon arrival at the MEDEVAC location abroad, as well as a local pediatrician to provide newborn care.

Travel back to post will be authorized for the mother and the infant only after a medical approval has been issued for each of them by M/MED/FP.

C. Travel From U.S. to an Assignment Abroad
A woman who is in the United States for training, home leave, or pending U.S.-to-post transfer, and who is at 28 weeks or greater gestation will not be cleared to go abroad until 4-6 weeks after delivery. MED may pay per diem, based on the given circumstances, for the woman to stay in the U.S. to deliver if she is on post-to-post orders, but is prevented from transferring due to this 28-week rule. Per diem cannot be approved for a pregnant woman or newborn transferring from a U.S. assignment to an assignment abroad, even if the departure is delayed due to this 28 week rule. An employee may receive Separate Maintenance Allowance (SMA) payments on behalf of his pregnant EFM spouse and any children who remain in the U.S. with the spouse provided that it reasonably appears that the employee and family members will be separated for at least 30 consecutive calendar days. Employees may apply for SMA benefits using form SF-1190 (Foreign Allowances Application, Grant and Report) and are urged to apply before the separation so that benefits may commence as soon as the employee and eligible family members are separated. (See Department of State Standardized Regulations, Section 262 and 263 for more details.)

Depending on the circumstances, a decision to place the EFM spouse and any family members on voluntary SMA and not on the employee's travel orders constitutes the initial election under DSSR 264.2(2). (See DSSR 262.4(a))

8. Travel Reservations
Travel cannot commence until MEDEVAC and fund cite telegrams have been issued, but reservations can be made beforehand. The ticket must be issued with an open return. The policies of American carriers require that the pregnant employee or covered eligible family member depart post not later than six weeks prior to the expected delivery date. Medical considerations, however, may dictate an earlier departure from post.

9. Per Diem
A. The Department's Office of Medical Services authorizes up to 90 days total of per diem for the combined period before and after delivery, usually six weeks each, to a pregnant employee or eligible family member MEDEVACED to the United States or elsewhere. Periods of hospitalization are not covered by per diem. Generally, per diem is not extended beyond six weeks after delivery. Per diem in excess of 90 days, but not to exceed 180 days, may be authorized by the Medical Director or designee or the Foreign Service medical provider when there is a clear medical complication necessitating early departure from post

or delayed return to post. Per diem for newborns is authorized at one-half of the applicable local rate, excluding periods of hospitalization.

B. To the greatest extent possible, obstetrical travel should be scheduled to coincide with other non-medical travel, such as home leave or transfer orders, to avoid the necessity of additional medical travel expense. No per diem may be granted while on home leave. Minimum home leave, when transferring to another assignment abroad, is 20 workdays and maximum is 45 workdays (Reference 3 FAM 3430) for employees and their eligible family members. When transferring to a domestic assignment, the maximum number of home leave days authorized is 25 workdays (3 FAM 3435.1).

C. Per diem will not be extended for delays in obtaining a passport for the newborn.

Note: HR/CDA/AD technicians mentioned in the following paragraphs are located in Room 4250, SA-3, phone: 202-663-0405, fax: 202-663-0449.)

10. Layette Shipment/UAB Shipment
If the employee is at post, a layette shipment is permitted when suitable layettes are not available at post. A layette shipment is a separate airfreight allowance not to exceed 250 pounds gross weight for a newborn child or an adopted child less than five years of age who is an eligible family member. Once post has determined and certified that suitable layettes are not available locally (14 FAM 613.5), post must submit a cable to employee's HR technician (HR/CDA/AD) requesting that the employee's original travel orders be amended to authorize a layette shipment. This telegram must include post certification of unavailability. After the orders are amended, the employee must contact the Office of Transportation and Travel Management Division (A/LM/OPS/TTM) in the Department to make arrangements for onward shipment (Phone: 202-647-4140/4141 or from outside the Washington, D.C. area, toll free 800-424-2947; fax: 202-647-4956; e-mail TransportationQuery@state.gov). The employee or eligible family member will arrange for a family member/friend/store in the U.S. to obtain a layette if s/he has not already done so before going to post. The family member/friend/store may also coordinate with A/LM/OPS/TTM for shipping. Air shipment of the layette may commence up to 120 days prior to an expected birth, and must commence no later than 60 days after the birth of the child.

If the employee has not yet arrived at post, the travel authorization will be amended to add the newborn child as an additional EFM, and to add the appropriate unaccompanied air baggage (UAB) shipping weight entitlement, usually 100 or 150 pounds depending on the total number of EFMs included on the travel authorization.

11. Information/Documents to Take With You
The MEDEVACed employee or EFM should carry the name and telephone number of employee's HR/CDA/AD technician and take with her a blank FORM OF-126 ("Foreign Service Residence and Dependency Report") and a blank diplomatic or regular passport application. She should also take medical records pertaining to the pregnancy, in English, including test results and prenatal care; and insurance information for the attending doctor's office in the United States. MED/Foreign Programs will provide a Form DS-1622 ("Medical History

and Examination for Foreign Service") for children 11 years and under before the employee/family member is medically evacuated. Read instructions carefully and provide any information requested in MED channel telegrams. Issues to address while in the United States:

12. M/MED Contact
Upon arrival in U.S., the employee mother or EFM must call M/MED Foreign Programs office located in State Annex 1, 2401 E. Street, NW, Room L-209, phone: 202-663-1662. This is necessary for arrival notification and administrative assistance.

13. Health Insurance
The Federal Employees Health Benefits program requires that all in-patient confinements must undergo pre- certification in the United States. Therefore, the employee mother or EFM or doctor must call her insurance company prior to admission to the hospital to give birth (or within two working days in the event of an emergency hospitalization) to receive full insurance benefits. To ensure maximum insurance coverage, employee mother or EFM should choose a preferred provider within the scope of her private health insurance. M/MED pays the deductible and co-insurance for covered pregnancies when a "Letter of Authorization" (Form DS-3067) is issued by Med/Foreign Programs after initial contact with Foreign Programs upon arrival in the U.S. on MEDEVAC. An employee serving under an FMA or Temporary appointment on intermittent non-work schedules (INWS) or LWOP status should review her medical coverage if she has elected self-coverage.

An employee on LWOP may make arrangements with her/his human resources office at post or in the appropriate bureau Executive Office to repay health insurance premiums when s/he returns to duty. It is the employee's responsibility to make sure that the baby is added to his/her health insurance policy. If the parents are both U.S. federal government employees who each have self-only coverage, two SF-2809s must be completed to terminate one self-only plan and change the other to family coverage. Questions regarding this or other health insurance issues on the addition of a child should be faxed to HR/ER/WLP, 202-261-8182 or an e-mail message sent to Shelly V. Kornegay.

14. Working in the Department Before/After the Baby is Born (State employees only)
An expectant mother who has her baby in the United States generally spends at least six weeks in the U.S. prior to the delivery of her baby, and 45 days after delivery. If she travels to the Washington D.C. area and desires to work at the Department during this time, a short-term detail in the employing bureau or in another bureau may be possible through the employing bureau's Executive Director and Human Resources officer. If the pregnant employee works a short-term detail in the Department, she will be considered on work status without charge to leave, and M/MED will continue to authorize per diem.

15. Child Care for Siblings
An employee in the U.S. for childbirth may be eligible for assistance with the cost of care of eligible children who accompanied employee from post through the Department's Child Care Subsidy Program. Family income must qualify and care must be provided at licensed facilities. Program requirements are found at http://hrweb.hr.state.gov/prd/hrweb/er/worklife/DependentC

http://hrweb.hr.state.gov/prd/hrweb/er/worklife/DependentCare/Childcare/c
hild_care.html16>
are/Childcare/child_care.html

16. Birth Certificate
The first step in getting the baby back to post is obtaining the birth certificate.
Hospitals typically start the paperwork. The process can sometimes be expedited
if the employee/EFM explains the special circumstances (i.e., the baby cannot
travel to post without a passport, which can only be issued with a birth
certificate). It is advisable to obtain two certified copies of the birth certificate,
one to be used for passport processing.

In the case of a child born overseas, the parents should apply at the ACS Unit
in the country where the baby was born for a "Consular Report of Birth Abroad,"
which is the record of the birth abroad of a U.S. citizen. Under U.S. law, the
document is full proof of U.S. citizenship and although not a birth certificate,
may serve as a birth certificate in the U.S. Both parents should also
simultaneously apply for a regular passport, to be issued immediately at post,
and a diplomatic (dip) passport to be issued by the Special Issuance Agency in
Washington, D.C. The processing time for the dip passport is not long, and is
usually expedited for overseas applications, especially in urgent situations. The
ACS unit should mail the application for the diplomatic passport to the Passport
Special Issuance Agency by overnight courier, and the passport will be returned
in the same manner.

17. Adding the New Baby as a Dependent
The new baby must be listed as a dependent in the Family Management System.
Send a copy of the birth certificate and completed, signed OF-126 "Foreign
Service Residence and Dependency Report" to the employee's (HR/CDA/AD)
technician. The technician will enter the baby into the employee's records. The
baby cannot be formally added to the employee's orders until medically cleared
(see Medical Clearances below). M/MED cannot medically clear the baby until
the baby is entered into the system. M/MED will> notify HR/CDA/AD that the
infant is medically cleared for travel, and the technician will amend the
employee's orders to include the newborn (does not apply to infants born at
post). A copy of the orders will then be forwarded to the Travel Management
Center.

18. Passport
The baby must have a passport (preferably diplomatic), and in many cases, a
visa as well, to travel to post. The baby cannot travel on the parent's passport.
Application for the passport will require the personal appearance of both
parents and the infant before an authorized acceptance agent in the country
where the newborn is located. If both parents cannot be present, the reason
must be explained in a notarized statement from the absent parent, who also
gives consent to issuance of the infant's passport.

For employees or eligible family members in the Washington, D.C. area, the
employee's HR/CDA/AD technician prepares form DS-1640 ("Request for
Passport Services") authorizing issuance of a no-fee Diplomatic Passport for
the baby and forwards it to Passport Services, Special Issuance Agency (202-
955-0198). There is also a passport desk located in the Employee Services
Center (Room 1252, hours: 9:00 a.m. to 2:45 p.m.).

For employees or eligible family members outside of the D.C. area, there are two options:

A. a regular passport may be issued in approximately six weeks at any regional passport office for $82 which includes a $52 passport fee and a $30 execution fee. Urgent cases can be processed quickly, but require payment of an additional $60 fee to expedite; or

B. a diplomatic passport may be obtained quickly at no cost, but additional time may be needed to allow for visa processing. For information regarding diplomatic passport issuance and visa requirements, please contact passport services at 202-955-0198 or e-mail them at diplomatictravel@state.gov prior to the baby's birth.

When the baby is born and has been added to the employee's orders, the HR/CDA/AD technician can fax or mail to the mother a completed Form DS-1640 authorizing issuance of a no-fee diplomatic passport for the child. Present the DS-1640 and a completed passport application including photos, at either a regional passport office or an authorized U.S. passport acceptance agency, such as a local post office or clerk of court (for help locating the nearest acceptance facility see http://travel.state.gov/.

Provide the acceptance agent with a stamped express mail envelope addressed to Passport Services, Special Issuance Agency, 1111 19th St., N.W. Suite 200, Washington, D.C. 20036, Attn: Diplomatic Travel Branch. See paragraph 16 above regarding passport applications for children born abroad.

19. Medical Clearances
MED provides medical clearance services for all agencies that participate in the Department of State's Medical Program. A medical clearance may be granted after the mother's obstetrician and baby's pediatrician provide M/MED/FP (Foreign Programs (202) 663-1662) with necessary medical information to accomplish the clearance action. The pediatrician must complete Form DS-1622 (Medical History and Examination for Foreign Service for Children Under 11 years). This must be done when the baby is a minimum of four weeks of age, but within 90 days of birth. The completed form must be forwarded to M/MED/FP by fax to 202-663-3247, if on MEDEVAC. If not on MEDEVAC, the form must be forwarded to M/MED/MR. To enroll a new baby as an eligible family member in the Department of State Medical Program, an OF-126 (Foreign Service Residence and Dependency Report) must be submitted to the HR/CDA/AD Technician. All other agencies must send a Memorandum of Eligibility to M/MED/MR.

20. Medical Records
Employees/eligible family members are reminded to hand-carry or fax pertinent medical records to the responsible physician at post for appropriate follow-up.

21. Return Travel
The newborn requires an airline ticket to return to post. Employee or EFM may call the Travel Management Center (TMC) (1-866-654-5593) at HST for reservations for mother and baby or visit the TMC, Room 1243, HST. Remember that travel to post may take place only after medical clearances have been issued (MEDEVACed mothers and their infants are cleared by M/MED/FP) and after the HR/CDA/AD technician has provided the Travel Management

Center with a copy of the amended travel orders. Depending on circumstances, the TMC may either mail the baby's ticket or provide a prepaid ticket at the airport on the day of travel.

22. Travel Vouchers

Employees are responsible for keeping track of travel voucher expenses. Vouchers must be completed by Department of State employees and submitted within seven workdays following completion of travel as required by 4 FAH-3 H4651.1-1a.

Within ten workdays following receipt of the completed travel voucher, post is requested to report to M/MED/EX the dollar amount of transportation, per diem, taxi, and miscellaneous expenses claimed on the voucher.

APPENDIX 2

POWER OF ATTORNEY – IN LOCO PARENTIS, ACTING AS PARENT.
To be used for instance, if the children are not under parental control, such as when a grandparent has them for the summer or, when one parent has to emergently depart and the other is not present and a third party, trusted co-worker, etc. needs this in case the children need medical care.

Example POWER OF ATTORNEY "in loco parentis"

KNOW ALL PERSONS BY THESE PRESENTS:
That we, _____, Social security number: _____ and _____, Social security number: _____, of the state of _____, a member of the Foreign Service of the United States of America currently residing in _____ serving at the Embassy of the United States, do hereby appoint _____, Social security   number   _____,   presently   residing   at _____ as our true and lawful attorney-in-fact to do the following acts *in loco parentis*, to assume and maintain guardianship of our child(ren),
_____ Social security number _____
_____ Social security number _____; to do all acts necessary or desirable for maintaining health, education and welfare; and to maintain customary living standards, including but not limited to the provision of living quarters, food, clothing, medical, surgical and dental care, entertainment and other customary matters; and specifically to approve and authorize:
1. Any and all medical treatment deemed necessary by a duly licensed physician;
2. to execute any consent, release or waiver of liability required by medical or dental authorities incident to the provision of medical, surgical or dental care to any of them by qualified medical or dental personnel.
3. travel to the United States and/or back to our residence of _____; to include any domestic or international travel.

We hereby give and grant individually to our said attorney full power and authority to do and perform all and any act, deed, matter and thing whatsoever in and about any of the aforementioned specified particulars as fully and effectually to all intents and purposes as we might and could do in my own persons if personally present; and in addition thereto. We do hereby ratify and confirm each of the acts of my aforementioned attorneys lawfully done pursuant to the authority herein above conferred.

WE HEREBY AUTHORIZE OUR ATTORNEY TO INDEMNIFY AND HOLD HARMLESS ANY THIRD PARTY WHO AACCEPTS AND ACTS UNDER OR IN ACCORDANCE WITH THIS POWER OF ATTORNEY.

We intend for this to be a LIMITED Power of Attorney. This Power of Attorney will continue to be effective if one or both become disabled, incapacitated or incompetent. This Power of Attorney is effective on the ___ day in the month of _____, 20___ and will remain in effect for a period of ____ months. This Power of Attorney will expire on the ___ day of _____, 20___.
We authorize by attorney-in-fact to hire legal counsel in order to carry out the provisions of this document or determine the existence of legal requirements, such as required filing or placement of notices, which may affect the validity of this document.

WE HEREBY RATIFY ALL THAT OUR ATTORNEY SHALL LAWFULLY DO OR CAUSE TO BE DONE BY THIS DOCUMENT.

This Power of Attorney shall become effective when we sign and execute it below. Further, unless sooner revoked or terminated by us, this Power of Attorney shall become NULL and VOID on the _____ day of _____, 20___.

Notwithstanding our inclusion of a specific expiration date herein, if on the above-mentioned expiration date or during the sixty (60) day preceding that specified expiration date, one or both should be or have been determined by the United States Government to be in a status of "missing", "missing in action" or "prisoner of war", then this Power of Attorney shall remain valid and in full effect until sixty (60) days after we have returned to the United States control following termination of such status UNLESS OTHERWISE REVOKED OR TERMINATED BY US.

IN WITNESS WHEREOF, we sign, seal, declare, publish, make and constitute this as and for our Power of Attorney in the presence of the Notary Public witnessing it at my request this date _____. State of _____, County of _____.

I, the undersigned, certify that I am a fully commissioned, qualified and authorized notary public. Before me personally, within the territorial limits of my warrant of authority, appeared _____ and _____ who are known to me by the people who are described herein, whose names are subscribed to, and who signed the Power of Attorney as grantors and who, having been duly sworn, acknowledged that this instrument was executed after its contents were read and duly explained, and that such execution was a free and voluntary act and deed for the uses and purposes herein set forth.

IN WITHNESS WHEREOF, I have hereunto set my hand and affix my seal this _____ day of _____, 20____.

_____
Grantor's Signature

_____
Grantor's Printed Name

IN WITHNESS WHEREOF, I have hereunto set my hand and affix my seal this _____ day of _____, 20____.

_____
Grantor's Signature

_____
Grantor's Printed Name

ACKNOWLEDGEMENT

STATE OF
COUNTY OF

Acknowledged before me this _____ day of _____, 20___

_____
(Notary Public)
My Commission expires

POWER OF ATTORNEY – ONE PARENT TO THE OTHER.

To be used for instance, if one parent is traveling without the second present (note clause 3), or if one parent is on long-term TDY.

Example POWER OF ATTORNEY "one parent to another"

KNOW ALL PERSONS BY THESE PRESENTS:

That , _____, Social security number: _____, of the state of _____, a member of the Foreign Service of the United States of America currently residing in _____ serving at the Embassy of the United States, do hereby appoint _____, Social security number _____, presently residing at _____ as my true and lawful attorney-in-fact to do the following acts to assume and maintain guardianship of my child(ren),

_____ Social security number_____; to do all acts necessary or desirable for maintaining health, education and welfare; and to maintain customary living standards, including but not limited to the provision of living quarters, food, clothing, medical, surgical and dental care, entertainment and other customary matters; and specifically to approve and authorize:

1. Any and all medical treatment deemed necessary by a duly licensed physician;
2. to execute any consent, release or waiver of liability required by medical or dental authorities incident to the provision of medical, surgical or dental care to any of them by qualified medical or dental personnel.
3. travel to the United States and/or back to our residence of _____; or any other travel, international and/or domestic, be it recreational or otherwise..

I hereby give and grant individually to my said attorney full power and authority to do and perform all and any act, deed, matter and thing whatsoever in and about any of the aforementioned specified particulars as fully and effectually to all intents and purposes as I might and could do in my own persons if personally present; and in addition thereto. I do hereby ratify and confirm each of the acts of my aforementioned attorneys lawfully done pursuant to the authority herein above conferred.

I HEREBY AUTHORIZE MY ATTORNEY TO INDEMNIFY AND HOLD HARMLESS ANY THIRD PARTY WHO ACCEPTS AND ACTS UNDER OR IN ACCORDANCE WITH THIS POWER OF ATTORNEY.

I intend for this to be a DURABLE Power of Attorney. This Power of Attorney will continue to be effective if I become disabled, incapacitated or incompetent.

I authorize by attorney-in-fact to hire legal counsel in order to carry out the provisions of this document or determine the existence of legal requirements, such as required filing or placement of notices, which may affect the validity of this document.

I HEREBY RATIFY ALL THAT MY ATTORNEY SHALL LAWFULLY DO OR CAUSE TO BE DONE BY THIS DOCUMENT.

This Power of Attorney shall become effective when I sign and execute it below. Further, unless sooner revoked or terminated by us, this Power of Attorney shall become NULL and VOID on the _____ day of _____, 20___.

Notwithstanding our inclusion of a specific expiration date herein, if on the above-mentioned expiration date or during the sixty (60) day preceding that specified expiration date, we should be or have been determined by the United States Government to be in a status of "missing", "missing in action" or "prisoner of war", then this Power of Attorney shall remain valid and in full effect until sixty (60) days after we have returned to the United States control following termination of such status UNLESS OTHERWISE REVOKED OR TERMINATED BY US.

IN WITNESS WHEREOF, I sign, seal, declare, publish, make and constitute this as and for our Power of Attorney in the presence of the Notary Public witnessing it at my request this date _____. State of _____, County of _____.

I, the undersigned, certify that I am a fully commissioned, qualified and authorized notary public. Before me personally, within the territorial limits of my warrant of authority, appeared _____ and _____ who are known to me by the people who are described herein, whose names are subscribed to, and who signed the Power of Attorney as grantors and who, having been duly sworn, acknowledged that this instrument was executed after its contents were read and duly explained, and that such execution was a free and voluntary act and deed for the uses and purposes herein set forth.

IN WITHNESS WHEREOF, I have hereunto set my hand and affix my seal this _____ day of _____, 20___.

_____
Grantor's Signature

_____
Grantor's Printed Name

ACKNOWLEDGEMENT

STATE OF

COUNTY OF

Acknowledged before me this _____ day of _____, 20___

_____

(Notary Public)

My Commission expires:

APPENDIX 3

Regarding parenting books, the most important tidbit I have is to read them while you're pregnant. This is the only chance you have because as a parent, you run out of time astonishingly fast. I read a lot less then I did pre-parent, but don't fall for the line that you won't get to read for years. The childcare books we have in our library, for references, (*and a few to have on hand, just in case). Since they are alphabetical by author, I put a (1) numbering system for my personal order of importance:

American Academy of Pediatrics (6)
The Complete and Authoritative Guide: Caring for Your Baby and Young Child
> A mouthful but a good reference, better I think than the Mayo clinic of the same. You do not need both. But do pick one for the 'official' party like from the pediatrics. This is very information dense, but well laid out and not alarmist.

Robert A. Bradley
Husband Coached Childbirth
> We thought this was great for historical context and basic information on how this method came to be. But never EVER forget (how could you with this book!?), that they have an agenda. This is the background, history and basic method for "natural" childbirth.

T. Berry Brazelton
Touchpoints
Touchpoints 3-6
> A very nice reference for where your child is developmentally and how to assess it. As an animal behaviorist, I liked these books for their information content and some very useful perspective, which sometimes can be severely lacking.

Carol Cooper
DK: The Baby and Child Question and Answer Book
Quick reference. Fast and easy.

Glade B. Curtis (1)
Your Pregnancy Week by Week
A no-nonsense informational and timely (what you need to know when) book that doesn't scare you if you read ahead (because we all want to know, ahead!). As an aside, I don't like the 'What to Expect' series, because to me it seems to borrow trouble and speak down to the mothers, but lots of people do. We're all worried for goodness' sake, we don't need MORE to worry about. Check them both out, and others, and go with what feels right for you.

Adele Faber & Elaine Mazlish (7)
How to Talk So Kids Will Listen & Listen So Kids Will Talk
These are slightly outdated books with timeless information. The chapter summary on one page for easy reference is very helpful.
Siblings without Rivalry
This is the second of the two Faber books that we found useful. There are these simple picture pages that sum things up wonderfully.

By the way, both these books are based on a fabulous book called *Between Parent and Child*, by Hiam G. Ginott, about communication that I was just given. All three are great — the two above for some basics and sort of tailored approach, but the original cannot be beat.

Tracey Hogg (3)
Secrets of a Baby Whisperer
This is our A#1 recommendation to new or expecting parents. We give this one away constantly to expectant friends — because it is middle of the road. Don't bother with her third book, the 'answers to all your questions' one, since no one can answer all your questions, and it is a knock-off compilation of the first two books. Now, I have given away the third book to expectant mothers, particularly ones I do not know well, with the recommendation that if parts interest them, to get the other two.
Secrets of the Baby Whisperer for Toddlers
And was I ever thankful for the timing of THIS one, when my son was two and daughter was being born. Ditto the always giving it away; usually as a

set now. I will swear that my children are (mostly)(generally) so well adapted because of these two books.

Mel Levine
A Mind at a Time

Information more than anything else – learning styles, how to work with your child's particular ones (young too!) and how to make up for short-falls. From this, I did learn that there are different methods that are appropriate for children and how to identify them in order to choose the right school for my children. I also learned how to defend my decision NOT to send them to the school that everyone else was sending their children! Who knew that I would need to know that!

Susan McCutcheon (2)
Natural Childbirth the Bradley Way

THIS is the how-to manual. Graphic, with pictures that are rather dated, and examples, but this was good for Husband and I who did not have a class, but had this book. And if Son had cooperated, it would have worked well! There are exercises, lessons and practice in an easy to follow format for both parents' participation.

Judith Martin (5)
Miss Manners Guide to Rearing Perfect Children

I actually prefer this book to the Post book. It is certainly more readable than Ms. Post's, but it is not as serious, so you have read more critically. Only give it a read if you like tongue in cheek dry humor. Ok, it's stinking hilarious. The subtitle says it all, "A primer for everyone worried about the future of civilization." The info is good, but in a dry, witty sort of way. Read it with a grain of salt, she is NOT exactly serious, but she is helpful.

Peggy Post (4)
The Gift of Good Manners

You think I'm kidding, don't you? I am so not kidding. Really really really. This will hold you in good stead for AGES – and all I have to say to mine now is "Manners" and it covers so much! This is useful, informative, and helpful. It explains WHY we should emphasize manners, not just what to do to get them. My favorite tip, for my cautious, sensitive son (who would be called shy by folks who didn't know he was assessing the situation rather than concerned by it), is to teach them that manners are a shield – if someone asks, "How are you?" you can answer, "Fine, thank you. And how are you?" and then they talk, instead of you! While it is still taking some practice, we have a tool for him to cope with new people and situations. It isn't just because it is polite.

Miriam Stoppard
DK: Complete Baby and Childcare
Lovely details, great tips and set up of the book, good case studies, but oh-so politically correct.
DK: Pregnancy and Birth Handbook
Again with the great set up and easy access. This is a very nice supplement to the week-by-week book, and has a lot of easy to read, quick to digest (read in bed!), accessible information. DK books are like that.

Teach Your Child
Very practical, explains milestones and development. Again, quite politically correct.

As an aside, the DK (Doring-Kindserley book, a website well worth bookmarking) books great easy reference. This is regarding structured, organized learning, not learning via play.

David Werner
**Where there is no Doctor*
This one could scare you if you let it; this is one of those 'just in case' books. That said, it has good information, although it can be a bit obscure sometimes. It is set up for those teaching local citizens of undeveloped countries about modern medicine, which can be helpful when you just need to know how to assess if it is an earache or ear infection and to call your Med Unit or not.

Reading list extras (check out at your local library, borrow or buy, read, and donate to local woman's shelter — you'd be surprised at how many young, or newly pregnant women show up there):

James Dobson
Dare to Discipline
Now, you have to read around the spewing bible-thumping (the man IS the head of Focus on the Family), but there is some good solid advice in this book. Some of it is extraordinarily far right wing, but some of it is really useful if you read critically. I might not agree with the man's politics, but I did glean helpful things from this and the next book.
Bringing up Boys
Again, I reiterate the above. Know your source, there is an agenda and bias

of course; this one more blatant than most. However, I recommend this for anyone with a boy! How can one not agree that the most important role model for a boy is a father!? That said, there are decidedly politically Incorrect comments regarding single mothers that might put you off.

Harvey Karp
The Happiest Baby on the Block
>...per a friend who tried this book, it has good advice on swaddling. He talks about the Fourth Trimester. "When you bring your soft, dimpled newborn home from the hospital, you may think your nursery is a peaceful sanctuary.... To him, it's a disorienting world part Las Vegas casino, part dark closet! Karp recommends a series of five steps designed to imitate the uterus. These steps include swaddling, side/stomach position, shhh sounds, swinging and sucking. The book includes detailed advice on the proper way to swaddle a child, the difference between a gentle rocking versus shaking and more. According to the author, virtually all babies will respond to these strategies although some trial and error may be needed to find the most effective calming method. A number of the steps letting kids nurse more frequently or encouraging babies to use pacifiers, for instance contradict other childcare experts. However, parents who are at their wits' ends because of a baby's incessant crying will find this book invaluable." (from the Amazon.com review)

The Happiest Toddler on the Block
>"A unique approach to the tantrums, melt-downs and overriding challenges that often accompany the demanding years from one to four. Viewing toddlers as primitive thinkers akin to prehistoric man, Karp divides his patients into developmental groups: the "Charming Chimp-Child" (12 to 18 months), the "Knee-High Neanderthal" (18 to 24 months), the "Clever Cave-Kid" (24 to 36 months) and the "Versatile Villager" (36 to 48 months). Parents may find the toddler years so frustrating, Karp suggests, because they don't speak their child's language. To deal effectively with the undeveloped brains of toddlers, one must understand "Toddler-ese," he says, a method of talking to youngsters that employs short phrases, repetition, a dramatic tone of voice and the use of body language. Although the author admits parents may feel foolish speaking in this manner, he nevertheless maintains that the approach soothes children by respecting their needs. Additionally, Karp offers suggestions for positive discipline (e.g., loss of privileges and time out)

and guides parents through early expected milestones, while acknowledging that a child's individual temperament (e.g., easy, cautious, spirited) will uniquely influence the pace of his or her development. While some readers may find the relentless cave-kid metaphors irksome, Karp's gentle, easygoing tone is soothing and offers new hope and strategies to those who may have given up on making sense of the toddler years." (again, from the Amazon.com review, but I whole-heartedly agree! It is Baby Whisperer and Animal Behaviorist all in one.)

For comparison purposes:

Gary Ezzo
Babywise
> A very strict, no compromise schedule school. Seems a little cold-hearted to me; but people do swear by it. It is the far right of the baby spectrum.

James Sears
The Baby Book
> "Attachment parenting" as a gentle, reasonable approach to parenting that stresses bonding with your baby, responding to her cues, breastfeeding, "wearing" your baby, and sharing sleep with your child. AKA, baby knows best and YOU, my friend, are S.O.L. (oops, did I type that out loud?).

APPENDIX 4

SHOPPING LIST FOR KID KIT AND MEDICAL KIT

Kid Kit	Medical Kit
First aid guide (easy)	(all items from Kid Kit PLUS:)
First aid foam	Poison kit w/ ipecac & charcoal
Children's Benadryl	Latex gloves
Bandages	Cotton balls
Hydrocortisone cream	3″ cotton gauze
Antibiotic cream w/pain relief	Kaoelectroltye electrolyte replenisher
Antifungal cream	KY liquid lubricant
Diaper rash ointment (w/zinc)	Children's immodium
Digital thermometer	Children's laxative
Alcohol wipes	No-battery flashlight
Baby orajel	Saline nasal spray, no preservatives
Antibacterial wipes	Roll of gauze
Sterile saline	Small splints
Infant/Children Tylenol	VetRap
Nose aspirator	Ace bandage
Beany Baby/small toy	NuSkin (liquid skin)
Insect repellant	Butterfly closure bandages
Sun screen	Medical tweezers
	Hydrogen peroxide
	Hemostat scissors
	Small cuticle scissors
	*suture material/scalpel/syringes
	Medical tape

*if possible

APPENDIX 5

SAMPLE FOOD INTRODUCTION CHART

First	Fruits	Vegetables	Dairy	1year+
Iron fortified rice cereal	Ripe banana	Ripe Avocado	Cottage cheese	
Single grain cereals	Cooked strained:	Cooked pureed:	Whole fat yogurt	
Whole grain cereals	Apricot	Broccoli	Clear juices	
Homemade cereal	Pineapple	Brussel sprouts	Apple juice	
Tahini	Mango	Cauliflower		
Cook beans or lentils	Peaches	Cooked sweet potato		
Hard cooked egg white	Apple	Summer squash		
Barley	Nectarines	Asparagus		
Brown rice	Papaya	Spinach		
Tofu	Cantaloupe	Carrots		
Ground nuts	Pears	Beets		
Thinned nut butters	Honeydew	Greens		
Millet	Kiwi	Green beans		
Ground seeds	Plums	Peas		
Bulgur cereal	Prunes	Kale		
Oatmeal	Watermelon	Eggplant		
Brewers yeast	Peeled, quartered grapes	White Potato		Cooked egg yolk
Oats		Rhubarb		Honey
Cooked whole grains	Blueberries	Rutabega		Orange juice
Cornmeal w/ germ	Berries	Turnips		Tomato, finely chopped
Powdered kelp		Cooked onion		Citrus fruits
Whole grain pasta				Strawberries

Please do take the time to find a food introduction chart that you trust. This is just one example, and I know you'll be reading more books than just this one!

APPENDIX 6

Tylenol/Motrin dosage charts

CHILDREN'S MOTRIN DOSAGE
Motrin is an every 6 hour medication. Motrin = ibuprofen

Weight	Age	Infant Motrin Concentrated Drops (50mg/1.25ml)	Children's Motrin (100mg/1tsp)	Children's Motrin Chewable Tabs (50mg)	Junior Strength Chewable Tabs (100mg)
	Under 6 mos	Not recom-mended	Not recom-mended	Not recom-mended	Not recom-mended
12-17 lbs	6-11 mos	1.25ml 2nd line	½ tsp		
18-23 lbs	12-23 mos	1.875ml 3rd line	¾ tsp		
24-35 lbs	2-3 years		1 tsp	2 tabs	
36-47 lbs	4-5 years		1 ½ tsp	3 tabs	
48-59 lbs	6-8 years			4 tabs	2 tabs
60-71 lbs	9-10 years		2 ½ tsp	5 tabs	2 ½ tabs
72-95 lbs	11 years+		3 tsp	6 tabs	3 tabs

CHILDREN'S TYLENOL DOSAGE
Tylenol is an every 4 hour medication. Tylenol = acetaminophen

Weight	Age	Infant's Concen-trated Drops (80mg/0.8ml)	Children's Sus-pension Liquid (160mg/5ml)	Children's Soft Chew Tablets (160mg/5ml)	Junior Strength Chewables (160mg each
6-11 lbs	0-3 mo.	½=0/4ml			
12-17lbs	4-11 mo	1=0.8ml			
18-23 lbs	12-23 mo	1 ½=1.2ml	½ tsp		
24-35 lbs	2-3 years	2=1.6ml	1tsp	2 tabs	
36-47 lbs	4-5 years		1 ½ tsp	3 tabs	
48-59 lbs	6-8 years		1 ½ tsp	4 tabs	2 tabs
60-71 lbs	9-10 years		2 tsp	5 tabs	2 ½ table
72-95 lbs	11 years		3 tsp	6 tabs	3 tabs
96lbs +	12 years+				4 tabs

NOTE: the closest you can give these medications is to rotate back and forth between Tylenol and Motrin every **three** hours.

APPENDIX 7

The latest updated Screening Report can be found at:

The National Newborn Screening and Genetics Resource Center web site: GeNeS-R-US, (Genetic and Newborn Screening Resource Center of the United States).

http://genes-r-us.uthscsa.edu/nbsdisorders.htm

The National Newborn Screening and Genetics Resource Center (NNSGRC) is a cooperative agreement between the Maternal and Child Health Bureau (MCHB), Genetic Services Branch and the University of Texas Health Science Center at San Antonio (UTHSCSA), Department of Pediatrics.

They provide information and resources in the area of newborn screening and genetics to benefit health professionals, the public health community, consumers and government officials.

INDEX